Leadership Lessons from the Volkswagen Saga

Steven B. Howard

Caliente Press

Leadership Lessons from the Volkswagen Saga

Steven Howard
c/o Caliente Press
1775 E. Palm Canyon Drive, Suite 110-198
Palm Springs, CA 92264
Email: Steven@CalienteLeadership.com | CalientePress@verizon.net

Book Layout ©2017 BookDesignTemplates.com

Quantity Sales Ordering Information:
Special discounts are available on quantity purchases by corporations, educational institutions, associations, and others. For details, contact the Caliente Press email address above.

Cover Design: Zachary Colman

Table of Contents

Dedication

This book is dedicated to

Alex Chan Hon Wai

Partner. Friend. Motivator.

As long as we keeping pushing each other,

we will continue to reach greater heights,

both individually and together.

Introduction

When I first read about the Environmental Protection Agency (EPA) announcement on Volkswagen's wrongdoing, I instinctively knew that this was not likely to be just another corporate scandal that gets swept away in a few months.

I wrote to myself: "this is a story with legs, long-term consequences, and numerous iterations to come."

I also knew the story would touch all of my professional hot buttons — leadership, corporate responsibility, corporate image management and corporate branding, accountability, and the desire to see those in positions of power punished if their actions are found to be illegal or done for personal benefit.

How right I was. And now, 17 months after this corporate cheating scandal became public, the story is still far from over.

The Volkswagen diesel emissions test cheating scandal and its various offshoots have had a far-reaching impact on a wide range of parties.

This impact has been financial, environmental, political, and regulatory. The parties affected include car owners, Volkswagen's leadership team and employees, shareholders, car dealers, government officials, regulatory agencies, the media, the automotive industry, and even the Made-in-Germany brand.

Since the emissions test cheating scandal was revealed by the EPA in September 2015, Volkswagen has been hit by vehicle recalls, fines in numerous jurisdictions around the world, legal challenges, class-action lawsuits, and criminal and civil investigations in several countries.

To date, Volkswagen has been assessed or agreed to over $24B in fines, penalties, and compensatory payments to car owners. One Volkswagen employee is serving an 18-month jail term in South Korea. Another is awaiting sentencing in the U.S. after a plea bargain arrangement. A third sits in a U.S. jail thousands of miles away from his home in Germany pending his own trail or plea bargain agreement. Five of their colleagues in Germany have been indicted on felony charges by a U.S. grand jury and have been warned not to leave the country.

As this book goes to press, Volkswagen and the U.S. Justice Department have just agreed to a $4.3B settlement on civil penalties and criminal fines. A settlement that includes Volkswagen pleading guilty to three federal felony charges and agreeing to provide assistance to the Department of Justice's ongoing investigations.

This has been closely followed by a $1.2B settlement agreed to (but not yet approved by the court) in relation to the use of illegal emissions test cheating software in approximately 85,000r 3-liter diesel-powered Audi, Porsche, and VW vehicles.

These two settlements are comparatively minor, however, to the $15.3B settlement agreement that was accepted and confirmed by a U.S. District Court Judge in San Francisco in October 2016 in relation to the use of defeat device in over 475,000 Audi and VW vehicles across seven consecutive model years.

However, any hopes by the Volkswagen leadership team and the company's shareholders that by agreeing to one of the largest consumer class-action settlements ever in the United States, along with pleading guilty to three federal offenses and being tagged with the largest fines ever assessed to an automaker, will quickly put the diesel emissions scandal behind it quickly are simply illusionary.

For one thing, several U.S. states and numerous governments and government agencies around the world are still seeking punitive and compensatory damages. Plus, the criminal investigation by the U.S. Department of Justice remains open and further criminal charges against either the company or its current and former executives may be forthcoming. And Volkswagen faces thousands of investor lawsuits in at least a half-dozen jurisdictions including in both its home market of Germany and in the United States.

The Volkswagen Saga is a story of deliberate corporate malfeasance that has impacted the automaker's car brands, leadership structure, governance, corporate reputation, current and future financial results, and its corporate culture.

It is a story full of leadership lessons on corporate governance, branding, crisis communications, corporate responsibility, and individual accountability relevant to leaders of any size organization

The Volkswagen scandal is now the benchmark for corporate cheating and corporate scandals. Just as Exxon Valdez oil spill in 1989 was constantly brought up as the benchmark for oil spills until the BP Deepwater Horizon explosion and subsequent massive oil spill in the Gulf of Mexico in 2010, this story will be dredged up as the yardstick for future corporate scandals. The former and current executives from ExxonMobil, BP, Enron and other corporate disaster and malfeasance stories of recent years must all be thrilled! They can finally escape the limelight of future media cycles.

The Volkswagen saga is a huge wake-up call for leaders at all levels of any company or organization. And it will continue to be so for years to come.

Iconic investor Warren Buffet once said, "It takes 20 years to build a reputation and only five minutes to ruin it." Poetically, the EPA announcement of Volkswagen's emission test cheating takes approximately five minutes to read.

Throughout the lengthy investigative, settlement, and corrective process that is now over a year old, millions of Volkswagen vehicles continue to over pollute in cities and countries around the world. As things stand now, this will not change for many more months to come.

There are four things to remember when thinking about the leadership lessons and implications emanating from this story:

This was not corporate negligence or a correctable mistake that took place, but rather deliberate malfeasance on a grand scale and over a seven year period of time (in fact it most likely would be continuing today had it not been for the testing conducting by West Virginia University).

Volkswagen did not overlook something in production and take a risk assessment that the cost of recalls outweighed fixing the problem during manufacturing. Rather, engineers at the company deliberately installed software into the management systems of over 11 million vehicles whose sole purpose appears to be to cheat the known procedures of emissions testing.

Despite lengthy internal and external investigations, or perhaps because of, only eight people have been charged, prosecuted, or arrested to date. And only one person has been sentenced to jail time, this being one poor Volkswagen soul in Korea.

Over 11 million Volkswagen vehicles on the road continue to spew dangerous nitrogen oxide (NOx) into the air we breathe almost three years after the excessive emissions were revealed by the on-road testing performed by the International Council on Clean Transportation and the scientists at West Virginia University.

As this book goes to press in February 2017, approximately 17 months after the scandal became publicly known, many questions remain, including:

Why did Volkswagen purposefully cheat on diesel emissions tests?

Will regulators in Europe or elsewhere penalize Volkswagen financially to the extent that U.S. regulators have?

Will anyone serve jail time for their criminal acts, other than the one person in South Korea serving an 18-month sentence?

And perhaps the two most important questions: Will Volkswagen survive? Is Volkswagen too big to be allowed to fail and collapse as a corporate entity?

The answer to the last question is undoubtedly: probably.

Volkswagen does employ over 610,000 workers around the world, which means well over a half million families would be hurt if the company collapsed. Plus there are thousands of dealers, suppliers, and business partners, all employing their own staffs and workers — and all having families of their own — whose economic futures would be bleak if the Volkswagen Group went under or was broken up into little pieces to be incorporated into other vehicle manufacturing conglomerates.

These questions are not the main purview of this book as these topics are not my focus and I am not in a position to answer them fully. I will, however, touch upon them occasionally in the text of this book since readers are as likely as I am to find these questions to be interesting and fascinating aspects of a story that continues to unfold.

Rather, the questions that intrigued me throughout the past 17 months are the ones leaders across all organizations should be asking, and then modifying them as necessary to apply to their own organizations:

Why did no one in Volkswagen voice concerns that the damage to the environment, and to the health of fellow humans, are critical concerns worth considering?

Did anyone ever ask if the potential damage to the Volkswagen brand image and corporate reputation was worth risking if the company was caught installing the emissions test cheating defeat device software?

How could those involved maintain the cheat device software deception over 8 years while so cold-heartedly and callously dismissing the impact of this cheating on public health and the environment?

Where were the internal voices of conscience and realism that should have spoken up and expressed their ethical and moral concerns? Was the Volkswagen workplace totally devoid of employees who take into consideration the health of fellow human beings? Is the engineering staff at Volkswagen so amoral that there was no individual or collective concern for the air pollutants their products would be emitting? Or did job security concerns overrule all other individual morals, ethics, and accountability standards?

And while these and many other questions remain unanswered, many lessons can already be extracted from the turmoil created by this scandal, including:

The need for individual punishments when their actions deliberately violate laws protecting the health and well-being of humanity.

The need for regulators to have sufficient funds to do their jobs professionally and thoroughly without having to rely on self-test or third-party submissions made by the firms they are regulating.

The need for emissions tests of vehicles to be performed around the globe under real-world driving conditions, not in fabricated laboratory tests performed under ideal conditions requested by automotive manufacturers.

The need for modern corporate governance structures and standards to be in place, even in the most closely held, cross-linked shareholding situations.

The need for individuals to be accountable and more willing to speak up when they know of corporate wrongdoing, no matter what the corporate culture or workplace climate.

The need for organizational leaders to understand that legalese and corporate speak are not the proper way to respond to a crisis, especially when said crisis impacts millions of customers. Doing so simply creates more drama and additional brand equity deterioration with customers, government officials, journalists, shareholders, interest groups, and concerned citizens.

These lessons are the topics we will explore in this book, with the caveat that some lessons, as well as new ones, will continue to evolve as this scandalous story lingers and regenerates itself for months and years.

Steven Howard

February 2017

Note: Due to the ongoing nature of the Volkswagen saga, I anticipate updating this book every six months or so for the next two years.

CHAPTER ONE

How the Scandal Unfolded

September 2015 begins promisingly for Volkswagen. The company is on track to surpass archrival Toyota as the number one manufacturer and seller of automotive vehicles (the key goal in its 2018 corporate strategy plan).

Additionally, its sporty Audi A3 hybrid is a finalist for the annual "Green Car of the Year" award from *Green Car Journal*, an award previously won by Volkswagen in 2010 by the automaker's Volkswagen Jetta TDI Clean Diesel car and in 2011 by its Audi A3 TDI Clean Diesel car. In 2014 its Audi A3 TDI and its seventh-generation Volkswagen Golf line-up were both finalists for the "Green Car of the Year" award, as was its Audi A6 TDI in 2013.

Across North America, Volkswagen and its car dealers are riding high as they sell the VW Golf range of cars, which *Motor Trend* magazine named "2015 Motor Trend Car of the Year." In fact, in announcing this award the previous November, *Motor Trend* wrote, "The Golf was a near-unanimous choice among our judges by virtue of its strong performance in each of our six Car of the Year criteria."

Earlier in the year the 2015 Golf and 2015 Golf TGI were also named the North America Car of the Year in their respective segments. This prestigious industry award is selected by 60 automotive journalists in the

U.S. and Canada and is presented each year in January in conjunction with the North America International Auto Show (NAIAS) in Detroit.

And in Europe, the VW Passat was named European Car of the Year 2015 at the Geneva Motor Show.

Topping all this good news is the September 9th announcement that Volkswagen has been named the world's most sustainable car company by RobecoSAM AG. In fact, Volkswagen is one of only two automakers listed in both the Dow Jones Sustainability Index World and the Dow Jones Sustainability Index Europe.

In its self-congratulatory press release on this achievement, Volkswagen writes, "For investors, the Dow Jones Sustainability Index is the most significant benchmark for measuring the development of the world's most sustainable companies."

The review by the "experts" at RobecoSAM analyzed the corporate performance of 33 automotive manufacturers. Volkswagen was given top marks with 91 out of 100 points. Remarkably, the company was scored 93 on economic sustainability, 91 on social sustainability, and 89 on ecological sustainability.

In the press release Volkswagen AG CEO Martin Winterkorn, who reportedly was already aware of the nitrogen oxide emissions testing issues the company was having with the U.S. Environmental Protection Agency (EPA), boastfully states, "This distinction is a great success for the entire team. It confirms that the Volkswagen Group is well on the way to establishing itself long term as the world's most sustainable automaker."

Ironically (as the world is about to find out), the RobecoSAM analysis highlighted one of Volkswagen's most important achievements being "sustainability is the foundation of Volkswagen's corporate policy."

The organization oozes confidence and has a stellar brand reputation for producing a wide range of vehicles for buyers seeking trustworthy

German engineering at both the affordable mass-market and the luxury pricing points. And the annual Oktoberfest is just around the corner!

In fact, one suspects the attitude in Volkswagen's Wolfsburg, Germany headquarters is undoubtedly one of *das leben ist gut* (life is good)!

Then the morning of September 18 dawns along the eastern seaboard of the United States, particularly in Washington, D.C.

As Volkswagen headquarters in Germany is shutting down for the day, the Environmental Protection Agency announces in Washington that it has issued a Notice of Violation of the Clean Air Act to Volkswagen AG, Audi AG and Volkswagen Group of America, Inc.

The Notice of Violation alleges that Volkswagen and Audi diesel cars equipped with 2-liter engines from the model years 2009-2015 include software that circumvents EPA emissions standards for nitrogen oxide (NOx). The EPA stipulates that the software is a "defeat device" as determined by the Clean Air Act and is installed in approximately 500,000 vehicles across the United States. This figure is later revised to 480,000 vehicles.

The EPA also reveals that the affected cars, which include many of Volkswagen's most popular models, can emit more than 40 times the legal limit of NOx, a pollutant known to cause respiratory problems in humans.

Nitrogen oxide (NOx) is a very nasty pollutant. When emitted into the air it quickly converts into nitrogen dioxide, a reddish-brown gas with a highly pungent smell. When nitrogen dioxide absorbs sunlight, which it does very well, it transforms into the yellow-brown pollution haze we see as smog.

This smog aggravates and exacerbates numerous human health problems, including asthma, bronchitis, and emphysema. If washed into the ground via rain, nitrogen dioxide can harm or kill both plants and animals, thus potentially getting into our food chain.

Within days of the EPA announcement Volkswagen is forced to confirm that approximately 11 million vehicles worldwide have the defeat device software installed, including roughly 8.5 million in Europe. The affected vehicles comprise models from across the Volkswagen Group product range and include 5 million VW cars, 2.1 million Audi cars, 1.2 million Skoda cars, and over 700,000 SEAT cars. In addition, there are 1.8 million commercial vehicles such as vans included in the 11 million total.

The impact on the environment and air quality from the Volkswagen emissions is much higher in Europe than the United States, simply because of the higher volume of cars sold there in a smaller geographic footprint. In some European markets, diesel cars (from Volkswagen and other car manufacturers) account for almost 50% of all registered vehicles. As a result, in some European cities the high amounts of nitrogen dioxide are particularly troublesome, especially from a long-term health perspective. This will become an important issue in Europe in the coming months when on-road emissions tests show that no automotive manufacturer meets the current Euro 6 standard for emissions when their vehicles are tested in actual driving conditions (they only meet the Euro 6 standard when tests are conducted in highly controlled laboratory environments).

The EPA actually sent Volkswagen this initial Notice of Violation in July. Why they waited until the middle of September to publicly announce the Notice of Violation is unknown, though media reports suggest Volkswagen was trying to work out some sort of arrangement with the EPA during the interim that would result in relatively minor fines in the range of $100M.

In March 2016 Volkswagen will admit as much. Citing one unidentified automaker as having paid a $100M fine in 2014 after certain violations of U.S. emissions laws, the company says in a statement that "Volkswagen was advised that in the past that U.S. emissions penalties were not especially high for a company the size of Volkswagen."

The statement, issued in response to a German shareholder lawsuit accusing Volkswagen of failing to properly disclose the potential costs of the scandal when it first exploded, added, "It was expected that the diesel matter could be resolved with the U.S. authorities by disclosing the software modification, agreeing on appropriate measures to restore vehicle compliance with the law, and the payment of potential fines in line with prior U.S. settlements."

Boy were they wrong!

The tone and verbiage of this statement, issued six months after their emissions test cheating was revealed, shows how little Volkswagen's leadership understood the seriousness of the scandal, particularly from the perspectives of the EPA, the California Air Resources Board (CARB), U.S. state environmental officials, and car owners.

This was not a "diesel matter" but deliberate action to cheat and violate the U.S. Clean Air Act (along with a host of U.S. state environmental protection laws).

This was not a "software modification." It was thousands of lines of software code written specifically to cheat on emissions tests, and to allow their vehicles to emit up to 40 times permitted pollutants into the air when driven on the roads by consumers, many of whom thought they were purchasing and driving environmentally friendly "clean diesel" cars.

This statement reads like Volkswagen's senior leadership team considered a fine in the neighborhood of $100M to simply be an affordable cost of business for getting caught. A mere slap on the wrist. Nothing more than a corporate speeding ticket. Pay the fine and move on.

Again, boy were they wrong!

Shockingly, this is actually the SECOND time Volkswagen has gotten caught installing defeat devices in vehicles sold in the U.S. market.

In July 1973 the EPA accused Volkswagen of installing defeat devices in the automaker's 1974 models. Volkswagen then had to admit it had also sold 1973 models with the same defeat devices, which comprised temperature setting switches that cut or turned off pollution controls at low levels.

The EPA believed that 25,000 vehicles fitted with this cheating technology had been sold, and it took Volkswagen to court for violating the Clean Air Act. Volkswagen accepted a $120,000 fine but admitted no wrongdoing.

As autumn blossoms in North America and Europe, further details of what is quickly labeled Dieselgate by the media become known. The public learns that the EPA actually began questioning Volkswagen about the diesel emissions data in the middle of 2014. Their discussions began after the EPA was tipped off by the International Council on Clean Transportation, a European non-profit organization that had gotten researchers at the West Virginia University's Center for Alternative Fuels, Engines, and Emissions to study diesel emissions on certain suspected vehicles.

For reasons that are not fully clear yet, Volkswagen took over a year before admitting that the company had installed illegal software designed to defeat EPA pollution tests.

Now that the cheating software has become public, Volkswagen's initial response is to blame a "handful of rogue engineers" for designing and installing the defeat device software. The company line is even repeated by Volkswagen Group of America President and CEO Michael Horn when he is called to testify at a Congressional inquiry in mid-October.

One early casualty of this rapidly deteriorating situation is Volkswagen AG CEO Martin Winterkorn, who resigns on September 23, despite holding firm to his assertion that "he didn't do anything wrong." He is replaced by Matthias Mueller, who moves over to the group CEO spot from his position as head of the automaker's Porsche brand.

Trying to get ahead of this rapidly moving story, Volkswagen announces it has commissioned the U.S. law firm Jones Day to lead an internal investigation into who is responsible for the diesel emissions test cheating scandal. The decision is made following a lengthy Volkswagen supervisory board meeting. The automaker says that the completion of the investigation will take "at least several months."

As Volkswagen scrambles to find a technical solution to reduce NOx emissions from its 2-liter diesel cars, and simultaneously attempts to keep the lid on what is rapidly escalating into a public relations disaster, the EPA strikes again.

On November 2, the EPA issues a second Notice of Violation alleging that a similar defeat device has been installed in certain light duty diesel vehicles equipped with 3-liter engines. This time Porsche AG and Porsche Cars North America are cited in the Notice of Violation, along with Volkswagen AG, Audi AG, and Volkswagen Group of America, Inc. The EPA notice says these vehicles, from the model years 2014 through 2016, emit NOx up to nine times EPA allowable limits.

A week later Volkswagen officials notify the EPA that, in fact, this latest defeat device has been installed in all its 3-liter models since 2009.

As other heads start to roll within the Volkswagen leadership group, media reports state that at least nine Volkswagen employees have been suspended pending the outcome of the internal investigation.

And, in an attempt to pacify car owners in the U.S., Volkswagen in November decides to offer $1000 in gift cards and vouchers to owners of the 2-liter diesel engine cars affected by the emissions test cheating scam. Car owners of vehicles containing the emissions test cheating software will get a $500 Visa debit card for use anywhere and a $500 gift voucher for service or merchandise at VW and Audi car dealers. This same "goodwill" program is later offered in January to U.S. owners of the 3-liter TDI diesel engines loaded with the defeat device software.

For the remainder of calendar 2015 Volkswagen continues its attempts to paint as rosy a picture of the diesel emissions test cheating scandal as possible.

New CEO Matthias Mueller tries to calm the nerves of anxious Volkswagen employees in November, telling workers at the Wolfsburg plant that the current emissions scandal is "technically and financially manageable." The coming months show that neither premise really depicts the whole picture of what Volkswagen truly faces.

For months, Volkswagen continues to adhere to the company line that only a handful of rogue engineers are responsible for this mess.

This position is received with a great deal of skepticism by customers, government officials, and media outlets. The more that is revealed, and the more that critical questions go unanswered by Volkswagen, the greater are the suspicions that Dieselgate may represent corporate malfeasance of the highest nature.

As the *Financial Times* writes in the early days of the scandal, "Most corporate scandals stem from negligence or failure to come clean about corporate wrongdoing. Far fewer involve deliberate fraud and criminal intent."

Yet that is exactly what appears to be the case here. A group within Volkswagen — whether this was a small group or a large group is still unknown — made decisions to deliberately cheat the diesel emissions tests required by the EPA and other regulatory bodies.

To make matters worse, whatever conversations Volkswagen is having with the EPA and the California Air Resources Board (CARB) during November and December are not working in its favor.

This becomes obvious when, on January 4, 2016 (the first business day of the new year), the U.S. Department of Justice files a 31-page complaint in the U.S. District Court for the Eastern District of Michigan on behalf of the EPA against Volkswagen AG, Audi AG, Volkswagen Group of America, Inc., Volkswagen Group of America Chattanooga Operations LLC, Porsche AG, and Porsche Cars North America for alleged violations of the Clean Air Act. The suit seeks both injunctive relief and the assessment of civil penalties.

Things on the public relations front do not get any better when new CEO Mueller tells NPR radio in early January that Volkswagen believes this is simply a matter of "not the right interpretation of American laws." He also responded to the NPR reporter with an "I cannot understand why you say that" comment when asked if there is an ethical problem deep inside the company.

Even worse, Mueller's response to the ensuing reply and question from NPR goes badly astray. The NPR reporter says: "Because Volkswagen, in the U.S., intentionally lied to EPA regulators when they asked them about the problem before it came to light." And in reply Mueller surprisingly states, "We didn't lie. We didn't understand the question first. And then we worked since 2014 to solve the problem. And we did it together and it was a default of VW that it needed such a long time."

Volkswagen and Mueller issue a retraction of that statement the following day, saying the comment was partially caused by Mueller answering a reporter's question in English (which is not his native language). Unfortunately, the damage has already been done and the cultural differences between the Germanic methodology of close-fisted management of issues and the transparency process of the American regulatory and legal systems could not be starker.

In a follow-up interview with NPR, Mueller shockingly says, "We have to accept that the problem was not created three months ago. It was created, let me say, 10 years ago. We had the wrong reaction when we got information year by year from the EPA and from the California Air Resources Board." This is one of the first public indications that Volkswagen is now aware that origins of the cheat device software go back a full decade.

Volkswagen subsequently gets hammered weeks later when CARB flatly rejects a submitted proposal from the automaker for fixing the 2-liter cars equipped with its illegal defeat device software. In announcing the rejection, CARB said the Volkswagen proposed plans contained "gaps and lack sufficient detail."

The statement went on to say, "The description of proposed repairs lack enough information for a technical evaluation; and the proposals do not adequately address overall impacts on vehicle performance, emissions, and safety."

In an accompanying statement, the EPA bluntly says, "EPA agrees with CARB that Volkswagen has not submitted an appropriate recall plan to bring the vehicles into compliance and reduce pollution. EPA has conveyed this to the company previously."

In a sign of the highly tenuous and fractious relationships between CARB and Volkswagen at the time, CARB chair Mary D. Nichols was equally blunt in the agency's news release. "Volkswagen made a decision to cheat on emissions tests and then tried to cover it up," she said.

She went on to say, "They continued and compounded the lie and when they were caught they tried to deny it. The result is thousands of tons of nitrogen oxide that have harmed the health of Californians. They need to make it right. Today's action is a step in the direction of assuring that will happen."

Mind you, this submitted solution was roughly at the same time that Volkswagen CEO Mueller was telling NPR that Dieselgate was merely a "misunderstanding and misinterpretation of U.S. laws." I got the feeling that CARB's scornful and caustic comments were partially delivered to ensure no such possible misunderstanding or misinterpretation of its reasons for rejecting this proposed fix.

As realization of the cost ramifications of the cheating scandal escalates, Volkswagen in early February announces delays of 4-6 weeks for publication of its 2015 financial results (due on March 10) and its annual meeting of shareholders (scheduled for April 21).

A month later these delayed dates are set as April 28 for publication of its 2015 financial results and June 20 for the annual meeting of shareholders, a full two months later than the originally scheduled date of April 21.

In another blow, the U.S. Federal Trade Commission (FTC) in March files a suit against Volkswagen for deceptive and false advertising.

The FTC suit alleges Volkswagen helped others, such as its dealers, deceive consumers by selling cars based on false claims that the cars were low-emission, environmentally friendly, met U.S. national and state emissions standards, and would maintain a high resale value.

"For years Volkswagen's ads touted the company's 'clean diesel' cars even though it now appears Volkswagen rigged the cars with devices designed to defeat emissions tests," FTC Chairwoman Edith Ramirez said in announcing the lawsuit. "Our lawsuit seeks compensation for the consumers who bought affected cars based on Volkswagen's deceptive and unfair practices," she added.

Also in March, Volkswagen Group of America President and CEO Michael Horn unexpectedly steps down "by mutual agreement" and with immediate effect "to pursue other opportunities." He had been with Volkswagen for 25 years and assumed the Volkswagen of America CEO role in 2014.

Having joined Volkswagen in 1990, Horn had held a series of senior executive roles, including heading VW sales in Europe, before stepping into the CEO role at Volkswagen of America headquarters in Herndon, Virginia.

Horn's sudden departure causes huge consternation among the 652 Volkswagen dealers across the United States. Horn was viewed by the dealers as one of the few Volkswagen executives who understood their plight and was willing to fight for them within the Volkswagen hierarchy.

The National Volkswagen Dealer Advisory Council said in a statement that Horn's departure "is a serious blow to the U.S. dealer network, the employees of Volkswagen of America, the workers at the Volkswagen plant in Chattanooga, and the entire Volkswagen community." It also added that "the change in management can only serve to put the company at more risk, not less."

One Volkswagen dealer is quoted by the Reuters news agency as saying Horn was "probably the most popular (head) we've had as long as I've been a dealer" and added that Horn knew the American market "better than most."

A few weeks later, around a dozen members of the Volkswagen National Dealer Advisory Council from the U.S., travel to Germany to hold frank face-to-face discussions with senior Volkswagen leaders. According to news reports this delegation meets with VW global brand boss Herbert Diess, newly appointed North America head Hinrich Woebcken, head of global sales Jürgen Stackmann, and North America sales head Ludger Fretzen to discussion key issues and concerns of the Volkswagen dealers in the U.S.

Media reports also say that this dealer delegation convinced Diess to attend the National Automotive Dealers Association (NADA) conference in Las Vegas the following month and have a sit-down meeting with Volkswagen dealers, something he was not previously planning to do.

A few days after these meetings, a lawyer in New Jersey says he is crafting a potential class-action lawsuit on behalf of Volkswagen dealers in the U.S. against Volkswagen alleging breach of contract and fraud. He says no action will be taken until after the dealers meet with Volkswagen leaders at the NADA event.

At the annual NADA event in Las Vegas, Diess meets with hundreds of Volkswagen auto dealers and promises to "redefine" the company's tarnished image and "relaunch" the VW brand. He also said Volkswagen would fast track much-needed products so dealers would have more non-diesel vehicles available to sell.

Also in mid-March first reports emerge that a whistleblower is suing Volkswagen in Michigan after being fired by the company over a data deletion row. The whistleblower claims that staff at the Volkswagen data center in Auburn Hills, Michigan were deleting and destroying data related to the diesel emissions test cheating scandal a full three days after the EPA announced the first Notice of Violation.

He also claims that he was fired because Volkswagen management feared he would leak this information to the U.S. Department of Justice. The lawsuit is quietly and confidentially settled in June "amicably to the satisfaction of both parties."

Meanwhile, the lawsuits by the U.S. Department of Justice, the Federal Trade Commission, and numerous state attorneys general are consolidated into one major case and transferred to the jurisdiction of the U.S. District Court for Northern California and Judge Charles Breyer.

At the end of March, sensing the frustrations of U.S. regulators and car owners who have now been in limbo for six months not knowing what to do with their cars, Judge Breyer gives Volkswagen 30 days to reach an agreement with the EPA, CARB, FTC, and others or face going to trial. This is later extended to the end of June when the parties tell Judge Breyer in late April they need more time despite significance progress made toward a settlement agreement.

By April the ongoing Volkswagen problems begin to cast a shadow over the entire German car industry. A survey by the Edelman Trust Barometer shows that German public trust has grown over the past year for every industry — except the German automotive industry which dropped to just 41% (from 61% in 2015).

In early May the Volkswagen AG board announces that preliminary results from the Jones Day internal investigation into the diesel emissions scandal have revealed no serious violations by former or current top executives. It is interesting to note that the announcement says no "serious" violations; it does not state that no violations were made by past or present executives.

At this time the Volkswagen board also reiterates that details of the internal investigation by law firm Jones Day will not be disclosed until late 2016 at the earliest, for fear that releasing details would disrupt an ongoing criminal investigation by the U.S. Department of Justice.

In June, around the time that news of the unfair dismissal lawsuit is withdrawn in the United States by the whistleblower in Michigan who claimed Volkswagen employees in Auburn Hills were destroying and deleting data related to the emissions test cheating scandal, German media and the *New York Times* report that several Volkswagen employees told investigators that in August 2015, just before the scandal broke, someone "in a supervisory position" told them indirectly to remove evidence of the emissions test cheating defeat device software.

The New York *Times* cites an anonymous source who claims the employee "was a member of Volkswagen's legal staff and has since been suspended from his job."

A German media report states that German prosecutors are indeed looking into a Volkswagen employee suspected of suppressing documents and obstructing their investigation by asking colleagues to "get rid of data." This request was partially carried out. However, the state prosecutor's office says it is optimistic that some of the data will be recovered.

Finally, on June 27th Volkswagen and its various opponents file the Proposed Settlement Agreement with Judge Breyer. This proposed $14.7B agreement calls for:

Volkswagen to spend up to $10B buying back or repairing roughly 475,000 VW and Audi vehicles with 2-liter diesel engines and paying their owners an additional $5001 to $10,000 each.

Volkswagen to spend $2B over 10 years to fund programs directed by the EPA and CARB to promote construction of electric vehicle (EV) charging infrastructure, development of zero-emission ride-sharing fleets, and other efforts to boost sales of cars that do not burn petroleum-based fuels.

Volkswagen to put aside $2.7B over three years to enable government and tribal agencies to replace old buses or to fund infrastructure to reduce diesel emissions.

In a separate agreement, Volkswagen also reached a settlement with 44 U.S. states, the District of Columbia, and Puerto Rico that will cost the automaker at least $600M.

Thus, the total price tag for the two agreements is $15.3B. Significantly, neither of these deals covers the 85,000 3-liter VW, Audi, and Porsche vehicles also equipped with emissions test cheating software. The terms and costs of that settlement are not likely to be known until after Thanksgiving, and perhaps not even until early 2017.

In the EPA news release announcing the terms of the settlement, EPA Administrator Gina McCarthy says, "Today's settlement restores clean air protections that Volkswagen so blatantly violated. And it secures billions of dollars in investments to make our air and our auto industry even cleaner for generations of Americans to come. This agreement shows EPA is committed to upholding standards to protect public health, enforce the law, and to fund innovative ways to protect clean air."

Deputy Attorney General Sally Q. Yates added, "By duping regulators, Volkswagen turned nearly half a million American drivers into unwitting accomplices in an unprecedented assault on our atmosphere. This partial settlement makes a significant first step towards holding Volkswagen accountable for what was a breach of its legal duties and a breach of the public's trust."

Yates also foreshadowed future Justice Department action in her remarks, saying: "And while this announcement is an important step forward, let me be clear, it is by no means the last. We will continue to follow the facts wherever they may go."

Judge Breyer says he will review the Settlement Agreement. In July he grants preliminary approval of the Proposed Settlement Agreement while simultaneously sending it out for public comment. He also schedules an October date for his eventual ruling of acceptance, rejection, or modification of the proposed agreement.

As summer spreads across the northern hemisphere, South Korea — Volkswagen's fourth largest export market — becomes another major concern for Volkswagen executives in Germany. At the top of their concerns is the 33% drop in sales in South Korea for the first half of the year compared to the first six months of 2014. And that was the good news!

In July South Korea bans the sale of 80 Volkswagen models by revoking their certifications. This results in a ship being stranded in Seoul's harbor that was delivering more than 3000 new Volkswagen vehicles to the market.

South Korea also fines Volkswagen 17.8B won ($16M) for allegedly fabricating documents on emissions or noise levels. This is in addition to the 14.1B won ($12.7M) South Korea authorities fined Volkswagen in November for outfitting diesel vehicles with the cheating software that distorts results of emissions tests.

In mid-July CARB rejects Volkswagen's proposed recall plan and fixes for the 3-liter VW, Audi, and Porsche vehicles equipped with the defeat device. In its letter CARB uses similar language as in January when the proposed 2-liter engine fixes were likewise rejected by the agency.

"VW's and Audi's submissions are incomplete, substantially deficient, and fall far short of meeting the legal requirements to return these vehicles to the claimed certified configuration," California's regulatory agency states. It also said it would not have enough data until at least December to make a determination on whether a fix would work for all the affected 3-liter diesel vehicles. The affected vehicles include the VW Touareg, Porsche Cayenne, and the Audi A8.

In one of the few pieces of good news for Volkswagen as the anniversary of the diesel emissions test cheating passes, the German Sunday newspaper *Bild am Sonntag* reveals that the Jones Day internal investigation has shown that current Volkswagen CEO Matthias Mueller had no knowledge of the automaker's diesel emissions test cheating before it became publicly known.

However, this is quickly offset by news that Volkswagen AG chairman Hans Dieter Poetsch has become a target of an investigation by German prosecutors for allegations involving securities law violations for "failing to notify shareholders quickly enough of the financial risks of the diesel emissions cheating scandal." Poetsch was the Chief Financial Officer of Volkswagen when the automaker was first informed of the EPA Notice of Violation of the U.S. Clean Air Act. He became chairman a few weeks after the emissions test cheating became public knowledge.

As the costs of the diesel emissions test cheating start to pile up, CEO Mueller demands a heightened belt-tightening at the automaker, including a 10% decrease in material costs and overheads in the 2017 budget.

Reports start to circulate in automotive trade journals that, as part of the company's cost-saving moves, Audi is likely to drop out of the World Endurance Championships (WEC) after 2017 and the VW flagship brand will quit the World Rally Championship even though it has won the manufacturer's title four years in a row.

Meanwhile, while Volkswagen remained Europe's biggest selling carmaker, its market share for the first nine months of 2016 dropped to 23.8% compared to 24.9% for the same period in 2015.

In mid-November Volkswagen AG and Audi confirm that both U.S. and European regulators are investigating fresh problems related to "irregularities" found in the carbon dioxide (CO_2) emissions levels in a number of Audi automatic transmission vehicles. These problems were discovered by the California Air Resources Board (CARB) earlier in the year. Volkswagen admits that Audi automatic transmission software in some models can change test behavior in a manner that minimizes CO_2 emissions during testing and return to normal settings when driven on the road. It looks like a new round of explanations and negotiations with the EPA and CARB are in store.

Later in the month, Reuters reports that the Jones Day investigators will now question Audi CEO Rupert Stadler regarding this new cheat software that lowers CO_2 emissions during testing on some Audi diesel and gasoline models. He had previously been questioned and, according to news reports, cleared over the NOx diesel engine emissions test cheating defeat device found in various Audi 3-liter cars.

Within days the first class-action lawsuit related to the Audi CO_2 issue is filed in the United States. "Throughout the yearlong Dieselgate scandal, Audi chose to continue to deceive consumers across the country with yet another emissions-cheating device installed in even more of its vehicles," stated attorney Steve Berman from the Seattle law firm representing vehicle owners in the suit. "This kind of flagrant disregard for federal environmental regulations and consumers' expectations is unacceptable, and we intend to hold Audi to the law on behalf of those who overpaid for Audi's noncompliant polluting cars."

The last two months of 2016 see a flurry of activity on the legal front for Volkswagen.

In late November and early December, U.S. District Court Judge Charles Breyer twice postpones scheduled hearings related to the 85,000 3-liter vehicles running with the emissions test cheating defeat device software installed. He states that both parties are very close to an agreement and prefers to let their negotiations process continue to work rather than initiate formal court proceedings.

Around the same time, the U.S. Federal Trade Commission requests Judge Breyer to force further questioning of Volkswagen officials regarding whether evidence, including mobile phones, was destroyed during the agency's probe into the diesel engine emissions test cheating. This comes after the automaker's designated witness answered "I do not know" or some variation thereof over 250 times, often in response to questions the FTC believed he "should have been able to answer."

"In the context of the massive scandal at the center of this case, 23 lost or bricked phones is a bright red flag, especially when they include phones that belonged to important individuals," the agency's lawyers said in their court filing. They added the agency "should not have to accept VW's assurance that there is nothing to see and that we should just move along."

Interestingly, in early December word leaks out of Wolfsburg headquarters that several Volkswagen executives have begun hiring U.S. criminal defense lawyers. This takes place as U.S. Department of Justice authorities travel to Germany to interview managers and to seek cooperation in their criminal investigation probe.

The timing of these interviews prompts concerns to surface that the DOJ may not be able to complete its criminal probe and reach a resolution with Volkswagen before the Trump Administration takes over in late

January. Whether this would be good or bad for Volkswagen is unknown, and speculation goes both ways.

However, Jeff Sessions, appointed as the new Attorney General by President-elect Trump, said in 2010 when he was a U.S. Senator that he would not back away from charging a major company if there was evidence of criminal conduct. At the time, the U.S. Department of Justice was investigating BP over the Deepwater Horizon oil spill in the Gulf of Mexico. Sessions, a former federal prosecutor in Alabama, also stated at the time that the Justice Department should not be swayed or influenced by concerns that criminal charges against BP might harm those who depend on the company for jobs. "They are not too big to fail," he stated. If he brings that same attitude to his role as head of the Justice Department Volkswagen and its executives may be in for a long and rough journey ahead.

Perhaps preferring to deal with the devil they already know, rather than with the unknowns of a new administration, CEO Mueller publicly states that he hopes an arrangement with the DOJ can be completed before the end of the year.

Finally, just before Christmas the Department of Justice announces the DOJ, EPA, and CARB have reached a $1B agreement with Volkswagen to resolve the outstanding civil issues surrounding the 85,000 3-liter Audi, Porsche, and VW vehicles equipped with the emissions test cheating defeat device software. This negotiated settlement includes:

A $225M payment by Volkswagen into an environmental trust fund to remediate the excess emissions produced by these cars.

A $25M payment by Volkswagen into a fund to support the use of zero emission vehicles in California.

Volkswagen will offer to buy back or terminate leases without penalty on the 2009-2012 affected models. Volkswagen will also offer to correct the defeat device software so that the vehicles meet emission requirements, subject to approval of the fix by U.S. regulators.

Volkswagen will recall and repair the 2013-2016 models to bring them into compliance, subject to approval of the fix by U.S. regulators. If the regulators do not approve the fix, Volkswagen will offer to buy the vehicles back and terminate any outstanding leases without penalty.

If all eligible car owners opt for the buyback option, the total cost to Volkswagen is estimated at around $1B.

This agreement only covers the lawsuits filed against Volkswagen by the U.S. Department of Justice on behalf of EPA and CARB. The class-action lawsuit on behalf of the 85,000 car owners for additional compensation remains outstanding as this book goes to press. If this settlement is similar to the $5001 to $10,000 compensation payments made to each of the 2-liter car owners in the previous settlement, then the costs to Volkswagen will increase by another $400M to $800M.

The year 2017 starts off with more bad news for Volkswagen. On January 4th U.S. District Court Judge Charles Breyer rules that Volkswagen and former CEO Martin Winterkorn must face American investor claims over the Dieselgate saga in California. The judge also rejected a request from VW brand chief Herbert Diess to have proposed securities fraud lawsuits discharged.

The automaker and its former and current executives had requested to have these cases dismissed, arguing that such lawsuits should be tried in Germany. However, Breyer said "because the United States has an interest in protecting domestic investors against securities fraud" the lawsuits should proceed as filed in a U.S. court.

The investors suing Volkswagen and its executives are mainly municipal and state pension funds that had invested in Volkswagen through American Depository Receipts traded on U.S. stock exchanges.

This is followed by a week later by an announcement from the Department of Justice and the Environmental Protection Agency that Volkswagen has agreed to pay $4.3B in civil and criminal fines, plus plead guilty to felony charges of defrauding the U.S. government, committing wire fraud, and violating the Clean Air Act.

As part of this plea bargain arrangement, Volkswagen must cooperate in the DOJ's continuing investigation, face new annual environmental management system audits, and let an independent monitor oversee its compliance for three years.

This penalty includes a $2.8B criminal fine and $1.5B for a civil settlement and far exceeds the $1.2B penalty levied against Toyota in 2014 over unintended acceleration in its vehicles. It is the largest fine ever imposed by the U.S. government on an automaker.

Additionally, the DOJ announced that six high-level Volkswagen managers in Germany had been indicted on charges of lying to environmental regulators or destroying computer files containing evidence. All six were also charged with one count of conspiracy to defraud the U.S. by making false statements to regulators. The six executives and the additional charges against them are:

Jens Hadler, head of Volkswagen engine development 2007-2011. Charged with conspiracy.

Bernd Gottweis, head of quality management and product safety 2007-2014. Charged with wire fraud.

Richard Dorenkamp, head of VW engines' after-treatment department 2003-2013 and leader of the team of engineers that developed the first diesel engine designed to meet U.S. standards. Charged with violations of the U.S. Clean Air Act.

Heinz-Jakob Neusser, head of Volkswagen engine development 20111-2013 and head of VW brand development 2013-2015. Charged with wire fraud and clean air violations.

Oliver Schmidt, head of VW's Engineering and Environmental Office in Michigan 2012-2015. Charged with wire fraud and clean air violations.

Jurgen Peter, an engineer in the quality management and product safety group 1990-present. Charged with wire fraud and clean air violations.

In announcing the settlement, the Department of Justice also outlined a deliberate and elaborate scheme inside Volkswagen to intentionally commit fraud and then attempt to cover it up. It also stated that at least 40 Volkswagen employees were allegedly involved in destroying evidence and deleting thousands of documents in an effort to hide the emissions test cheating from U.S. regulators.

"Volkswagen obfuscated, they denied, and they ultimately lied," proclaimed Attorney General Loretta Lynch. Hinting that charges against additional Volkswagen employees, including even higher-ranking executives, may still be in the works, Lynch added, "We will continue to pursue the individuals responsible for orchestrating this damaging conspiracy."

This announcement occurred just days after the U.S. Federal Bureau of Investigation arrested Oliver Schmidt, one of the six indicted Volkswagen managers, as he was transiting through Miami International Airport on his way to Germany after a holiday in Cuba. Schmidt was formerly Volkswagen's top emissions compliance executive in the United States and, according to an FBI affidavit presented in court, played a central role in Volkswagen's attempted cover-up of its diesel emissions test cheating.

Following this arrest, senior Volkswagen managers were warned by the company not to travel to the USA in case other charges are pending. Additionally, the five other indicted managers, all resident in Germany, were advised that leaving Germany is risky as they could be arrested and extradited to the USA. However, they remain relatively safe if they remain in Germany as the German constitution only permits extradition of German citizens to other European Union countries or to an international court.

A few days after the announcement of Volkswagen's guilty plea to criminal charges, Germany's *Bild am Sonntag* newspaper reports that former Volkswagen CEO Martin Winterkorn knew about the automaker's emissions test cheating issues two months earlier than previously stated. Citing confidential documents the newspaper says Winterkorn was presented with evidence about the emissions testing defeat device software in July 1015 by Oliver Schmidt.

However, later that week Winterkorn denied knowing about the cheating software before late August 2015 in testimony before a German parliamentary committee. He declined to be more specific about when he was actually informed about the emissions test cheating because it was a matter still under investigation by German prosecutors. "I too am looking for satisfactory answers. It is incomprehensible why I wasn't informed early and unambiguously," he told committee members during a two-hour hearing.

A week later prosecutors in Germany announced they are expanding their probe into Volkswagen's emission testing cheating. An announcement from the prosecutor's office in Braunschweig said they have increased the number of suspects being investigated from 21 to 37 individuals. They also said they now have evidence that former CEO Winterkorn may have known of the cheating earlier than he has publicly acknowledged. As such, they are now investing Winterkorn for possible charges of fraud, in addition to suspicion of a securities market violation.

As part of their investigation, prosecutors raided 28 locations, including offices and private homes, in Germany. No word was given on how long the investigations would continue and when any charges might be forthcoming.

Around the same time, Volkswagen announced that Christine Hofmann-Dennhardt, the woman recruited a year earlier from Daimler to join the management board and head its integrity and legal affairs, would be leaving "by mutual consent." The announcement from Volkswagen cited "differences in their understanding of responsibilities and future operating structures within the function she leads" for her sudden departure.

In late January 2017, a lawyer for Volkswagen tells a U.S. District Court hearing that less than 67,000 of the 475,000 VW and Audi 2-liter diesel vehicles with emissions test cheating software have been returned to dealers as buybacks or lease terminations. He says that figure is expected to rise to around 96,000 by the end of January.

Finally, at the end of January Volkswagen agrees to a $1.2B settlement plan covering the 85,000 3-liter Audi, Porsche, and VW 3-liter vehicles fitted with the emissions test cheating defeat device software. Car owners who opt for fixes will receive between $7,000 and $16,000, while owners who participate in the buyback offer will receive $7,500 on too of the value of their vehicles. However, if the fix proposed by Volkswagen is not approved by EPA and CARB, the automaker will be forced to buyback all affected vehicles and the total cost of the settlement could reach as high as $4B.

This coincides with the revelation that Volkswagen says it delivered 10.3 million cars in 2016. With Toyota producing only 10.21 million cars in 2016, and selling 10.17 million globally, this makes Volkswagen the "world's biggest carmaker" for 2016. This must be a bittersweet victory for the Volkswagen executive team in Wolfsburg as they finally achieve the main goal of the 2018 corporate strategy plan.

Of course, we have to believe and trust the validity of the self-reporting numbers stated by Volkswagen. After all that has gone on in the past 17 months, and all that has been revealed about the lack of veracity and accuracy in other corporate releases during this time period, sceptics are bound to take this announcement with the proverbial grain of salt.

Meanwhile, while all this has been happening, Volkswagen is simultaneously facing additional scrutiny and legal actions in Europe, Asia, Latin America, and Australia.

EUROPE

Regulators and law enforcement officials in Europe react quickly when the news of the emissions test cheating becomes public.

Europe, of course, is Volkswagen's home market, which accounts for approximately 40% of its worldwide vehicle sales and where it sells roughly one of every four vehicles purchased. The Volkswagen Group is, by far, the most dominant carmaker across Europe with a portfolio comprising eight automotive marques from six countries: the German brands Audi, Porsche, and VW, the Italian brand Lamborghini, Bugatti from France, the Czech Republic car Skoda, Spain's SEAT, and the famed luxury Bentley brand from the United Kingdom.

In a little over a week after the EPA announcement of Volkswagen's misdeeds, the German Federal Motor Transport Authority (KBA) gives Volkswagen a 10-day deadline to submit a plan laying out what and when its vehicles will meet emission standards.

By the end of September Volkswagen confirms that commercial vehicles and cars from its Spanish unit SEAT are included in the 11 million vehicles fitted with the cheating software.

In early October, German prosecutors raid the Volkswagen company headquarters in Wolfsburg in search of evidence related to the emissions test cheating scandal.

And on October 12 the European Investment Bank (EIB) announces it is investigating how Volkswagen used $5.2B in loans it has received from the bank. EIB President Werner Hoyer said EID, a nonprofit public lending institution, may have to demand immediate payback of the loans depending on what the investigation reveals. An unspecified percentage of the loans by EIB to Volkswagen were reportedly intended for the development of low-emission engines. "The EIB could take a hit," states Hoyer as the bank "has to fulfill certain climate targets with our loans."

Meanwhile, apparently not satisfied with Volkswagen's response, the KBA in mid-October orders a nationwide recall of all Volkswagen vehicles in the country fitted with the defeat device software (estimated at 2.8 million). As per EU rules, this means this recall will automatically be applied to all 8.5 million cars with the defeat device software installed across the entire 28-country European Union.

Other legal matters are moving rapidly for Volkswagen across many fronts in Europe. A prosecutor in Verona, Italy leads a raid at Lamborghini's headquarters in Bologna. By late October investigations have commenced in at least four European countries — France, Germany, Italy, and Spain — into the Volkswagen emissions test rigging. This includes the German state of Lower Saxony (which is a major shareholder in Volkswagen and holds seats on the Volkswagen AG supervisory board) filing a criminal complaint after prosecutors discover that a file, said to include internal government memos on the emissions scandal, has gone missing.

In what may (or may not) prove to be a related issue, a Norwegian shipowner seeks $50M in compensation from a marine unit of Volkswagen for rigging performance tests of ship engines.

As is the case in any major scandal, politicians and lawmakers also start to get involved. Germany's environment minister urges tougher emissions testing throughout the European Union. He says Germany and the rest of the EU need to act quickly to implement real-world road testing and in calling automakers to account. A few weeks later, Germany's Chancellor Angela Merkel says Volkswagen needs to deal with the diesel emissions test cheating scandal "in a transparent manner."

In late October the Financial Times reports that the European Union's top environmental officer, EU environmental commissioner Janez Potočnik, warned his EU colleagues in 2013 that automakers were rigging European emissions tests. In digging around, I found that in 2013 the European Commission's Joint Research Service (JRS) published a study showing that emission levels of diesel vehicles were significantly higher than many believed.

In the report, the JRS also identified that defeat devices could be used in laboratory tests:

> *Sensors and electronic components in modern day light-duty vehicles are capable of "detecting" the start of an emissions test in the laboratory, (with) some vehicle function may only be operational in the laboratory if a pre-defined test mode is activated. Detecting emissions tests is problematic from the perspective of emissions legislation, because it may enable the use of defeat devices that activate, modulate, delay or deactivate emissions control systems with the purpose of*

either enhancing the effectiveness of the systems during emissions testing or restricting the effectiveness of these systems under normal vehicle operation and use.

While the JRS report did note that such defeat devices were generally prohibited, it highlighted that exceptions existed to "protect the engine against damage and to ensure safe vehicle operation." Such exceptions, the report noted, "leave room for interpretation and provide scope, together with the commonly applied test procedures, for tailoring emissions performance."

The close relationships between the auto industry and the EU regulators will become one of the key stories emanating from the Volkswagen scandal, along with public and media queries into why Europe's emissions regulations, particularly for diesel engines, are not as tight and as tough as those found in the United States.

Meanwhile, Volkswagen continues to face numerous battles on many fronts throughout Europe. For instance, in Switzerland approximately 600 car owners file criminal complaints connected to the emissions test cheating scandal. And Daimler-Benz CEO Dr. Dieter Zetsche calls Volkswagen's use of emissions test cheating devices "a blow to our industry" and damaging to the Made in Germany brand.

Then in early November Volkswagen shares fall to their lowest level in five years after the automaker announces that an internal investigation has revealed "unexplained irregularities" in the carbon dioxide (CO_2) emissions in 800,000 of its vehicles. The additional CO_2 emissions result from incorrect fuel consumption data previously supplied by Volkswagen. As the company's announcement said these vehicles were "predominately diesel engines," the possibility was raised for the first time that some

Volkswagen vehicles with gasoline-powered engines may now have previously unidentified excess emissions problems.

On the next day Moody's downgrades Volkswagen's credit rating from A3 to A2 and includes a negative outlook. The credit rating agency says the downgrading reflects mounting risks to Volkswagen's reputation and future earnings.

Volkswagen quickly asks European finance ministers to charge the company, not car owners, for any additional taxes related to fuel usage or CO_2 emissions due as a result of its underreporting of these figures. Many countries in Europe provide tax incentives and rebates to consumers to encourage the purchase of low-emission cars, and these enticements may be in jeopardy due to Volkswagen's incorrect fuel consumption data submissions.

Weeks later German prosecutors launch a tax evasion probe at Volkswagen, in connection with the ongoing diesel engines emissions test cheating scandal. In Germany vehicles are taxed according to fuel consumption. The prosecutors will investigate whether owners of the affected Volkswagen diesel engine vehicles underpaid on taxes, a matter which the prosecutor's spokesman says is "not small."

In early December, as estimates of the costs of the emissions test cheating scandal continue to rise, Volkswagen secures a $30B bridging loan to cover potential Dieselgate costs. This is practically the only good news to come Volkswagen's way in the last three-and-a-half months of the year.

More bad news surfaces when Reuters reports that German prosecutors are now investigating Volkswagen's former CEO Martin Winterkorn on fraud allegations. And the year closes with news that Volkswagen is being suspended from the FTSE Good Index and banned from re-entry for at least two years. This index is popularly known by investors as the FTSE Ethical Index.

Also, just before the end-of-year holiday season gets underway, the European Parliament announces plans to establish a committee to investigate Volkswagen's emissions scandal and whether regulatory oversight of the car industry in Europe is too lax. In typical bureaucratic fashion, some 45 members will sit on the committee. The inquiry, which will get underway in March, could last up to a year and will investigate alleged contraventions of European Union law and alleged "maladministration" in the application of the law.

As a new year gets underway, Volkswagen continues to get hit left, right, and center from politicians, lawmakers, investors, prosecutors, the media, and European regulators. As Tom Cruise says sarcastically in the movie A Few Good Men, "the hits just keep on coming."

Shortly after the start of the new year, European Industry Commission head Elzbieta Bienkowska writes to Volkswagen CEO Mueller demanding that European customers of Volkswagen should be compensated in the same way as those in the United States.

Investor lawsuits across Europe against Volkswagen for the company's share price drop since September start to stack up and pick up steam. A Dutch foundation, the Volkswagen Investor Settlement Foundation, says it has won the support of dozens of institutional shareholders for its efforts to seek a deal with Volkswagen and have such an agreement applied worldwide based on a Dutch law covering global collective settlements.

At the end of February the German car regulator KBA says that Volkswagen failed to notify U.S. and California environmental regulators in 2004 about a defect in an emissions-related part.

In April Volkswagen must delay a recall of 160,000 Passat and Skoda cars in Europe when its software update fix aimed at correcting the emissions violations fails to work properly. Checks by the German Federal Motor Transport Authority (KBA) show that fuel consumption in some 2-liter diesel engines actually increases following the software update.

Later that month KBA orders almost all of the car industry's major players, both German and foreign owned, to make changes to their motors to reduce levels of hazardous emissions. The regulator says tests show actual emissions are up to 50 times legal limits.

British politicians and law enforcement officials also start to join in the "jump on Volkswagen" game. A British transport minister tells a U.K. Parliament transport committee that the country's Serious Fraud Office is looking into the issue of compensation in Britain for owners of the 1.2 million cars in the United Kingdom affected by the Volkswagen diesel emissions scandal.

As the postponed Volkswagen annual general meeting of shareholders nears, German investor group DSW calls for an independent audit of Volkswagen's emissions test rigging scandal, to be conducted in addition to the automaker's probe being led by the Jones Day law firm. "When you have an independent investigation you can be sure that the findings will be publicized. With internal investigations you do not know whether everything has been made transparent," states DSW spokesman Jurgen Kunz.

Around the same time Volkswagen says the "huge amount of information and data" being examined in the internal investigation being led by Jones Day will not be published until later in the year. Previously Volkswagen had indicated the findings would be made public before the annual meeting of shareholders.

To no one's surprise, Volkswagen's majority stockholders close ranks at the annual meeting of shareholders defying the ire of minority investors and DSW. The three main shareholders — the Porsche-Piech families, the Lower Saxony regional government, and the Arab Gulf state of Qatar — which control 89% of the voting stock in Volkswagen AG, back the company's management over criticisms and complaints from the small investors calling for the independent inquiry into the emissions test cheating scandal and how this has been handled by the carmaker's senior executives.

After having its motion defeated at the Volkswagen annual meeting of shareholders, DSW announces it will go to court to push for an independent investigation of the Volkswagen diesel emissions scandal. DSW says in a statement it is convinced that such an investigation is the right tool for cleaning up the scandal.

Having slumped for eight consecutive months, Volkswagen's European market share hits a five-year low. The group's share of Europe's car sales in April falls to 25.4% and its market share for the first four months of 2016 is 23.9%, its lowest since 2011.

Around the time of its postponed annual meeting of shareholders, Volkswagen learns that former CEO Martin Winterkorn is now under investigation in Germany for alleged stock market manipulation. German prosecutors in Braunschweig say the investigation of Winterkorn and another current board member is focused on "sufficient real signs" that Volkswagen executives did not alert investors and the market as soon as they were made aware of the possible financial damage that could result from the EPA's first Notice of Violation of the U.S. Clean Air Act.

The Braunschweig prosecutor's statement says this new probe was opened on behalf of Germany's Federal Financial Supervisory Authority, the country's main financial watchdog. Volkswagen releases a statement saying this new probe offers no fresh facts on former CEO Winterkorn.

In subsequent weeks media reports in Germany name the second (and current) board member as Herbert Diess, the relatively new VW brand chief. Diess said he is not planning to step down even though he is now a subject of the investigation.

July arrives with some good news for Volkswagen. The German Ministry of Transport announces that Volkswagen will not have to pay any fines for the millions of emissions test cheating diesel cars sold in the country. However, Volkswagen will be required to "return the cars to a legally compliant condition" according to the German Transport Minister Alexander Dobrindt.

That good news is immediately offset within a week when German prosecutors notify Volkswagen management that they will be seeking punitive damages in addition to the four criminal investigations already underway. If Volkswagen is forced to pay punitive damages in Germany the costs could be enormous, potentially running as high as the profit Volkswagen earned on each of the 11 million vehicles sold worldwide with the emissions test cheating software.

The prosecutors in the German city of Braunschweig also state in July that they have widened their probe into the diesel emissions test cheating, with 21 current and former Volkswagen staff now under investigation. In March prosecutors had indicated that only 17 people were under investigation.

This news is followed two days later by a committee of U.K. lawmakers saying Britain should consider prosecuting Volkswagen over the diesel emissions scandal. The British Transport Select Committee also says Volkswagen should be punished to avoid a repeat of the scandal.

Then, truck maker MAN, owned by Volkswagen AG, is one of five European truck manufacturers cited by the European Union's Competition Committee for price fixing and operating a secret system aimed at delaying the installation of pollution-curbing exhaust pipes and engines. MAN avoided being fined, however, as it had revealed the existence of the cartel.

At the same time, Europe's Commissioner for Justice begins working with European Union consumer groups to pressure Volkswagen into compensating customers across Europe as it proposes to do in the United States. Volkswagen has rejected all calls to do so for the 8.5 million affected vehicle owners in Europe, where different legal rules weaken the chances of car owners winning any kind of payout. Options will be discussed when the Justice Commission organizes a meeting with consumer groups in Brussels in September.

The bad news for Volkswagen continues into August. First, a district judge in Germany dismisses Volkswagen's objections and rules that local owners of tainted diesel vehicles had a right to return their cars for a full refund because of Volkswagen's "massive fraud."

Next, the German state of Bavaria announces plans to sue Volkswagen for damages. Bavaria's state pension fund lost approximately $784,000 after Volkswagen AG shares plunged following the diesel emissions test cheating scandal announcement. Bavaria is the first of Germany's 16 federal states to seek legal action against Volkswagen AG over the scandal.

On top of this, the district court in Braunschweig sends 170 investor lawsuits, claiming up to 4B euros ($4.5B) in damages against Volkswagen, onward to the regional court for selection of a model plaintiff. The model plaintiff's case will represent and then be applied to the other suits filed by hundreds of private and institutional investors who held, or continue to hold, shares in Volkswagen AG.

Investors suing Volkswagen will need a great deal of patience and fortitude. It seems the wheels of justice in Germany turn mightily slowly. A similar set of investor lawsuits filed against Deutsche Telekom AG by roughly 17,000 shareholders in 2001 has still not been resolved.

Investors also start targeting Porsche Automobil Holding SE, the major shareholder in Volkswagen AG. Several media outlets in German and abroad report that this publicly listed company may face an investor test case over how quickly it informed investors of the implications of the Volkswagen diesel emissions test cheating.

Car owners also start to contemplate legal action against Volkswagen. According to Handelsblatt, a leading business newspaper published in Dusseldorf, some Volkswagen car owners in Germany have started to plan legal action, believing that the software updates installed to fix diesel emissions are harming vehicle performance.

A British government statement in October 2016 indicates that Volkswagen's legal woes in Europe may only be beginning. In responding to the U.K. Transport Committee's Special Report on the diesel emissions test cheating scandal, the government statement said, "Prosecuting authorities from across Europe have met to discuss and coordinate their investigations. (U.K.) officials have been part of these coordinating efforts and continue to monitor the progress of these investigations."

The official statement also said, "The government will continue to fight for compensation for U.K. customers and continue our work to ensure that Volkswagen's serious action of cheating type approval tests is met with the appropriate consequences."

These consequences apparently need to be severe for the lengthy statement also said, "The government wants to ensure that the

Volkswagen Group faces appropriate legal consequences for its manipulation of emissions tests and is continuing to consider how best to do this. We have not ruled out opening our own investigation."

In late October, European Union consumer champion Vera Jourova asks for proof that Volkswagen can fulfill the company's pledge to make vehicles comply with limits on nitrogen oxide (NOx) by the fall of 2017. "We need VW to guarantee, in a legally binding way and without any time limit, that the repairs will work and do not have any negative impact," she writes in a letter to a Volkswagen official.

Trying to head off what appears to be a landslide of new legal, regulatory, and civil actions in Europe, Volkswagen says in early November that the software allowing its diesel vehicles to evade emissions testing does not violate European law. In an email statement the automaker proclaimed, "The software contained in vehicles with an EA-189 engine in the view of Volkswagen represents no unlawful defeat device under European law. The efficiency of the emissions cleanup system will not be reduced in these vehicles which however would be a prerequisite for the existence of an unlawful defeat device in the legal sense."

The Volkswagen statement draws criticism from Lower Saxony premier Stephan Weil, a member of the Volkswagen Group supervisory board. His office releases a statement saying, "This manipulative action is inexcusable in the opinion of the prime minister, regardless of whether the software is legal due to varying national legislation."

In mid-November, litigation funding company Bentham Europe announced plans to bankroll a potential 100B euro ($110B) damages claim against Europe's biggest truck makers after they admitted to operating a 14-year price-rigging cartel. The truck manufacturers include Daimler, Volvo, and Volkswagen's MAN truck unit.

Later in November the Mayor of London writes to Volkswagen requesting the automaker to reimburse Transport of London £2.5M ($3.1M) in lost congestion charge revenues from its vehicles which were known to be contributing to pollution levels. He also requested Volkswagen to "fully compensate" the approximately 80,000 London residents who "bought VW cards in good faith, but whose diesel engines are now contributing to London's killer air." It is estimated that London's dirty air kills up to 9,500 people per year.

Meanwhile, Paris faces its worst winter pollution in a decade and in December the city bans half of all cars from traveling within the city limits each day. It also makes public transportation free for three consecutive days. Similar action is also taken in Lyon. Around the same time, London's mayor announces that the city will no longer buy diesel buses for its famed public transportation network.

In Switzerland, prosecutors open criminal proceedings and seize evidence from a Swiss car importer after an appellate court rules Swiss investigators must conduct their own investigation of the Volkswagen emissions test cheating scandal. Over 2000 criminal complaints have been filed in Switzerland related to the emissions test cheating scandal.

The European Commission finally gets serious about the NOx emissions from diesel engine vehicles and undertakes legal action against seven countries, including Germany, Spain, and the United Kingdom for failing to police car emissions. The move reflects the growing frustration in the European Parliament and elsewhere over how national governments have failed to clamp down on the widespread air polluting emissions of automotive manufacturers exposed by the Volkswagen Dieselgate scandal.

"Abiding by the law is the first and foremost duty of car manufacturers," Elzbieta Bienkowska, the EU Internal Market

Commissioner said in the statement announcing the European Commission's actions. "But national authorities across the EU must ensure that car manufacturers actually comply with the law," she added.

A week later media reports surface about the results of lab tests conducted by the European Commission's Joint Research Center which show the latest Audi diesel engine emits double the statutory permitted levels of NOx. The results, which have still been made public, threaten to embroil Audi, the main profit contributor to Volkswagen AG, into another cheat device scandal.

Finally, good news arrives for Volkswagen a few days before Christmas when the German Federal Motor Authority (KBA) clears the automaker to begin repairing all vehicles in Germany (and hence the other 27 European Union member states) with the emissions test cheating software installed. In a statement Volkswagen said the KBA "confirmed that implementing the technical solution for the affected models will not adversely affect fuel consumption, engine performance, or noise emissions."

Officials in Britain, however, put a damper on any festive spirits in Volkswagen's Wolfsburg headquarters with two end-of-the-year declarations.

First, the U.K. government's chief medical officer says diesel cars should be phased out to reduce the tens of thousands of deaths caused each year by air pollution.

On the same day, the U.K. Transport Minister says over a million Volkswagen drivers in the country have been "taken for a ride" over the diesel emissions scandal and must be compensated by the automaker. He also revealed that Volkswagen has agreed to reimburse the U.K. government £1.1M ($1.4M) for the cost of vehicle emission tests on other automotive manufacturers conducted by the government earlier in the year.

Pressure continues to mount on Volkswagen to compensate car owners in Europe as 2017 gets underway. In the first week of January German consumer rights champion myRight files the first legal test case in Germany against Volkswagen. The suit seeks to force Volkswagen to repurchase vehicles with the emissions test cheating defeat device software at the original sales price.

The second week of January starts off with a British law firm commencing legal action against Volkswagen in that country. Their suit seeks thousands of pounds of compensation for each U.K. drive affected by the Dieselgate scandal. The firm says over 10,000 drivers have already signed up to the legal action.

In mid-January Poland's Office of Competition and Consumer Protection, the country's consumer protection watchdog, initiated proceedings against Volkswagen for misleading customers over emissions. This action could result in a fine of up to 10 percent of Volkswagen's sales turnover in the country.

Also in January a German court rules that Volkswagen must buy back, at full purchase price, a German customer's diesel car equipped with the emissions test cheating defeat device software. The judges in the rule said Volkswagen acted "indecently" by installing the software and they compared the automaker's deceit to previous cases in Europe where winemakers mixed antifreeze in wine and food manufacturers used horse meat in lasagna. Volkswagen said it would appeal the ruling.

Volkswagen announces it is halting production at one of its biggest factories in Germany for 11 days in January and February due to shrinking demand for its Passat saloon and estate models. The factory in Emden in Northern Germany employs about 9000 workers.

Another bad month of news for Volkswagen ends in January with a report from the German newspaper Berliner Zeitung that Germany's Federal Motor Transport Authority (KBA) raised suspicions in November 2015 that Volkswagen was using prototype vehicles for carbon dioxide (CO_2) emissions testing. The newspaper reports that KBA told Volkswagen that it would begin choosing test models randomly and appoint new experts to carry out testing because of its doubts about the independence of the automaker's CO_2 testing procedures.

ASIA

China is Volkswagen's largest national market, with annual vehicle sales around 2.7 million. The company has two joint ventures in China: FAW-Volkswagen, which manufactures Audi and VW passenger cars for sale in China, and SAIC Volkswagen, which manufactures cars for China under the VW and Skoda marques.

In mid-October 2015 the Chinese Environmental Protection Agency announces an investigation into Volkswagen's imported and locally produced vehicles. The Chinese authorities want to know if these vehicles are in compliance with the country's emissions standards.

Around the same time, China's General Administration of Quality Supervision, Inspection and Quarantine (AQSIQ) says it is "highly concerned" about the methodology used by Volkswagen to trick emissions tests and that it would take appropriate follow-up measures.

In early November China's top quality watchdog announces a recall of 5906 Volkswagen luxury brand Bentley cars due to a battery defect that could lead to overheating.

In late November, the South Korean government tells Volkswagen to recall 125,500 diesel vehicles over faked emission tests. The South Korean Environment Ministry also fines Volkswagen 14.1B won ($12.3M).

In January South Korea's antitrust regulator is probing Volkswagen over its advertising claims on emissions from its cars, according to a report from the Yonhap news agency. It also reports that the Korea Fair Trade Commission is investigating if Volkswagen ran false ads by claiming its cars met the European Union's strict Euro 5 emissions standards.

In February things get even tougher for Volkswagen in South Korea, as prosecutors raid the offices of Volkswagen and Audi as part of their probe into the emissions scandal. This is seen as a sign by some that criminal charges may be forthcoming in South Korea.

In India, the Ministry of Heavy Industries says Volkswagen cars in that nation are also fitted with a similar defeat device as in the U.S., and that emission levels of these cars are nine times higher than permitted levels in the country. The Ministry asks the country's Road Transport Ministry to take action against Volkswagen.

The following month the central excise department of Pune, India penalizes three Volkswagen firms in the country a total of Rs460M ($7.4M) for allegedly evading taxes by undervaluing cars sold in India between 2010 and 2014. The three firms are Volkswagen India, Skoda Auto India, and Volkswagen Group Sales. A Volkswagen spokesperson said the company would appeal the fines.

In April Volkswagen stops the sale of the diesel variation of its Vento sedan car in India over inconsistent carbon monoxide emissions. Models with a manual gearbox were found to be exceeding threshold emissions limits during tests conducted by the Automotive Research Authority of India (ALAI). Around the same time, Volkswagen recalls nearly 104,000 vehicles in China to replace a missing part, without which the brake pedals may dislodge.

In May Audi Volkswagen Taiwan Co. is fined NT$55M ($154,000) by a Taiwanese regulator over false advertising concerning the emission levels of certain vehicles.

In early June news reports indicate that Volkswagen's South Korea division is alleged to have manipulated 37 emissions and noise level tests submitted to the South Korean National Institute of Environmental Research to secure importation of its vehicles. Later in the month, a South Korean court issues an arrest warrant for a Korean-based Volkswagen executive in connection with the ongoing investigation into the automaker's emissions test cheating. It is the first known arrest warrant leveled against a Volkswagen executive anywhere in the world in connection with the scandal.

The following month Volkswagen says it will halt the sales of most of its vehicles in South Korea. Sales were already down 33% in the first half compared to the first six months of 2014.

In August South Korea formally suspends sales of 80 Volkswagen Group models and fines the company another 17.8B won ($16.1M), accusing the company of forging documents on emissions or noise-level tests. Affected car models are under the Audi, Bentley, and VW brands. The ban was announced before a ship in Seoul's harbor carrying 3000 brand new Volkswagen vehicles for the South Korea market could be unloaded.

In November the South Korean government announces it plans to ban the sales of 10 car models made by Nissan Motor Co., BMW, and Porsche after it found these automakers had also manipulated documents to make their vehicles road certified. The automakers face a combined $5.6M in fines and are given until mid-December to "clarify their positions." The ban goes into effect in December.

In early December the South Korean Fair Trade Commission (FTC) fines Volkswagen $31.9M for falsely advertising its diesel-engine vehicles as environmentally friendly. It is the largest such fine ever assessed in South Korea for false advertising. Government authorities in the country also said criminal complaints will be filed against current and former executives of Volkswagen.

As in Europe, the winter brings health-damaging levels of air pollution to China. Beijing and 22 other Chinese cities impose various emergency measures, including ordering cars off the roads and closing schools after air pollution levels soar to 10 times safe levels. Flights are also canceled or delayed due to poor visibility.

On January 5, 2017 a South Korean court sentences a Volkswagen executive to 18 months in jail for falsifying documents that enabled the automaker's vehicles to be imported into the country and certified as roadworthy. Two other employees were also convicted on related charges. A week later prosecutors in Seoul indict seven current and former executives of Volkswagen's Korean operations on charges of fabricating official documents and alleged violations of the country's Clean Air Conservation Act.

LATIN AMERICA
While Latin America is not yet a primary market for Volkswagen, the automaker has not escaped legal and regulatory woes in this region.

In November 2015 Brazil assesses Volkswagen $13M in fines over the emissions scandal.

In February 2016, Mexico's Profepa environmental protection agency imposes a 168M peso ($8.9M) fine on Volkswagen Mexico for importing and selling 2016 model vehicles in the country without the mandatory environmental certificate showing emissions standards compliance. Volkswagen Mexico blamed an administrative error for the oversight.

In November Volkswagen announces it will have a historian investigate the automaker's practices in Brazil during the country's military dictatorship between 1964 and 1985. This follows a civil lawsuit filed by former employees the previous year claiming 12 Volkswagen workers were arrested and tortured in a Volkswagen factory near Sao Paolo.

Also that month Volkswagen announces it will invest $2.2B in Brazil by 2020 to overhaul its production facilities and to pave the way for a new family of vehicles for the Latin America market. However, word also comes out that Volkswagen is planning to eliminate 5000 jobs in Brazil and 2000 jobs in Argentina within the next five years.

The following month Volkswagen announces that its Truck & Bus division will invest $447M in Brazil over the next five years in order to offer new products, modernize its manufacturing plant, and develop connectivity services.

AUSTRALIA
Australia is a relatively small market for Volkswagen, but it ranks high in consumer protection litigation and media attention.

Australia's consumer watchdog, the very powerful Australian Competition and Consumer Commission (ACCC) warns a few weeks after the scandal broke that Volkswagen could be fined up to A$1.1M ($780,000) for each pollution cheating device installed and used in the country. Media reports estimate that over 40,000 vehicles made by VW and Audi could contain the defeat device software.

The first class-action lawsuits against Volkswagen and Audi in Australia are filed in early November 2015, a mere seven weeks after the

EPA public announcement of the first Notice of Violation. At the same time these two suits are being filed on behalf of the approximately 100,000 diesel car owners of these two brands, the ACCC says it will start its own investigation of Volkswagen and warns of possible legal action against the automaker.

The ACCC follows through on that threat in September 2016. Saying that Volkswagen's Australian subsidiary has been lying about the emissions of its diesel vehicles, the ACCC files a lawsuit in Australian federal court. The ACCC says it wants Volkswagen Group of Australia to make public declarations of misconduct, pay unspecified financial penalties, and issue corrective advertising in relation to the company's actions over a five-year period.

Timeline Highlights

Here are the key events in the unfolding of the Volkswagen Saga. For a more detailed timeline please see Chapter 11 at the end of the book.

2009 Volkswagen begins to install defeat device software into vehicles in order to dupe diesel emissions laboratory tests and bypass tougher U.S. Environmental Protection Agency (EPA) rules capping nitrogen oxide (NOx) emissions.

2013 Researchers from the International Council on Clean Transportation (ICCT) and West Virginia University (WVU) discover significant irregularities and deviations between the NOx emitted by two Volkswagen vehicles (a 2012 VW Jetta and a 2013 VW Passat) during on-road tests and those recorded in laboratory tests. The on-road emissions are also much higher than what is permitted by the U.S. Clean Air Act.

2014 ICCT shares its findings with the EPA and the California Air Resources Board (CARB).

After being informed of the abnormalities found by ICCT and WVU, EPA and CARB begin their own investigations and request Volkswagen to explain the huge aberrations between the two testing methods.

Volkswagen initially argues that the third-party tests by ICCT and WVU are flawed. They also blame the problem on technical issues. Back-and-forth discussions and written correspondence on this matter between these two powerful regulators and Volkswagen go on for well over a year.

2015

Sept 18   The United States Environmental Protection Agency (EPA) makes public the Notice of Violation of the U.S. Clean Air Act issued to Volkswagen two months earlier. The EPA also says Volkswagen installed a "defeat device" software on more than 475,000 cars with 2-liter, four-cylinder diesel engines that enabled them to cheat on U.S. emissions tests. This software reduced nitrogen oxide (NOx) emissions when the cars were placed on test machines, but then allowed higher emissions and improved engine performance during on-road driving.

Sept 22   Volkswagen admits that about 11 million vehicles around the world with various configurations of its diesel engines have been fitted with the "defeat device" software. It sets aside 6.5B euros ($7.2B) to deal with expected costs of the scandal, including anticipated recalls to fix or replace the cheating software.

Sept 23   Volkswagen Group CEO Martin Winterkorn resigns, taking full responsibility for the "irregularities" found by U.S. inspectors while simultaneously insisting he did nothing wrong. Winterkorn had run the company since 2007.

Volkswagen shares have dropped by over one-third in value since the EPA public announcement five days earlier.

Sept 25   Volkswagen appoints Matthias Mueller, the head of the Volkswagen Group's Porsche unit, as the new group CEO.

Sept 29   Volkswagen announces it has commissioned the U.S. law firm Jones Day to conduct an internal investigation into the cheating scandal.

Oct 7   Volkswagen names Hans Dieter Poetsch, its CFO, as its new supervisory board chairman. The appointment fills a position that had been vacant since April when former chairman Ferdinand Piech resigned. Deputy chairman Berthold Huber had been acting as interim chairman since April.

Oct 8   CEO and President of Volkswagen of America Michael Horn testifies before Congress. He apologizes for the scandal, which he says he learned about 18 months earlier when the West Virginia University study was published. He recites the corporate line that blames "a couple of rogue engineers" for the defeat device software.

Oct 15   The German motor vehicle authority orders a recall of all Volkswagen cars with the test cheating software. By European Union rules this means all 8.5 million cars with the defeat device software must be recalled across the 28-country EU.

Oct 28   Volkswagen reports a loss of $1.83B for the third quarter, after taking a $7.5B reserve to cover anticipated costs of the scandal.

Nov 2   The EPA and the California Air Resources Board (CARB) say Volkswagen has also installed the emissions test cheating software on thousands of Audi, Porsche, and VW cars with 3-litre, six-cylinder engines. Volkswagen rejects the new allegations, which are issued by EPA in a second Notice of Violation of the U.S. Clean Air Act.

Nov 9   Volkswagen admits that the 3-liter engines do in fact have the illegal defeat device software install. It also reveals that this software has been installed in over 85,000 VW and Audi vehicles sold in the U.S.A. since 2009.

Dec 23   Volkswagen drops its "Das Auto" global advertising slogan, which has been in place for almost 10 years.

2016

Jan 4   The U.S. Department of Justice, on behalf of the EPA, files a $48B civil complaint in federal court against Volkswagen AG, Audi AG, Volkswagen of America Inc., Volkswagen Group of America Chattanooga Operations LLC, Porsche AG, and Porsche Cars North America Inc. for allegedly violating U.S. environmental laws, including the stringent Clean Air Act.

Jan 12   The California Air Resources Board (CARB) rejects Volkswagen's plan to fix the 2-liter diesel engines impacted by the original emissions test cheating software with scathing language. CARB said it was rejecting the proposed repairs because they lacked enough information for a technical evaluation and do not adequately address overall impacts on vehicle performance, emissions, and safety.

Mar 10   Michael Horn, President and CEO of Volkswagen Group of America, steps down with immediate effect to "pursue other opportunities."

Mar 29   The U.S. Federal Trade Commission (FTC) sues Volkswagen, saying the automaker's "Clean Diesel" advertising campaign made false claims that its vehicles were low-emission, environmentally friendly, and would maintain a high resale value.

Apr 22   Volkswagen AG reports a full-year loss of $1.74B after taking a $17.8B charge to its 2015 financial results to cover the increasingly growing costs of the diesel scandal. It also delays publication of the internal probe by law firm Jones Day until late in the year.

June 28 Volkswagen and the U.S. Department of Justice (on behalf of the EPA and the FTC) file a Proposed Settlement Agreement with U.S. District Court Judge Charles Breyer in which Volkswagen agrees to buy back 2-liter vehicles it cannot fix, pay compensation to car owners, and set aside funds to promote infrastructure for electric vehicles. The cost to Volkswagen could be up to $15.3B and this settlement does not cover the 3-liter vehicles also fitted with defeat device software. Judge Breyer accepts the Proposed Settlement Agreement for review and schedules a July date for preliminary approval by the court.

July 26 U.S. District Court Judge Charles Breyer grants preliminary approval of the Proposed Settlement Agreement between Volkswagen and the U.S. Department of Justice. He opens the agreement for public commentary and schedules October dates to hear public comments on the agreement and to grant final approval or amendment by the court.

Aug 25   Volkswagen reaches a tentative agreement with its dealer network in the U.S. to compensate them for losses incurred as a result of the emissions test cheating scandal. The value of the settlement is later revealed to be $1.21B.

Sept 9   Long-time Volkswagen engineer James Robert Liang pleads guilty to one count of conspiracy to defraud the U.S. government. As part of his negotiated plea agreement he will cooperate in the ongoing U.S. Department of Justice criminal investigation. He could be sentenced up to five years in prison and up to a $250,000 fine in January.

Sept 18   A German court says it has received a total of 1400 investor lawsuits against Volkswagen seeking damages and payments totaling 8.2B euros ($9.2B).

Oct 25   U.S. District Court Judge Charles Breyer signs an order approving the court settlement between the U.S. Department of Justice (on behalf of the EPA and FTC) and Volkswagen AG that includes Volkswagen spending up to $10B to buy back affected VW, Porsche, and Audi vehicles, paying compensation to U.S. car owners, and establishing to funds to provide infrastructure development for electric vehicles. According to Reuters Volkswagen will begin buying back the affected vehicles around the middle of November.

Nov 4   Volkswagen says the software allowing its diesel vehicles to evade emissions rules does not violate European law.

Nov 6   *Bild am Sonntag* reports that the California Air Resources Board (CARB) has discovered several Audi vehicle models running illegal software to bring carbon dioxide (CO2) emissions within legal limits under laboratory test conditions. The software has apparently been found in both gasoline and diesel Audi models with automatic transmissions produced up until May 2016. The paper also reports that Audi has suspended several engineers after being informed of this matter by CARB earlier this year

Nov 13   Volkswagen admits that Audi automatic transmission software can change test behavior in a manner that minimizes CO2 emissions during testing and return to normal settings when driven on the road.

Dec 19   Volkswagen Canada agrees to pay up to C$2.1B ($1.57B) to settle a class-action lawsuit. The agreement calls for VW and Audi brands to buy back and pay restitution to about 105,000 Canadian owners of vehicles with 2-liter diesel engines fitted with the emissions test cheating defeat device software. Volkswagen also agreed to pay a C$15M ($11.2M) fine to Canadian Competition Bureau.

Dec 20   Volkswagen agrees to a $1B settlement to fix or buy back the 85,000 3-liter VW, Porsche, and Audi vehicles fitted with the emissions test cheating defeat device software in the U.S. The resolution reportedly includes Volkswagen buying back 20,000 older Audi and VW sports utility vehicles (SUVs) and a software fix for 65,000 newer Porsche, Audi, and VW cars and SUVs. Talks are continuing with regards to additional compensation to be provided to affected car owners.

2017

Jan 5   A South Korea court sentenced a Volkswagen executive to 18 months in jail for falsifying documents enabling Volkswagen vehicles to be imported into the country. Two other employees were convicted on related charges.

Jan 7   A Volkswagen executive, Oliver Schmidt, who had headed the automaker's regulatory compliance office in the U.S. from 2014 until March 2015, was arrested by FBI agents at Miami International Airport before he could board a flight to Germany. He was charged with conspiracy to defraud the U.S. government.

Jan 11   The U.S. Department of Justice (DOJ) and the Environmental Protection Agency (EPA) announce that Volkswagen has agreed to a $4.3B settlement to resolve the U.S. government's civil and criminal investigations. Volkswagen also pleaded guilty to three federal felony charges and has agreed to cooperate with the DOJ's ongoing investigations.

Additionally, the DOJ announced that six Volkswagen executives and employees have been indicted by a federal grand jury on conspiracy and other charges related to the diesel emissions test cheating scandal. This includes Oliver Schmidt, who was taken into custody by FBI agents a few days earlier.

CHAPTER TWO

The Defeat Device Software

The Volkswagen diesel emissions test cheating scandal dates back to 2005 when, according to *Car and Driver* magazine, the VW brand chief Wolfgang Bernhard and engineer Rudolf Krebs began developing a new diesel engine for the U.S. market. According to the *Car and Driver* article (October 12, 2015), cost-cutting pressures within Volkswagen prevented a $335 piece of equipment to be included in the engine's design.

The defeat device software was reportedly created in 1999 by Bosch AG at the behest of Audi AG. According to an article in *Green Car Reports* (May 5, 2016), several engineers who worked on the software at Audi were "subsequently transferred to VW's own diesel programs." The article also states that when at VW these engineers worked on one of the 2-liter engines that was later found to include the defeat device software. It is also interesting to note that Martin Winterkorn was head of Audi in 1999 before becoming CEO at Volkswagen AG in 2007.

While Volkswagen has mostly stuck to its claim that the defeat device software was the responsibility of a "handful of rogue engineers," it now appears that knowledge of this software was probably more widespread. John German, a former EPA official and senior fellow at the International Council on Clean Transportation, the environmental group that played a key role in uncovering Volkswagen's emissions test cheating, is quoted in the *New York Times* (December 13, 2015) as saying the idea that a few rogue engineers in the engine design team are responsible for the diesel emissions test cheating "does not pass the laugh test."

We will not know the extent to which "who knew what and when" until the findings of the Jones Day investigation are released. Of course, with all the legal activity surrounding the diesel emissions test cheating scandal, Volkswagen's leaders may elect to never publicly release any or all of the Jones Day findings.

However, evidence has been mounting throughout the past 17 months that more than a handful of Volkswagen employees were aware of the existence and use of the defeat device software. This includes various media reports in April 2016 that a PowerPoint presentation dating back to 2006 has been uncovered by the Jones Day investigators that reportedly shows details on how to cheat laboratory emissions tests.

Additionally, Volkswagen has stated that the Jones Day report, originally promised for release in April 2016, would be delayed until at least the end of the year due to the volume of data and information being reviewed. According to media reports, this includes over 1500 laptops being reviewed by up to 450 investigators. Obviously, more than a handful of rogue engineers were using these 1500 laptops. Also, it would not require 450 investigators to look into the activities of a few engineers, rogue or not.

The Jones Day investigation has also been slowed by what insiders claim are dozens of code words for the cheat software that were used internally at Volkswagen.

Now, two months into 2017 and the Jones Day report still has not been released, nor has Volkswagen given any indication of when we can expect it to be released.

This is disconcerting for, as more and more details leak out regarding the findings of the Jones Day investigators, the less likely it appears that only a handful of "rogue" engineers were involved.

Additionally, we know that the U.S. Department of Justice suspects at least 40 Volkswagen employees have been involved in the destruction of data related to the diesel emissions test cheating software. How does this correlate to the findings of the Jones Day investigators?

What is also remarkable is that engineers at Volkswagen reportedly made improvements in the defeat device software in late 2014 or early 2015, well after company officials were responding to inquiries from CARB and EPA. This certainly takes the concept of continuous improvement (another key platform of the 2018 corporate strategy) to a new level.

This revised and improved cheating software was reportedly installed in 280,000 vehicles in the United States in early 2015 under the guise of service action recalls.

One suspects that such recalls had to be approved at some level of Volkswagen management in both the U.S. and Germany. Service recalls do not fall under the domain and authority of rogue engineers.

In October 2015 Volkswagen admitted to the EPA that its 2016 diesel engines, which had not yet been approved for importation by the EPA, "have a new type of engine software also designed to help the exhaust systems run cleaner during government tests." This new software makes a pollution control catalyst heat up faster, thus improving performance in lab tests.

Thus, it is apparent that the creation of deliberate cheating software to bypass U.S. emissions testing continued at Volkswagen well into late 2015, even though the automaker had been notified by EPA and CARB of irregularities in test results some 15 months earlier.

Had the Diselgate scandal not become public when it did, chances are an entire new model year of vehicles would now be on U.S. roads and likely emitting higher than permissible NOx particles into the air.

THE FIRST CONVICTION REVEALS MORE DETAILS

In September 2016 we learned more details of the defeat device software when long-time Volkswagen engineer James Robert Liang pleaded guilty in U.S. federal court to a single charge of conspiring to defraud the United States, commit wire fraud and violate the U.S. Clean Air Act.

Liang's guilty plea is part of a plea arrangement that requires him to cooperate with the ongoing criminal investigation by the U.S. Department of Justice. Most observers see this plea deal as an indication that the Justice Department will seek to charge others, especially since Liang pleaded guilty to a conspiracy charge.

Liang started working for Volkswagen in the automaker's diesel development department in Wolfsburg, Germany in 1983. In 2008 he was transferred to the United States to assist with the launch of Volkswagen's "clean diesel" vehicles. One of his roles, while working at the Volkswagen test facility in Oxnard, California, was as "leader of diesel competence," a position which reported directly to Volkswagen headquarters in Germany.

According to the 25-page indictment of Liang issued by a federal grand jury, which led to his guilty plea, Liang and other staff within Volkswagen reportedly knew in 2006 that Volkswagen's efforts to design its new "clean diesel" vehicles would not pass U.S. emissions standards while also delivering desired on-road performance. So they created and implemented the software defeat device program, making this a decade-long conspiracy to cheat on U.S. emissions testing.

The indictment says Liang conspired with current and former Volkswagen employees to mislead U.S. regulators about the software that enabled Volkswagen to circumvent national emissions standards and rules. In detailing a 10-year conspiracy by Volkswagen employees in both the U.S. and Germany the indictment also cites emails between Liang and co-workers that openly admit to the cheating.

As part of the plea agreement, Liang admitted that he and his (as yet) unnamed co-conspirators "misrepresented" that the Volkswagen diesel vehicles met U.S. emissions standards during certification meetings held with the EPA and the California Air Resources Board (CARB). He also admitted to hiding the existence of the defeat device software from both regulators.

Liang's lawyer said his client was "one of many at Volkswagen" involved in the scheme to design and implement the defeat device software.

Also according to documents filed in court, Liang and his fellow engineers at Volkswagen were also the team that enhanced the defeat device software. This came about after a rapid increase in warranty service claims by car owners caused by complaints about parts and components breaking down.

In analyzing the root cause behind these claims, Volkswagen engineers came to the conclusion that it was a result of the vehicles operating too long in "test mode" and not switching quickly enough to "road mode."

So Liang and his teammates upgraded the defeat device software so that it was more efficient at recognizing when the cars were either being tested or actually driven on the road. The upgraded software was pushed out to unsuspecting customers under the guise of service recalls that would help improve vehicle performance.

In the plea agreement Liang also admitted that he and his co-conspirators continued to lie to both the EPA and CARB even after these regulatory agencies began to ask questions about the emissions test results and actual vehicle emissions data.

The indictment references emails between Liang and other Volkswagen employees asking how to respond to CARB's concerns about the large discrepancies between the emissions of vehicles in laboratories and on the road. One email, written in German and sent to Liang and others in 2015 seeking suggestions on how to respond to CARB is said to include the sentence, "The key word creativity would be helpful here."

Later, Liang and other employees receive a group update email saying CARB was still waiting for answers and "we still have no good explanations!!!!!"

Liang faces up to five years in prison and a $250,000 fine. Sentencing was scheduled for January 11, 2017 but has since been postponed until May. We can probably expect additional Justice Department action on criminal charges or other plea arrangements to be announced before then.

HOW THE CHEATING SOFTWARE WORKS

The defeat device cheating software is designed to recognize when a vehicle is undergoing an emissions test in a laboratory or service bay. The software is able to sense vehicle test situations by monitoring speed, engine operation, air pressure, the lack of rear wheel axle movement during engine operations, and even the position and movement of the steering wheel.

When vehicles are placed in operation under a typical laboratory test condition, which usually requires placing the vehicle onto a stationary test rig, the software puts the engine management system into test mode.

Under the test mode conditions the engine runs below normal power and performance.

When the software detects such a test situation, it instructs the engine's management system to implement the engine's full pollution control and emissions filtering processes. This, however, leads to increased fuel consumption and, if engaged during actual road usage, impacts the car's all-important miles per gallon figures.

However, when the software detects that the vehicle is being operated on the road, it switches the engine management system out of test mode and reduces the pollution-filtering operations.

Thus, the software is designed to fully operate the emissions control systems only when it detects laboratory and service bay tests.

Also, since laboratory emissions tests are known to run for approximately 15-20 minutes, the software can also shut down the emissions particle filtering processes after the engine has been engaged for this length of time.

In many ways the cheating system was a clever solution and an innovative software program. Too bad it was blatantly illegal, not to mention the fact that it also meant these vehicles were emitting massive amounts of dangerous NOx pollutants into the air we breathe. As such, it is the antithesis of corporate social responsibility in anyone's book and should never have been allowed in over 11 million vehicles.

Some media reports say Volkswagen at one time actually developed a fix for new diesel vehicles which might have allowed their diesel engines to legitimately pass U.S. emissions tests. Instead, however, Volkswagen engineers updated the defeat device software and continued to game the emissions testing system.

But is Volkswagen solely to blame? Why did the automotive industry regulators, particularly in Europe and North America, remain oblivious to this emissions test cheating for over seven years? Why did numerous industry publications declare such cheating vehicles to be well-designed "green cars of the year" or "European car of the year"? Do industry journalists and publications simply take car manufacturer technical reports and self-assessed emissions data at face value carte blanche?

Over the past year the public has learned a tremendous amount about how automotive manufacturers manipulate and game laboratory emissions and fuel consumption tests.

Regulators are seemingly ill-equipped to monitor the automotive industry and thus allow all kinds of shenanigans by automakers so that laboratory tests produce better results.

For instance, no passengers or luggage (or their simulated weight) are used in laboratory tests, thus reducing the weight of the vehicles and correspondingly improving fuel consumption results. Additionally, consistent speeds are typically used in laboratory tests, rather than the stop-and-go traffic most drivers encounter. Also, air-conditioning and heating systems are not engaged during laboratory tests, even though few drivers use their vehicles without one or the other.

Other tricks included raising tire pressure and mixing fuel with motor oil, which enables an engine to run more smoothly while producing fewer emissions. Automakers are also known to improve aerodynamics by removing wing mirrors and taping up doors during emissions tests. One media report even stated that some automobile manufacturers use special tires made specifically to perform better on the test rig platform.

Additionally, laboratory tests are conducted in controlled temperature environments, a far cry from the excessive heat or frigid cold temperatures in which vehicles are typically driven.

Another method is to control the operating temperatures of emissions-reducing recirculation systems and particulate filters during laboratory tests. Auto manufacturers apparently shut down the filter systems in their vehicles at different temperatures in order to prolong the life of the parts involved. The result is that these systems will run at full effectiveness in temperature-controlled official laboratory tests, but will not be effective in everyday driving conditions outside optimum temperature ranges.

In other words, such laboratory emissions tests are actually far from replicating real-world driving conditions and true vehicle usage. Which means that these laboratory tests are basically open-book tests designed to enable vehicles to pass emissions restriction laws and rules enacted by lawmakers and regulators. As such, they have no basis in reality and no correlation to real-world driving conditions. Simply put the laboratory test results produced are more contrived fiction than fact.

WHY ISN'T THIS AN EASY FIX?

There are three reasons why it has not easy for Volkswagen to come up with a quick technical solution to bring its diesel engine vehicles up to emission control standards. After all, if it were, one thinks that Volkswagen would have installed this fix in the first place, rather than relying on its cheating defeat device software to get its vehicles through laboratory emissions tests.

First, Volkswagen's 2-liter, four-cylinder TDI diesel engine is a complicated piece of equipment and engineering. Its pollution emissions system comprises an exhaust particulate filter and three catalytic converters for oxidation, oxides of nitrogen (NOx), and hydrogen sulfide.

Basically the system uses a NOx trap and a diesel particulate filter to clean the engine's exhaust. The NOx trap absorbs the harmful, smog-causing oxides of nitrogen, while the particulate filter traps soot.

When the NOx trap becomes saturated with oxides of nitrogen the system runs a slightly modified cycle that pumps a bit of extra fuel into the exhaust system to burn off the trapped NOx.

Other diesel engines sold around the world use a selective catalytic reduction (SCR) system. This system requires a special urea solution, which adds cost, complexity, and additional regular maintenance. On the other hand, it works and legitimately passes U.S. emissions tests without the need for an illegal defeat device software solution.

The SCR system uses an oxidation catalytic converter in conjunction with a diesel particulate filter and a special SCR catalyst. It injects specific amounts of an aqueous urea solution into the vehicle's exhaust system, which then reacts with the SCR catalyst to dramatically reduce NOx by chemically converting it into nitrogen and water.

Volkswagen's engineering team was aware that the urea exhaust treatment system would help their new diesel engines meet U.S. emissions standards. But the $335 per vehicle price tag was deemed too high in 2005 since a company-wide cost-cutting exercise was underway. This decision led to the use of the defeat device software solution.

The second issue is that the range and variety of vehicles affected is staggering. The nearly half a million Volkswagen vehicles in the U.S. affected by the defeat device software comprise over a dozen different models from three distinct brands and four entirely different combinations of engines and emission systems. All spread over up to seven model years. And that's just for the 2-lier diesel engines. The problems with the 3-liter diesel engines are an entirely different matter. And, of course, there are different models and variations in Europe and other parts of the world that need fixing as well.

Thirdly, both Volkswagen and its car customers are worried that applying and installing any new hardware or software components may cause the vehicles to lose performance or reduce their miles-per-gallon efficiency. Many Volkswagen car owners are enamored with their vehicle's torque and power and thus are genuinely concerned that any fixes or solutions might impact these.

In fact, one of the early solutions derived by Volkswagen for its VW Passat and Skoda cars sold in Europe actually increased fuel consumption and thus CO_2 pollution output, when initially installed and tested. As a result, a planned recall of 160,000 vehicles had to be postponed until this unintended consequence could be rectified.

Additionally, Volkswagen's rapidly cobbled together first proposed solution for its 2-liter diesel engines did not pass mustard with CARB. In fact, CARB was scathing in its rejection of this proposed solution in February 2015, saying Volkswagen's proposed solution contained "gaps and lack sufficient detail." The statement went on to say, "The description of proposed repairs lack enough information for a technical evaluation, and the proposals do not adequately address overall impacts on vehicle performance, emissions, and safety."

Fortunately for Volkswagen, the less-restrictive environmental pollution laws in Europe means that it will be easier to install fixes in the 8.5 million cars affected on that continent.

However, while it may be easier and less costly for Volkswagen to fix its diesel engines in Europe, progress to date has been slow going. As of this writing, Volkswagen has repaired less than 10% of the 8.5 million affected models in Europe. In late September the automaker was still saying that the majority of these 8.5 million vehicles should be repaired in 2016, with an unspecified number to be fixed by early 2017. However, as of late September 2016, Germany's KBA motor vehicle authority had granted approval to proposed fixes designed to fix the problems in only about 5.1 million vehicles, leaving a significant gap to be closed.

The automaker received an early Christmas present in mid-December when KBA finally granted approval for repairs on all vehicles sold within Europe fitted with the illicit emissions test cheating software.

So, why Volkswagen was not able to achieve any of its optimistic targets for fixing impacted vehicles in Europe, it appears that European car owners will finally receive their repairs and remedies during 2017.

CHAPTER THREE

Wide-Spread Impact

The Volkswagen diesel emissions scandal and its various tributaries and offshoots have had a far-reaching impact on a wide range of parties. This impact has been financial, environmental, regulatory, political, emotional, and eye-opening. The parties affected include car owners, Volkswagen's leadership team and employees, shareholders, car dealers, government officials, regulatory agencies, the media, the automotive industry, and even the Made-in-Germany brand.

In addition, the Volkswagen saga has impacted the automaker's car brands, leadership structure, governance, corporate reputation, current and future financial results, and (hopefully) its future corporate culture. These topics will be specifically covered in subsequent chapters.

I say "hopefully" in the paragraph above because only a change in the Volkswagen corporate culture — along with corresponding changes in its leadership and governance structures — will likely prevent future cheating and deliberate malfeasance from happening again. I will explain why in chapter five on Corporate Governance Lessons.

For now, let's review some of the direct impacts this scandal has had on the key constituents listed in the opening paragraph above.

CAR OWNERS

Volkswagen's vehicle customers who own the affected cars have gone through over a year of angst, anxiety, uncertainty, and, in many cases, downright anger over being misled about the environmental credentials of the cars they purchased and drive.

For many people, an automobile is the second largest investment or expense in their lives, after home ownership. As such, these are considered purchases. Car brands and models are often a reflection of an individual's taste, preferences, lifestyle, and projected persona. Such reflections are not to be screwed with, particularly if an automaker wants to develop long-term brand loyalty.

Volkswagen car owners have seen the resale value of their vehicles drop dramatically since the diesel emissions test cheating became public. They have been exposed to scores of media reports about potential fixes, possible buybacks of their vehicles by Volkswagen, and even direct compensation. They have had to endure months of uncertainty as to whether any solutions created by Volkswagen will impact the performance of their cars or the enjoyment they get from driving their vehicles.

And this has been the same, although at different levels of uncertainty, for Volkswagen car owners in dozens of countries around the world.

Greater certainty for car owners in the U.S. came only in late October 2016 when Judge Breyer accepted the negotiated agreement settlement. In most other markets uncertainty for car owners remains unabated.

For Volkswagen car owners outside North America there has also been the inconvenience and personal time required to take their vehicles to dealers to have solutions installed once their vehicles have been recalled.

VOLKSWAGEN EMPLOYEES

The company's employees have also experienced over a year of angst, anxiety, and uncertainty. Rumors continue to swirl about potential layoffs and other cost reductions (such as reduced shift work) to enable Volkswagen to pay the fines and other costs associated with this scandal.

Additionally, their individual and collective beliefs in Volkswagen's leadership has been severely dented, if not completely shattered.

Hundreds of employees have been subjected to investigator interviews and queries. Those and may others have had their computers dissected and inspected and their emails scrutinized.

Another worrisome indicator for employees of the belt-tightening to come came in November 2015 when the supervisory board of Volkswagen announced it will cap spending on property, plant, and equipment at around 12B euros ($12.8B) for 2016, an 8% reduction on its previous capital expenditure plan of around 13B euros.

Concerns that workers may have to bear the brunt of the compensation load for the company's wrongdoing has led Bernd Osterloh, the head of the automaker's powerful works council, to declare, "Do not make guinea pigs for economic experiments out of the 215,000 employees at the Volkswagen brand." The works council represents Volkswagen employees in all matters except wages.

An IG Metall union official said that under the current labor agreement between the union and the automaker that Volkswagen is contractually and legally prohibited from laying off any union workers. But this contract is subject to renegotiation and has not staved off employee jitters and worries.

These fears continue to have a firm foundation in fact, as Volkswagen has already announced that 3000 office jobs would be eliminated by the end of 2107. Volkswagen has said these job cuts would come through normal employee attrition, early retirement programs, transferring office workers to vacant positions, and by allowing temporary employment contracts to expire.

Of course, any variance from these stated plans will be an additional nail in the coffin of trust between Volkswagen workers and the company's leadership.

Things became more ominous around the time the $15.3B Settlement Agreement was accepted by U.S. District Court Judge Breyer. In October 2016, Volkswagen HR chief Karlheinz Blessing, a member of the nine-person Volkswagen AG supervisory board, said he expects up to 25,000 staff to be cut at the automaker over the next decade as older workers retire. While reaffirming that no forced dismissals are forthcoming, he said that cuts in production jobs were anticipated since the assembly of electric car engines requires fewer workers than current combustion engines.

At the same time, the company's works council, which has almost half the seats on the Volkswagen management board, said it would not back retrenchments without a commitment from Volkswagen's leaders to fix targets and quotas for products, output, and investment. This was in response to VW brand head Herbert Diess's announced plans to cut annual costs in the VW division by 3.7B euros ($4.1B) through 2021 via a revised "future pack" with employees.

In November 2016, a senior Volkswagen manager attending the launch of an updated version of the VW Golf hatchback in Germany told a reporter from the Reuters news agency, "It's undeniable that cost discipline has become the name of the game at VW."

VOLKSWAGEN LEADERSHIP

The first casualty of the diesel emissions test cheating was CEO Martin Winterkorn. Herr Winterkorn had been at the helm of Volkswagen for nine years and was the highest paid CEO on Germany's blue-chip DAX stock market in 2014.

The shakeup of the leadership team continued a few weeks later with the announcement of Hans Dieter Poetsch, the automotive group's Chief Financial Officer, as the new Volkswagen AG Chairman. He filled a position vacated by Ferdinand Piech, who had resigned six months earlier. Poetsch, in turn, was replaced as CFO by Frank Witter.

In subsequent months the automaker also brought in two outsiders to its management board: Christina Hohmann-Dennhardt, the compliance chief at rival Daimler to handle integrity and legal affairs, and Thomas Sedran, the interim CEO at Opel in 2012-13 and the former head of the General Motors Chevrolet and Cadillac brands in Europe, to run group strategy.

These are significant changes to the top tier leadership of the Volkswagen Group. But are they enough? We will discuss the impact of these changes in chapters four (Corporate Leadership Lessons) and five (Corporate Governance Lessons).

SHAREHOLDERS

Investors in Volkswagen AG saw their shareholdings free fall over 23% in the first two weeks after the scandal broke publicly, reducing Volkswagen's market value by over 25B euros ($27.5B)

Within another few weeks, it had dropped by more than 40% from its pre-scandal levels.

Naturally, shareholders were not impressed by such losses in their portfolios. This is especially true for some of the larger pension fund investors, several of which have filed lawsuits against Volkswagen in attempts to recover some or all of their losses.

Some of the most activist shareholders — such as Hermes EOS and Norway's Norgen Bank Investment Management (NBIM) — are also not impressed with the governance structure of Volkswagen AG. Dr. Hans-Christoph Hirt, co-head of Hermes EOS publicly encouraged Volkswagen shareholders to vote against the discharge of both the management and supervisory boards of the automaker at the annual general meeting in June 2016. Meanwhile, NBIM publicly criticized the ownership structure of Volkswagen AG, saying too much power is concentrated in the Porsche-Piech family and that this puts minority shareholders at a disadvantage.

At the Volkswagen AG annual general meeting in June 2016, DSW, which represents shareholders in Germany, tried to force through a proposal mandating an outside investigation into the Volkswagen diesel emissions test cheating circumstances and history. Naturally, with the three main shareholders in Volkswagen owning 89% of the voting rights, this valiant effort was easily defeated and dismissed.

Shareholders also had their own anxiety and angst to deal with as they confronted numerous media rumors in March that Volkswagen might not pay a dividend in order to stash away more cash for scandal-related costs. This eventually proved not to be true.

In fact, the supervisory board discussions to eliminate the 2016 dividend payment may have actually been part of an internal power play to dilute the Lower Saxony government's voting powers. This will be covered in chapter five on lessons for corporate governance.

VOLKSWAGEN CAR DEALERS

Dealers in the U.S. were already on edge with Volkswagen before the emissions test cheating scandal blew up in their faces.

To begin with, media reports say that Volkswagen dealers invested over \$1B in new facilities over the past decade to support the automaker's ambitions of selling 800,000 VWs in the United States by 2018 (and one million cars in total including Audi, Porsche, and Bentley models).

That target was already out of reach when the scandal hit. Volkswagen car sales in the U.S. had actually fallen in each of the previous three years and were hovering around the 350,000 level for 2015.

According to an article in *Automotive News* (March 16, 2016) dealers had also been complaining about mismanaged supplies and model allocations. In early 2016 they also became worried about "ominous signals" from Volkswagen's newly installed leadership team concerning the automaker's commitment to the U.S. market.

The new chief of the VW brand Herbert Diess fueled speculation about Volkswagen's commitment to the U.S. market when he pondered out loud at the Detroit Auto Show in January 2016 whether VW could continue to compete with mass-market brands like Honda and Toyota. He even suggested that the Volkswagen Group might be better off with a strategy that focuses on near-premium products only for the U.S. market, which would mean lower volumes for both VW and its heavily invested dealer network.

At the end of August, nearly a year after the test cheating story broke, Volkswagen told a U.S. court that it will pay compensation to its network of 652 dealers hit by the scandal. Volkswagen revealed in a court filing in October 2015 that the price tag is in the neighborhood of \$1.2B. Each dealership will receive around \$1.85M, with the payments spread out over 18 months. This is in addition to other incentives and reimbursements that Volkswagen has already shelled out to dealers for vehicles that were unable to be sold.

GOVERNMENT OFFICIALS AND REGULATORS

Regulators around the world, but most significantly in the European Union and the United States, have egg on their respective faces for not knowing about the deliberate diesel emissions test cheating by Volkswagen, despite the fact that the cheat device software had been installed in vehicles for seven consecutive model years.

In fact, it wasn't even government regulators who detected the cheating by Volkswagen. It was the non-profit organization International Council on Clean Transport (ICCT) which, in collaboration with the Center for Alternative Fuels, Engines and Emissions department at West Virginia University, which figured out that the laboratory test results were significantly different than the on-road real-world emission test results. They then alerted EPA and CARB of their findings and suspicions in 2014.

Surprisingly, the EPA did not conduct its own tests to verify or validate the ICCT results. Instead, it basically sent a "please explain" request to Volkswagen in May 2014.

This enabled Volkswagen to enter into a series of back-and-forth discussions and communications with EPA and CARB for over a year. Meanwhile, EPA and CARB continued to allow these cars to keep emitting illegally high levels of NOx into the air across the country. Why?

While EPA now looks like a hero for leveraging the U.S. Department of Justice to force a punitive settlement with Volkswagen, it should also be held accountable for allowing these emissions to continue unabated for over 30 months since being notified by ICCT.

In Europe, while the environmental regulations on NOx emissions are not as stringent as in the United States, the European Union regulators acted much faster upon learning (from the EPA announcement) of Volkswagen's diesel emissions test cheating defeat device. Within weeks, KBA, the German Federal Motor Transport Authority, ordered a recall of all affected cars in Germany (estimated at 2.8 million). This had the effect of being applied across all of the European Union. So, in essence, all 8.5 million vehicles in Europe were subject to recall within a month of European Union regulators becoming aware of the issue.

However, the recalls do not take effect until KBA has approved the fixes created by Volkswagen. Thus, while the recall requirement happened quickly, the actual recalls and corrective measures are taking well over a year to be implemented.

This fast reaction by European regulators — especially KBA — however, does not diminish their own accountability for not finding the cheating in the first place. Many are quick to blame the cozy relationship between national regulators in Europe and the automotive industry for this failing. And there is plenty of evidence to support such suspicions.

"The issue is a systemic one" across the industry, according to Nick Molden of Emissions Analytics. He is quoted in the *Guardian* newspaper (October 9, 2015) as saying, "The VW issue in the U.S. was purely the trigger which threw light on a slightly different problem in the EU — widespread legal over-emissions."

Adds Friend of the Earth air pollution campaigner Jenny Bates in the same article, "With further manufacturers implicated, this is yet more evidence that this scandal goes way beyond VW, and should cause decision-makers to question the very future of diesel vehicles on our roads. This is a massive health disgrace and the failure to prevent vehicles breaking pollution rules will have cost lives."

Yet, over a year later, very little has been done by regulators in Europe to enforce the emissions and air pollution rules and regulations already on the books.

Not too surprisingly, the European Automobile Manufacturers' Association (ACEA) jumped into the fray and tried to stave off European

Union action on real-world, on-road emissions testing. The industry association proclaims that a "tougher European emissions testing regime could mean small diesel car models are withdrawn." It claims implementing real driving emissions laws would mean new technology to curb pollution and that this *could* (emphasis mine) add weight and costs to vehicles.

Is there widespread test-gaming in the automotive industry? Undoubtedly yes. And any movement to reduce such test gaming over the short term will have significant impact and consequences for car manufacturers. However, it would also have significant positive health impact and consequences for the citizens these emissions and air pollution rules, and the enforcement regulators, are supposedly protecting.

In fact, research from Transport & Environment (T&E) in the U.K. shows that, as of September 2016, not a single car brand meets the Euro 6 air pollution limits when driven on the road. This diesel emissions standard is only achieved under laboratory test conditions.

T&E evaluated emissions test data from approximately 230 car models with diesel engines. Their tests, based on real-world driving conditions, showed that cars made by Fiat, Suzuki, and Renault emit up to 15 times that allowed by the European standard for nitrogen oxide (NOx).

"We've had this focus on Volkswagen as a 'dirty carmaker,' but when you look at the emissions of other manufacturers you find there are no really clean (diesel) carmakers," said Greg Archer, clean vehicles director at T&E in an article in the *Guardian* newspaper (September 19, 2016). He adds, "Volkswagen is not the carmaker producing the diesel cars with the highest nitrogen oxides emissions and the failure to investigate other companies brings disgrace on the European regulatory system."

The European Union parliamentary inquiry into both the Volkswagen diesel emission test cheating and the regulatory oversight of the automotive industry across the EU may last into the spring of 2017 or perhaps even longer. Hence European citizens should not anticipate any resolution to this cozy situation any time soon.

THE MEDIA

The media, especially automotive trade journals, have lost credibility as well from the Volkswagen saga. After all, how can we believe all of these "prestigious awards" they give out, many with big-name jurors on their selection panels, when it is now obvious that these publications do no investigation at all into the validity of car maker claims?

Sure, I understand that trade media are not investigative journalists. And, of course, they do not want to do anything to upset their valuable advertisers and automotive industry subscribers.

But how can we take them seriously now that we have found out several of their "Green Cars of the Year" and other category award winners were actually spewing out noxious and dangerous pollutants at up to 40 times permitted levels? Should consumers and car buyers put any faith at all in their awards?

And the same goes true for any future pronouncements from RobecoSAM, the group that gave Volkswagen the title of "the world's most sustainable car company" just nine days before the EPA announcement of the first Notice of Violation. How many no longer trust their sustainability investment advice?

AUTOMOTIVE INDUSTRY

The Volkswagen saga is only the latest in a long line of scandals to hit the automotive industry. From the gas tank exploding Ford Pintos of the

1970s to the millions of Takata air bags being recalled today, this is an industry teeming with scandalous safety and environmental issues.

It is also an industry plagued with cheating. In the first year since the Volkswagen Dieselgate scandal broke, several other auto manufacturers have been caught out or admitted wrongdoing with regards to emissions data, fuel consumption figures, pollution control equipment, or safety issues, including:

Mitsubishi Motors admitting that it incorrectly reported gas mileage consumption figures on almost all its vehicles sold in Japan since 1991, a 25-year period, as well as on two mini vehicles it produced for Nissan Motor Co.

Renault recalling 15,000 vehicles with faulty pollution filtering systems.

Citroën, Fiat, Honda, Hyundai, Jeep, Mazda, Mercedes-Benz, Mitsubishi Motors, Nissan, Renault, Volvo and other car brands emitting more greenhouse gasses than advertised, according to independent studies of real-world driving conditions as opposed to laboratory testing.

Suzuki Motor Corp disclosing it has been using improper methods to test fuel economy on more than 2.1 million vehicles.

Five automakers (plus Volkswagen) raided by German antitrust regulators as part of a probe into steel price fixing allegations. Reports suggest the six car manufacturers may have formed a cartel to keep the price of steel used to make car parts low.

Fiat Chrysler is under a U.S. federal fraud investigation of allegations that the make of Dodge and Jeep vehicles inflated sales figures.

In the past year Fiat Chrysler has also faced financial penalties for safety problems that included lapses with recalls covering millions of vehicles and regulatory reporting failures.

Honda and Chrysler fined $70M each by the U.S. Department of Transportation for failing to forward consumer complaints to the National Highway Traffic Safety Administration (NHTSA) as required by law. Honda's civil penalty is due to failure to report 1729 deaths and injury claims to NHTSA between 2003 and 2014. Fiat Chrysler America was fined after acknowledging significant failures in early warning reporting dating back to the beginning of the mandatory program in 2003.

Toyota Motor Corp reportedly agrees to a settlement of up to $3.4B to resolve a federal class-action suit brought by U.S. owners of pickup trucks and sport utility vehicles (SUVs) whose frames could rust through. The proposed settlement covers about 1.5 million Tacoma compact pickups, Tundra full-size pickups, and Sequoia SUVs alleged to have received inadequate rust protection that could lead to serious corrosion impacting the structural integrity of the vehicles.

Nissan, BMW, and Porsche facing allegations in South Korea of falsifying documents to obtain road certifications.

And a Bloomberg report in November 2015 says that Volkswagen failed to report at least one death and three injuries involving its vehicles to the U.S. National Highway Traffic Safety Administration's database designed to save lives by spotting possible vehicle defects. A week prior to the Bloomberg report Volkswagen said it was commissioning an outside audit of its compliance with U.S. safety laws.

Interestingly, the current defeat device scandal is not Volkswagen's first brush with either the EPA or the U.S. Clean Air Act. In 1974 the automaker paid a $120,000 fine to settle a complaint filed by the EPA over the use of defeat devices that disabled certain pollution control systems in four Volkswagen models produced in 1973.

Also, for years the German government lobbied its European Union counterparts against higher regulations on emissions. The German automotive industry employs over 750,000 workers and is a major driver of export income for the German economy.

"The car industry is crucial for the German economy," Deputy Finance Minister Jens Spadru is quoted as telling a conference just weeks after the scandal exploded. "It (the scandal) can have a big impact on the German economy," he added.

This is a heavyweight industry. And it knows how to throw its weight around.

Hence it is not too surprising to read in the *Wall Street Journal* (November 12, 2015) that "German Chancellor Angela Merkel intervened on behalf of German automakers with California environment authorities about the state's tough emissions rules, saying they were hurting German manufacturers, according to a spokesman for California's environment agency." The article, quoting from a report published in the German magazine *WirtschaftsWoche* describes a meeting at the Beverly Hills Four Seasons hotel on April 14, 2010 between California Governor Arnold

Schwarzenegger, Chancellor Merkel, and California Air Resources Board head Mary Nichols:

> *Instead of addressing the governor, Ms. Merkel addressed Ms. Nichols.*

> *Ms. Merkel's "first comment to me after the doors closed was a complaint...that California with its very strict nitrogen oxide limits is hurting German car makers," Ms. Nichols said, according to the magazine.*

> *Ms. Nichols said she was surprised that Ms. Merkel had such specific knowledge of the problems with nitrogen oxide emissions that German manufacturers faced.*

> *"I never experienced a similar intervention against our environment laws by a politician either before or after," Ms. Nichols is quoted as saying.*

AN ISSUE OF TRUST

Should consumers trust any of the data being given to them by automakers and their dealers? One wonders.

In fact, research shows that consumers have very little trust in the automotive industry.

The annual Edelman Trust Barometer survey in Germany in 2016 showed a remarkable collapse in the trust of the automotive industry. In the survey, consumers were asked to "please indicate how much you trust businesses in each of the following industries to do what is right." The automotive industry sector dropped from a 61% score in 2015 to a 41% level in 2016.

This is a shocking result, especially since the automotive industry had seen steady increases from a 51% level in 2012 to a high of 62% trust level in 2014. Whereas the automotive industry was tied with the technology sector for top honors in Germany in 2014 and 2015, it sank to third lowest in the 2016 survey results.

An Autolist survey of 2,387 vehicle owners across all 50 U.S. states in December 2015 and January 2016 showed that the Volkswagen scandal had a significant impact on how American drivers viewed both Volkswagen and the automotive industry.

The survey results showed a 12% decline in trust levels for the auto industry and an 18% decline in perceptions of German engineering quality.

Not surprisingly, Volkswagen took an enormous hit in this survey as well, with drops of 27% in the perception of the quality of Volkswagen automobiles, a 28% decrease in willingness to consider buying a Volkswagen vehicle, and a stunning 47% drop in how Volkswagen's environmental consciousness is viewed.

In addition, 62% of survey respondents felt the Volkswagen emissions scandal was "very severe" in terms of the environmental impact and 66% said it was "very severe" in terms of the legal impact.

Interestingly, consumers saw the BP oil spill in the Gulf of Mexico as a more severe environmental disaster by only a 3 to 1 margin.

The lack of consumer trust in the automotive industry has not gone unnoticed by some lawmakers. In June 2015 Britain's Transport Secretary Patrick McLoughlin said that the entire car manufacturing industry must work on restoring public trust. "Following the Volkswagen emissions scandal, the whole of the automotive industry must work hard to restore public confidence by being transparent about the systems they employ and advancing plans for introducing cleaner engine technology," Minister McLoughlin said.

Regulators will also need to play their role in helping to restore the public's trust in the auto industry. They can start with insisting on making real-world, on-road emissions testing the standard for reporting of emissions and fuel consumption.

It is somewhat surprising that there has not yet been a greater and more vocal call for revamping the regulation of the automotive industry, particularly from environmentally conscious consumers and political groups. I suspect the long, drawn-out, and nasty U.S. election process over the past two years has put such calls on hold until later this year. However, we can no longer allow the automotive industry to continuously put profits before public health. Reform is certainly in order.

Such reforms need to include mandatory compliance with emissions rules based on independent, transparent, and real-world driving conditions. If nothing else, Dieselgate has taught us naïve and unaware consumers that official laboratory tests have almost nothing in common with actual driving conditions and accurate emissions levels.

It is obvious that Volkswagen is not the only automotive manufacturer gaming the system. The entire automotive industry appears to have a long history of deceiving regulators, manipulating pollution standards, and stage-managing fuel consumption data. While done in the pursuit of sales and profits, these shenanigans and trickeries have been detrimental to public health, the air we all breathe, and our environment.

In chapter eight we will look at the lessons for corporate responsibility. A question for the automotive industry — how can consumers and governments trust this industry to act on climate change? When will this industry put public health before profits?

MADE IN GERMANY BRAND

The quality and sophistication of Germany's highly regarded engineering competency have long been badges of honor for the country. The Made in Germany label represents quality engineering and high-quality technical solutions.

These positive brand attributes have helped German companies offset high labor costs by enabling them to charge higher prices products perceived to be more upscale, reliable, premium, and technologically savvy.

Unfortunately, several research studies have shown that the Volkswagen saga has put a dent in both the Made in Germany brand and in German pride.

This was acknowledged in February 2016 by Germany's Vice Chancellor Sigmar Gabriel, who is also the country's economy minister. "Industrial production stands for quality that one can trust," he said. "These champions project a positive image for Germany that is good for all of us. And when it doesn't work, as currently is the case with Volkswagen, then it risks causing collective damage to the Made in Germany label that goes beyond the company."

The crisis is also a national embarrassment for Germany, which for years has showcased Volkswagen as a model of the country's engineering prowess and expertise.

IS VOLKSWAGEN TOO BIG TO FAIL?

When I first heard of the EPA's announcement of its first Notice of Violation, my immediate feeling was this could be the end of Volkswagen as we know it. With potential fines in the tens of billions of dollars, this was always going to become a mammoth financial hurdle for the company. I envisioned the possibility of the company being broken up into little pieces, with the various brands of Audi, Porsche, SEAT, VW, Bentley, and Ducati being sold off to the various bidders.

And that could still happen, if the European Union or its member states ever impose a U.S.-style settlement agreement or significant civil fines or criminal penalties on Volkswagen.

But the truth is, Volkswagen probably is too big and too important for government authorities to allow it to fail. In 2016 it ranked as the seventh largest company on the Global Fortune 500 list (based on revenue).

The company has a global workforce of over 610,000 people, which means well over half a million families around the world are dependent on salaries and income from Volkswagen for their daily subsistence and discretionary spending.

Add to that the thousands of suppliers to the company, all employing thousands of more workers whose families rely on the continued existence of Volkswagen for their own existence.

Now add many hundreds of car dealers around the world, again with thousands of employees whose incomes are important to thousands of more families.

And then there is the global economy to consider. The demise of Volkswagen would impact global shipping, major supplier industries such as steel, parts and component manufacturers, real estate markets, and even the agricultural businesses supplying food to these hundreds of thousands of families dependent on this giant automaker.

So yes, Volkswagen probably is too big to be allowed to crumble into history along the likes of Enron, EF Hutton, and other corporate bad boys.

But this does not mean it is too big to be punished for its sins.

European Automotive Industry Supervision

Air pollution has been called the single largest environmental health risk in Europe. A report published in November 2015 by the European Environment Agency (EEA) estimates that air pollution is responsible for over 430,000 premature deaths annually across Europe.

The EEA report cited particulate matter (PM), ground level ozone (O_3), and nitrogen dioxide (NO_2) as the three most problematic air pollutants impacting human health across the continent. Those living in cities were the most exposed to air pollutants at levels deemed unsafe by the World Health Organization (WHO).

With the air quality standards in Europe significantly lower than WHO guidelines, the EEA report stated that meeting WHO air quality standards would result in 144,000 fewer premature deaths. It also pointed out that 93% of nitrogen dioxide (NO_2) exceedances occur close to roads. The EEA report estimated premature deaths attributed to NO_2 exposure at 75,000 per year. With almost half of all vehicles in Europe running on diesel, the connection between the EEA report and the nitrogen oxide (NO_x) emissions of diesel vehicles becomes obvious.

104 • STEVEN B HOWARD

One would think that European Union parliamentarians, as well as their national legislative colleagues, would make reducing these premature deaths a priority. But, of course, any solution — such as stricter enforcement of vehicle emissions rules — would have economic consequences.

As the European Commission's own website states, the automotive industry "is crucial for Europe's prosperity. The sector provides jobs for 12 million people and accounts for 4% of EU's GDP."

In January 2016 the European Commission, the executive arm of the 28-member European Union, announced proposals to take control of automotive regulation in Europe, including new powers to impose fines and recall vehicles.

"With our proposals today we will raise the quality and independence of vehicle testing and improve oversight of cars already in circulation," EU Industry Commissioner Elzbieta Bienkowska said in a statement.

The proposals are part of a massive overhaul of the European Union's car approval system, and would give the European Commission powers over national car regulators. Under the proposed rules car manufacturers found cheating on pollution tests could face a fine of 30,000 euros ($32,600) per vehicle. Additionally, non-compliant cars could be taken off European roads.

Included in the proposed rules are requirements for automakers to submit data on the software protocols for all vehicles, as this would help EU regulators spot emissions test cheating defeat device software. The new legislation would also grant authority to European Commission scientists to perform random vehicle checks.

This is a good test to see if government and regulatory attitudes have changed after the embarrassing revelations of the Volkswagen cheating scandals and subsequent disclosures that no automotive manufacturers meet the EU emissions rules during on-road testing. However, a year later, these proposals are still going through negotiations between EU lawmakers and continue to face tremendous scrutiny and lobbying from national governments and the powerful automotive industry.

In early December 2016 the European Commission began legal action against Britain, Germany, Luxembourg, and Spain for failing to catch and penalize emissions test cheating by automotive manufacturers. Three other member states were cited for not having sufficient rules and regulations in place.

The move comes after mounting pressure on the European Commission from the European Parliament and others to clamp down on what many see as excessive collusion between the powerful automotive industry and national governments.

This action aims to force member nations to remove diesel cars from the roads and prevent them from spewing dangerous levels of nitrogen oxide (NOx) pollutants into the air. "This goes beyond Volkswagen," an EU source told the Reuters news agency.

This initial step by the European Commission is called an infringement procedure, which enables the European Union executive to ensure the 28 member nations abide by EU-wide regulations. The seven nations cited have two months to respond, failing which the Commission may take them to the EU court in Luxembourg.

The action comes after several national investigations have revealed that many carmakers in Europe use questionable techniques to help them pass national emissions tests. This includes probes in Britain, France, Germany, and Italy which have revealed the use of defeat devices in cars licensed to operate in these countries.

By the carmakers counter claims of illicit activity by saying there is an exemption which allows emission control systems to be turned off when necessary for safety or to protect engines. It is a large legal loophole widely exploited by the automotive industry, particularly since the car manufacturers get to say what constitutes "a need to protect an engine."

However, Europe's Industry Commissioner Elzbieta Bienkowska has repeatedly said the letter of the EU law is clear and that member states should respect the spirit of these laws.

In this action the European Commission accused Germany, Luxembourg, Spain, and the U.K. of failing to introduce adequate penalties that would deter future emissions test cheating similar is to Volkswagen's use of the illegal defeat device software in its vehicles (which Volkswagen claims is not an illegal defeat device under EU law).

According to ClientEarth lawyer Alan Andres, "By the government's own admission, pollution from diesel cars is one of the main reasons the UK is breaking legal air pollution limits, and the government has been ordered repeatedly to tackle illegal levels of NOx pollution as soon as possible. Yet the government has inexplicably failed to take action even where the car industry has knowingly put people's health at risk for years. This kind of deception demands a strong response by authorities, and since the government failed to provide it, the EU is stepping in."

The European Commission also accused Germany and the U.K. of failing to disclose the details of suspicious findings uncovered in their respective national investigations of emissions test cheating. The EU regulators say sharing such information is vital to carrying out the Commission's supervisory role.

Lastly, the European Commission also claimed that the Czech Republic, Greece, and Lithuania lack provisions in their respective national legislations for assessing fines against automakers that violate emissions rules.

While the European Commission actions are admirable, there are two major factors playing significant roles in why Europe's many regulatory bodies have been slow to respond to the excessive emissions levels of vehicles exposed by the Volkswagen saga. One is internal to the European Commission and the other is external.

First, the internal issue.

Leaked documents and correspondence between the European Commission's enterprise departments (known as DG Enterprise) and its environmental policy and enforcement division (known as DG Environment) depicts a battle between these two branches of the European Union executive.

The DG Environment sector wants to see the Real Driving Emissions (RDE) tests implemented as quickly as possible, while the DG Enterprise section argues for delays in implementation that are of benefit to the automotive industry. In one piece of correspondence from 2012, the DG Enterprise side stated that "the probability of rejecting vehicles by the RDE test procedure...has to be kept low."

Naturally, the DG Environment folks are more concerned with enforcing EU emissions standards and warned that the proposed delay would "violate EU pollution regulation."

I suspect the DG Enterprise team will most likely win this internal battle. For one thing, looking at the European Commission's website, there is zero mention of the environment, clean air, or sustainable living on the home page listing of its top priorities. However, "Jobs, Growth and Investment" is shown as the #1 priority. Listed as the third priority is "Energy Union and Climate."

Clicking on the Energy Union and Climate item for more details, we see the goal to be "making energy more secure, affordable and sustainable." Again, no reference to environmental protection, clean air, or sustainable living. It seems like the DG Environment branch is fighting a rearguard action within the European Commission.

Now for the external issue — the level of collusion and closeness between the automotive industry and national regulators.

As mentioned before, the automotive industry is a heavyweight and powerful sector of the European economy. It directly employs over 12 million people across the 28 member states in the European Union. And it indirectly employs millions more in supplier, distribution, and support industries. In a region where economic growth has been stagnant to slow for many years, few politicians or regulators want to put such a large employer at risk.

One example of the typical collusion seen between a national regulator and a major automotive manufacturer was revealed in the German magazine *Stern* in November 2016. According to German Transport Ministry documents leaked to *Stern,* Volkswagen worked closely with the ministry to defuse the 2015 CO_2 emissions problem the automaker learned it had just two months after the diesel engine emissions test cheating surfaced.

In November 2015 Volkswagen had publicly admitted that the carmaker's employees had lowered CO_2 emissions figures on 800,000 vehicles. As in the Dieselgate problem, the emissions discrepancies showed up between laboratory testing and real-world, on-road driving tests. However, a month later Volkswagen revised the figure of impacted vehicles to just 36,000 cars based on "thorough internal tests and measurement checks."

But that may not have been the whole story. According to the *Stern* article, in between these two announcements two lawyers from Volkswagen met with the Transport Ministry to advise regulators that the automaker was changing its official position. Instead of blaming its own employees for a mistake, Volkswagen would claim "that up to now it could not be decided what reasons lay behind the too-high CO_2 figures."

In addition, a leaked transcript of the meeting has the lawyers telling the ministry that Volkswagen was backing away from a previous commitment to measure emissions according to "tougher standards." According to the transcript, the ministry officials present at the meeting "took note of this consentingly."

Additionally, earlier in 2016 the German newspaper *Bild* exposed a joint cover-up by the German Federal Motor Authority (KBA) and the auto industry. Apparently, KBA discovered in April 2016 that CO_2 emissions are significantly higher than officially stated on 30 of the 54 vehicles it tested. *Bild* cited emails in its report showing that the auto industry influenced the KBA report on these tests. The magazine also reported that KBA chief Ekhard Zinke signed one email using the salutation of "with industry-friendly regards."

Additionally, in the United Kingdom, Norman Baker, the Transport Minister in 2010-2013, claimed that Prime Minister David Cameron delayed imposing new emissions limits in Britain following a personal request from German Chancellor Angela Merkel in order to protect the German motor industry.

Chairwoman of the UK transport select committee Louise Ellman said Minister Baker's claims raised serious questions over the effectiveness and independence of the country's automotive testing regime. "There is certainly a major question about the influence of the motor industry against the interest of the public," she said on BBC radio.

The importance of the automotive industry across Europe is staggering, so much so that national governments are willing to forsake additional annual revenues by allowing automakers to game the emissions testing process and their all-important reported fuel consumption figures.

While questions are raised, little action has been taken by either the European Commission or national legislatures. The proposals from a year ago by the European Commission continue to face debate as national governments and the auto industry resist change.

In many European countries cars are taxed based on the levels of CO_2 they emit, among other factors. By knowingly allowing car manufacturers to report lower CO_2 emissions than what is actually emitted in real-world driving conditions, governments deprive themselves of increased tax revenues. The German environmental group DUH estimates this lost revenue at 2.2B euros annually.

In addition, car owners reportedly pay an extra $450 to $500 per annum in fuel costs than what they could have expected based on the purposely higher rated fuel economy figures automotive manufacturers are allowed to report.

Emissions testing procedures and actual on-road emissions levels are topics that are not going to fade away anytime soon in Europe.

In fact, a report in late December on new emissions tests conducted by the European Commission's Joint Research Center adds more fuel to these fiery discussions. According to media reports on the yet-to-be-released study, tests conducted in August 2016 on several diesel engine vehicles revealed elevated NOx emissions on models from Ford Motor Co. and Citroën.

In addition, the study reportedly concludes that a car from Audi produced higher NOx emissions outside of routine test conditions, which may indicate the use of a defeat device not previously disclosed.

A spokeswoman for European Union Industry Commissioner Elzbieta Bienkowska said in December 2016 the Joint Research Center report was undergoing an internal assessment as it had only recently been provided to the European Parliament's emissions investigation committee. At the time of this writing the report has yet to be published and the impact on Audi and its parent Volkswagen AG, if any, are unknown.

Interestingly one report I read said the Joint Research Center had tested the Audi 2-liter EA-288 TDI engine, the successor to Volkswagen's EA-189 "clean diesel" engine at the heart of the Dieselgate scandal. The engine produced higher NOx emissions under certain conditions outside normal emissions test procedures, conditions that are becoming more standard in nature since the revelation of Volkswagen's defeat device software.

Even more interesting, the emissions tests conducted by the Joint Research Center (JRC) technicians included both a cold-engine test and a warm-start test. Under the warm-start test, NOx emissions reportedly rose to twice the legal EU limit. "If a vehicle has a significantly higher (NOx) values during a warm test in the European test cycle than in a cold test, then there is strong reason to suspect that there is a defeat device, because you can't explain this technically," Alex Friedrich, a former German government environmental official, is quoted as saying.

The JRC report is said to state that Germany's Federal Motor Transport Authority (KBA) did not perform the warm-start test when certifying this engine, even though it has performed such a test on other Audi models and on other automotive manufacturer models. KBA has yet to disclose why the warm-start test was not conducted on this particular engine.

Is this another sign of collaboration and collusion between Volkswagen and KBA? At this point it is too early to say. But the indicators are publicly piling up higher and faster as the Volkswagen saga continues.

Where does the European Union go from here? Regulation of the automotive industry continues to be a contentious subject between European Union parliamentarians and their national governments.

A plan for the European Commission's Joint Research Center to conduct emissions tests separately from national authorities was proposed after the Dieselgate scandal became headline news. However, according to a report in the *Guardian* newspaper (November 28, 2016), the pledge by the EU to "organize and carry out" emissions tests was deleted from regulations being drafted for discussion by EU ministers.

Julia Poliscanova, a spokesperson for the green campaign group Transport and Environment, is quoted in the *Guardian* report as saying, "There is a Mexican standoff going on, with governments afraid to act against their own fraudulent carmakers for fear it will put their domestic industry at a competitive disadvantage. This scandalous stalemate results from national governments prioritizing the interests of domestic carmakers above citizens' need to breathe clean air. National vehicle regulators in Europe have been captured by the car industry."

Regulatory action (and implementation) is needed in Europe sooner than later. An International Council on Clean Transportation (ICCT) study released in November 2015 showed that the disparity between the amount of CO_2 an average car emits during a laboratory test and when actually driven on the road is increasing. The gap was in the nine percent range in 2001 but has leaped to 42% in 2015 according to the ICCT study results.

A decision on new European Union emissions testing rules and regulations is expected in February 2017, but may well be delayed as further behind-the-scenes discussions and horse-trading takes place between lawmakers and the automotive industry.

In the meantime, the European Commission issued an 11-page guidance in late January 2017 on how EU member states should be policing automotive manufacturers. While not legally binding, the guidance is an attempt to clarify how existing EU rules should be implemented and could form the basis for future legal action against EU countries that do now crack down on excessive, health-damaging vehicle emissions.

CHAPTER FOUR

Corporate Leadership Lessons

There is little doubt that the company's notoriously rigid, top-down culture created an impression in Volkswagen engineers and others that they had to succeed — or else. They thus decided it was better, and smarter, to cheat than to fail. Wrong. So very wrong.

Volkswagen, meaning its leadership, employees, and shareholders, enjoyed for many years the fruits and benefits of the short-term results that this culture produced: rising vehicle sales, stalwart corporate and leadership reputation, escalating profits and corresponding rise in share price, and a VW brand that in 2014 was ranked #31 in the world by Interbrand, ahead of Canon, Ford, Gucci, Philips, Citi, Siemens, and SONY.

Now these same leaders (minus a few that have since exited the company), employees, and shareholders are going to pay massively over the near term for what this same corporate culture reaped.

As the *Washington Post* declared in an editorial in July 2016, "Volkswagen deserves to pay for tricking drivers and regulators. The company brazenly defied the law, unfairly undercut its competitors, cynically betrayed its customers, and damaged the country's air quality."

Management guru Simon Sinek writes, "Leadership is not about being in charge. Leadership is about taking care of those in your charge."

The leadership team at Volkswagen, unfortunately, was overly concerned about being in charge and being seen to be in charge. As such, they failed to take care of the 610,000 employees in their charge, as well as failed to take care of their dealers and customers around the world.

That's an appalling inscription for their leadership tombstones.

CORPORATE CULTURE AND WORKPLACE CLIMATE

As part of its performance-driven culture, Volkswagen was obviously a top-down driven organization that punished employees who could not keep up with the pace required for attaining rigidly set goals.

This type of management style, often called autocratic leadership or authoritarian leadership, is predisposed to having all strategic objectives and timelines created by executives at the top, with little or no input from those who will be tasked with implementing these strategies and achieving the non-negotiable deadlines.

Autocratic leaders typically make decisions based on their own ideas and judgments and rarely accept advice from followers (and almost never seek advice from outsiders).

While this streamlined, command-and-control approach may seem efficient and productive, it has been discredited in favor of greater organizational cooperation and employee empowerment.

Whether it is called autocratic leadership or authoritarian leadership, a leadership style characterized by top-level, individual control over all decisions, with little input from team members, is fraught with peril and unintended consequences.

One of the biggest problems with command-and-control, top-down corporate cultures is the appearance, but not the reality, of open, two-way communication between bosses and their employees. This false sense of openness, based on the credo of being "straightforward communicators," starts at the top and cascades throughout all levels of the organization. Unfortunately, in most command-and-control structures the straightforward communication flows in only one direction — from the top down.

The best description I read of how this tightly wound control structure and corporate culture at Volkswagen caused the organization to go so badly astray comes from Jeffrey Rothfeder, writing in *The New Yorker* (July 1, 2016):

> *These actions (creating the cheating software) were manifestations of a malady that is not unusual in companies with top-down cultures. In these environments, executives often perceive themselves and their organizations to be open and communicative hotbeds of collegiality and collaborative innovation. Organization experts, such as Keith Ferrazzi, the author of "Who's Got Your Back," describe this as a delusion of infallibility arising from centralized power. If leaders of these companies are so adept at management — as their sweeping responsibilities indicate and as everyone in the organization appears to tell them they are — how could the lower levels of their businesses be dysfunctional?*
>
> *Indeed, Volkswagen's conceit was that individual brands had autonomy, and that new ideas would bubble up from these separate groups, ultimately to be shared with other teams who would adopt them in perhaps a different form for their own purposes. But this notion, like the diesel fix itself, was a sham. Because of the pressure to meet timelines and to curry favor with higher-ups, which was the only path to promotion at the automaker, vehicle-model teams shared virtually nothing, keeping secrets about mechanical breakthroughs or new design elements from one another —*

even subverting one another when the opportunity arose. "Everyone in that company was adversarial," the consultant who worked with Volkswagen told me.

The stories emanating from Volkswagen sources and observers that one reads in numerous media articles do not paint a pretty picture of the corporate culture of the company, particularly under the leadership of Chairman Piech and CEO Winterkorn.

One gets the feeling that the Volkswagen culture was plagued with a sense of "we know best" and an attitude of "we can do whatever we want." The only moral codes seem to be "the ends justify the means" and "don't get caught."

According to *Süddeutsche Zeitung* newspaper, within Volkswagen "there was a culture of we can do everything, so to say something cannot be done was not acceptable. Instead of coming clean to the management board that it cannot be done, it was decided to commit fraud."

FEAR AND LOATHING

Bob Lutz, former General Motors CEO, is one industry icon who lays the blame for the Volkswagen scandal squarely at the feet of Chairman Piech. In a no-holds-barred column in *Road and Track* (November 4, 2015), Lutz blames the "tyrannical leadership style" of Piech for creating a climate that resulted in the diesel emissions test cheating.

As often happens, the "leadership" style of the chairman cascades down to the CEO and then continues to spill over to lower leadership ranks. Numerous reports show this to be true in the case of Volkswagen.

As an example, five former Volkswagen executives interviewed by Reuters (October 11, 2015) described a management style under CEO Martin Winterkorn that "fostered a climate of fear, an authoritarianism that went unchecked partly due to a company structure unique in the German motor industry."

"There was always a distance, a fear and respect," one former Volkswagen executive told Reuters. "If he (Winterkorn) would come and visit or you had to go to him, your pulse would go up. If you presented bad news, those were the moments that it could become quite unpleasant and hard and quite demeaning."

This climate of fear reportedly flowed down throughout the organization. Industry observer Bertel Schmitt, writing in *Forbes* (February 2, 2016) illustrates this with a colorful example:

> *"Under the despotic regime of Volkswagen sales chief Christian Klinger, a young Austrian upstart who drew his power from having married into the Piech family, and who was quietly disposed of in the course of Dieselgate, managers abroad had to sell, and suggestions of what to produce were not welcome.*
>
> *Klinger's favorite line I am told was "we need to prod the pigs in production," but he hated to be prodded. Suggested changes to the model policy were seen as excuses for failure, and firings followed."*

Schmitt adds in his column, "In the past decade management by megalomania became *de rigueur* at Volkswagen."

In an earlier column for *Forbes* (December 12, 2015) Schmitt writes that Winterkorn and Klinger, who held the second highest position at Volkswagen behind the CEO, were said to "have been at the center of the fear culture at Volkswagen."

Writing about the corporate culture at Volkswagen in *The New Yorker* (July 1, 2016), Jeffrey Rothfeder, author of *Driving Honda* and *The*

People vs. Big Tobacco, quotes a source saying Volkswagen "is fueled by intimidation at every level, which creates a borderline, or sometimes over the borderline, unethical culture."

From my perspective, as one who trains and develops leaders at all levels of organizations, the root cause of the Volkswagen saga is bad leadership, not rogue engineers.

The way the corporate culture at Volkswagen has been depicted, along with examples of leadership actions that clearly illustrate the "tyrannical leadership style" described by former GM CEO Bob Lutz, reminds me of the courtroom scene in the movie *A Few Good Men*.

Jack Nicholson, playing the character of Colonel Nathan Jessup, blames his men for implementing a Code Red disciplinary action against a fellow Marine (PFC Sanchez) against his orders. However, only moments before he states in his sworn testimony that his men do not disobey orders. So how could he have given an order that PFC Sanchez was not to be harmed? He couldn't, which leads to his fall in the movie's denouement.

The same seems to apply to Volkswagen. How could a small batch of "rogue engineers" go against a corporate culture that stood for ethical conduct and lawful compliance with environmental air protection standards? They really could not. Making this a sign that such an ethical culture was either absent or subdued at Volkswagen.

However, in a culture of strict obedience and adherence to achieving the corporate strategy of becoming the #1 automaker in the world, the concept of cheating and defrauding is not an ethical or moral question, merely a viable option where the end justifies the means.

"Volkswagen needs a fundamental cultural change," declared Bernd Osterloh, a labor executive and member of the Volkswagen supervisory board shortly after the diesel emissions test cheating became publicly known. "We need in the future a climate in which problems aren't hidden but can be openly communicated to superiors. We need a culture in which it is possible and permissible to argue with your supervisor about the best way to go."

While his statements are future focused, they also serve to confirm the status quo of the existing corporate culture within Volkswagen which bred the diesel emissions test cheating scandal, and all of the other immoral, unethical, and illegal activities cited below.

Interestingly, when S+P downgraded Volkswagen's credit rating in October 2015, a month after the scandal broke, it cited management and governance deficiencies for its actions, not Volkswagen's ability to pay debt or to financially cover the costs of the emissions test cheating scandal.

One of the four guiding values at Volkswagen under CEO Winterkorn was for leaders to "lead, demand and promote." Unfortunately, it seems like too much emphasis was placed on the "demand" part of that leadership principle.

A HISTORY OF UNETHICAL AND IMMORAL BEHAVIOR

While senior leaders may set the tone and architecture of the corporate culture, other leaders and supervisors create the workplace climate that reinforces how this culture is implemented, breathed, and lived. A look at the history of Volkswagen shows how this has played out, particularly in terms of unethical, immoral, and illegal behavior.

For most observers, where there is smoke there is fire. And there is plenty of smoke emanating from across the Volkswagen group to prompt questions about what kinds of values and morals exist with this corporate culture:

Truck maker MAN, owned by Volkswagen AG, is one of five European truck manufacturers cited by the European Union's Competition Committee for price fixing and operating a secret system aimed at delaying the installation of pollution-curbing exhaust pipes and engines. MAN avoided being fined as it had revealed to authorities the existence of the cartel.

Volkswagen is one of six automakers being investigated as part of a probe by the German antitrust regulator into allegations of steel price fixing. Reports suggest the six may have formed a cartel to keep the price of steel used to make car parts low.

Volkswagen is fined by Mexico's environmental protection agency for importing and selling 2016 models without the mandatory environmental certificate showing emissions standards compliance. Volkswagen blames an administrative error for the oversight.

South Korea suspends sales of 80 Volkswagen Group models and issues a $16.1M fine, accusing the automaker of forging documents on emissions and noise-level tests. Volkswagen is alleged to have manipulated 37 emissions and noise-level tests submitted to the South Korean National Institute of Environmental Research in order to secure importation of its vehicles.

Audi chairman Rupert Stadler throws a $14,000 beer drinking competition party for about 30 top executives in May 2016, while Volkswagen is in the midst of negotiations with lawyers representing the U.S. Department of Justice, EPA,

CARB, and the Federal Trade Commission. The party features plenty of beer as well as a Bavarian brass band flown in to perform. Three months later Stadler is ordered to reimburse the cost of this party to the company.

Volkswagen announces in November 2015 that an internal investigation has revealed "unexplained irregularities" in the carbon dioxide (CO_2) emissions in 850,000 of its gasoline and diesel powered vehicles. The additional CO_2 emissions result from incorrect fuel consumption data previously supplied by Volkswagen to authorities and car buyers.

KBA, the German Federal Motor Transport Authority, says in February 2015 that Volkswagen failed to notify U.S. and California environmental regulators in 2004 about a defect in an emissions-related part.

Bloomberg reports that Volkswagen failed to report at least one death and three injuries involving its vehicles to the U.S. National Highway Traffic Safety Administration's database designed to save lives by spotting possible vehicle defects.

Twelve former employees accuse Volkswagen of allowing its workers to be detained and tortured under Brazil's military rule from 1964 to 1985.

The central excised department in Pune, India penalizes three Volkswagen firms in the country $7.4M for allegedly evading taxes by undervaluing cars sold in India between 2010 and 2014. The three firms are Volkswagen India, Skoda Auto India, and Volkswagen Group Sales.

In 2007 a Volkswagen human resource executive was convicted of 44 criminal offenses and given a two-year suspended sentence and fined approximately 300,000 euros ($330,000). Among the charges were bribery, undue influence and breach of fiduciary duty. Specifics included kickbacks to Volkswagen managers from bogus companies doing real estate business with Volkswagen, favors to members of the worker's council, and the use of prostitutes at company expense in company-owned apartments.

In 2008, a Volkswagen labor leader and a manager were both convicted in a second bribery scandal that included claims of bribing labor leaders in exchange for favorable votes on policy between 1995 and 2005. The allegations also included organization of "side programs" involving prostitutes and extra benefits for worker representatives on the company's supervisory board. Four others were also convicted or accepted fines.

A Houston, Texas television station investigation in March 2016 showed that Volkswagen reports far fewer customer defect complaints to the U.S. National Highway Traffic Safety Administration than other automakers. Volkswagen Group of America responds by saying it is undertaking a third-party audit of its reporting processes.

Volkswagen executives are told in December 2016 to pay back millions of euros for use of company planes for private and family holidays. Executives were allowed to use company planes for personal travel under a generous expense package that only charged them the equivalent of commercial airfares.

Newspaper reports in Germany and Britain say that some have asked to refund over 1M euros ($1.1M) each after the automaker decided to crack down on the practice. According to German newspaper *Bild am Sonntag,* several of the executives billed for personal use of the company planes are still in senior positions at the company.

The German newspaper *Berliner Zeitung* reports that Germany's Federal Motor Transport Authority (KBA) notified Volkswagen in November 2015 that it suspected the automaker of using prototype vehicles to lower carbon dioxide (CO_2) emissions tests. KBA reportedly informed Volkswagen that it begin choosing test models randomly and appoint new experts to carry out testing because of its doubts about the independence of the automaker's CO_2 testing procedures.

And, of course, there is the 1973 case of the EPA accusing Volkswagen of installing defeat devices in the automaker's 1974 models discussed earlier.

Individually, each of these actions might be written off as errors in judgment by a few individuals. But when looked at collectively — and when one considers both the breadth of these morally questionable actions across a wide swath of the Volkswagen Group and the depth to which some of these illegal actions occurred — one begins to paraphrase Shakespeare and conclude that there is certainly something rotten in Wolfsburg.

Even in their year-long internal investigations and "negotiations" with the EPA after being informed of the irregularities between laboratory results and on-road testing of their vehicles, Volkswagen was apparently less than forthcoming. We see evidence of this in the September 18, 2016 EPA letter to Volkswagen issuing the first Notice of Violation:

> *The California Air Resources Board (CARB) and the EPA were alerted to emissions problems with these vehicles in May 2014 when the West Virginia University's (WVU) Center for Alternative Fuels, Engines & Emissions published results of a study commissioned by the International Council on Clean Transportation that found significantly higher in-use emissions from two light duty diesel vehicles (a 2012 Jetta and a 2013 Passat). Over the course of the year following the publication of the WVU study, VW continued to assert to CARB and EPA that the increased emissions from these vehicles could be attributed to various technical issues and unexpected in-use conditions. VW issued a voluntary recall in December 2014 to address the issue. CARB, in coordination with EPA, conducted follow up testing of these vehicles both in the laboratory and during normal road operation to confirm the efficacy of the recall. When the testing showed only a limited benefit to the recall, CARB broadened the testing to pinpoint the exact nature of the vehicles' poor performance, and to investigate why the vehicles' onboard diagnostic system was not detecting the increased emissions. None of the potential technical issues suggested by VW explained the higher test results consistently confirmed during CARB's testing. It became clear that CARB and the EPA would not approve certificates of conformity for VW's 2016 model year diesel vehicles until VW could adequately explain the anomalous emissions and ensure the agencies that the 2016 model year vehicles would*

not have similar issues. **Only then did VW admit it had designed and installed a defeat device in these vehicles in the form of a sophisticated software algorithm that detected when a vehicle was undergoing emissions testing.** (Emphasis added)

VW knew or should have known that its "road calibration" and "switch" together bypass, defeat, or render inoperative elements of the vehicle design related to compliance with the CAA (Clean Air Act) emission standards. This is apparent given the design of these defeat devices. As described above, the software was designed to track the parameters of the federal test procedure and cause emission control systems to underperform when the software determined that the vehicle was not undergoing the federal test procedure.

It appears that this corporate habit of subterfuge and obfuscation may have been condoned from the very top of the organization. In September 2016 we learn that the lack of transparency and full disclosure in dealing with the EPA may have been signed off by CEO Winterkorn. The German publication *Bild* reports that it has an internal Volkswagen memo dated July 20, 2015 that reportedly announces two Volkswagen employees would soon be meeting with CARB and that the "issues with Volkswagen's diesel engines should only be partially disclosed." The paper also states that this approach had been confirmed by Volkswagen CEO Martin Winterkorn on July 28th.

Bild also reports that the meeting between Volkswagen and CARB took place on August 5th and that Volkswagen employees admitted that the emissions levels of the automaker's vehicles did not meet U.S. standards and that engineers at the company were working to repair the situation.

Long-time automotive industry observer Bertel Schmitt, writing in *Forbes* (September 14, 2016), quotes a high-level executive in Volkswagen on the potential for the darkest secrets of the automaker to be revealed saying, "Volkswagen would collapse like the proverbial house of cards. Lopez, GM sourcing data, prostitutes for labor leaders, Pischetsrieder, Bernhardt, Porsche takeover, CO_2, the list of skeletons in their closet is long."

The Lopez referenced by Schmitt's internal Volkswagen source is José Ignácio Lōpez de Arriortuá, a high-performing purchasing manager at General Motors who was recruited to Volkswagen in 1993. Known for his ability to strong-arm suppliers, Lōpez was accused of bringing confidential GM documents with him to Volkswagen. A criminal investigation of allegations of corporate espionage ensued. Volkswagen denied any wrongdoing and the criminal charges against Lōpez were dropped when he resigned from Volkswagen and reportedly gave several hundred thousands of dollars to charity.

In contrast, one recent incident that clearly displays the type of corporate culture found at Daimler. According to media reports a Daimler executive in China got into a parking-lot dispute with a Chinese citizen on the outskirts of Beijing. Local media reports in China claim that the Daimler executive used a derogatory phrase during the argument and even said it applied to "all you Chinese." He also allegedly injured one man when he used pepper spray once a crowd began to congregate.

Daimler did not waste any time in publicly apologizing for the incident and removing the company executive from his senior-level position within Daimler Greater China. In an official statement, Daimler said:

> *"The nature of the dispute and in particular the manner in which it was conducted, irrespective of any comments*

alleged to have been made, is adjudged to be not only of concern to the public but viewed by us as detrimental to the standing of our company, unbecoming of a manager of our brand and prejudicial to our good name."

While this may have been a private dispute between its executive and a local citizen, Daimler was quick to realize that actions of employees can have direct impact on the corporate brand. It was also quick to take action not in keeping with its solid corporate culture, and no doubt its actions in this incident will be story told throughout the organization that helps to cement greater understanding of the Daimler corporate ethos.

A corporate culture is formed over time through patterns of behavior that are practiced, prohibited, or tolerated by the organization's leaders and workforce over time. When the leaders in an organization permit or tolerate individual or collective action that is at the edge of acceptable conduct, the likely results are actions that eventually cross the line into unethical or unsafe activities. This is particularly true when such "acceptable conduct" occurs on the periphery of ethical delineation over long periods of time. When this happens the definition of what is customary and normal behavior moves ever closer to (or past) the demarcation of ethical and principled conduct.

It would seem that Volkswagen has long lived on the fringes of ethical, moral, and legal codes. I suspect that the "borderline unethical culture" of Volkswagen described by the source in the *New* Yorker article has long been a problem at the automaker.

When the U.S. state of New York filed its lawsuits against Volkswagen AG, Audi AG, and Porsche AG, the state's Attorney General Eric Schneider was particularly seething in his description of the Volkswagen corporate culture and workplace climate:

"The cover-up of cheat devices Volkswagen AG used to cheat on diesel emissions tests was orchestrated and approved at the highest levels of the company, up to and including former CEO Martin Winterkorn.

The allegations against Volkswagen, Audi, and Porsche reveal a culture of deeply-rooted corporate arrogance, combined with a conscious disregard for the rule of law and the protection of public health and the environment."

The New York complaint, based on internal Volkswagen documents, emails, and witness statements, reportedly depicts a corporate culture at the automaker that allowed a "willful and systematic scheme of cheating."

Volkswagen's culture must change. As current CEO Mueller said, the "days of isolationism and the illusion that we know everything must end." Great words. We await the actions that will put this change into permanent place.

WHY STRATEGIC PLANS FAIL

Research shows that over 70% of all change initiatives worldwide fail to achieve their intended results. Surprisingly, this figure has remained fairly constant for several decades.

Why are organizations, including Volkswagen, so poor at implementing strategic plans?

One key reason, according to Bridges Business Consulting International, is that "leadership teams habitually underestimate the implementation challenge and what is involved." In our estimation, this also goes back to the corporate culture created by the leadership team, especially in control-and-command type leadership cultures.

Too often the post-mortems on failed strategies reveal these causes:

Strategy is often set by those who do not have to execute it.

Strategy is frequently set by those who do not understand how to execute it.

Strategies are often overly optimistic on what is required to execute successfully.

Leaders want strategies executed immediately, or as quickly as possible, without understanding the ramifications of expedited deadlines.

Leaders often fall in love with their own ideas without fully understanding what it takes to implement those ideas.

As you can see, it is often the way leaders approach problems, and how they determine the solution required, that often cause strategic plans to go astray. The failure of Volkswagen to build diesel-powered engines that could legitimately pass U.S. emissions testing for NOx can be linked to each of the five causes above.

CORPORATE ARROGANCE

One of the frequent adjectives used to describe Volkswagen and its leadership team is arrogant.

And with good reason. Here's what Chairman Poetsch said to stakeholders, the media, and the world at the annual shareholders meeting in June 2016:

"We sincerely regret that the diesel issue is creating a shadow on this good company."

A shadow? Nine months into the scandal and the Chairman of Volkswagen AG still considers this saga to be a mere shadow passing overhead? At this juncture, it is more like a shroud covering a great portion of the company. Or, at a minimum, the shadow of a shroud.

The company is about to agree to a $15.3B settlement in the United States that covers only part of the scandal and equates to roughly 25% of its market value. Volkswagen still faces highly likely criminal charges and yet Chairman Poetsch continues to refer to this scandal as the "diesel issue," as if it were a fuel-related problem and not a corporate scandal of immense proportion, size, and scope.

Words matter. And the words that Volkswagen continues to use in an effort to downplay the magnitude of this cheating scandal will either be considered as arrogance, a corporate lack of understanding, or both by consumers, regulators, the media, and the general public.

The "we know best" arrogant attitude within Volkswagen can also be seen in how the automaker reacted in February 2015 to the global recall of Takata airbags. Rather than immediately participate in this regulator mandated recall like the rest of the automotive industry, Volkswagen wrote to the U.S. National Highway Traffic Safety Administration requesting the agency to re-evaluate the scope of the Takata airbag recall.

Volkswagen told the NHTSA that the recall was unnecessary and should not be applied to its 850,000 vehicles in the U.S. because the vast majority of these vehicles used Takata inflators from the supplier's factory in Freiburg, Germany.

Even when being harshly punished by the U.S. government regulators, executives at Volkswagen cannot help sounding brash and arrogant, as in this comment from Hinrich Woebcken, CEO of Volkswagen Group of America: "Our relationship with U.S. authorities is not that bad. They are saying that you obviously did a good job of introducing diesels to the U.S. market. Now you can do the same with electric vehicles."

Funny, I never got the same impression at all that this was a message being communicated by anyone at the Department of Justice, Environmental Protection Agency, or the California Air Resources Board.

One thing which CEO Mueller told shareholders is definitely right:

"Our most important currency is trust."

In his remarks to speech to shareholders at the meeting in Hanover, he acknowledged the difficulty in winning back public confidence and said he knows that he and his leadership team must make this a priority. I would suggest to the Volkswagen leadership team that trust and arrogance, particularly at this point in time for this particular automaker, are currently polar opposites.

CHANGING THE CORPORATE CULTURE

CEO Mueller was slightly more conciliatory and forward-looking than Chairman Poetsch in his remarks to the roughly 3000 shareholders attending the annual meeting of shareholders in June 2016 saying, "What's done cannot be undone. But what does lie in our power is ensuring we act in a responsible manner. What our experience over the past few months has shown is that long-term success is only possible where law-abiding and values-driven behavior forms the basis for our daily actions and decision making."

Of course, the institutional and private investors in the audience advocating for an independent probe into the emissions test cheating scandal might have considered such an outside investigation to be "acting in a responsible manner." Words are great. Actions are greater.

Speaking of actions, Mueller told shareholders that Volkswagen is creating more clearly structured and systematic processes for the testing and release of engine management systems. He also said workflows and structures used for approving the software for engine management systems were being reorganized with more clearly defined and binding powers and responsibilities.

The company also said that its vehicle emissions tests will now be evaluated externally by an independent third party. "We have decided that emissions tests at our company will, as a general principle, be externally evaluated by independent third parties in (the) future," Mueller said. "Real-world random testing of vehicle emissions behavior on the road will also be introduced."

He went on to add, "I strongly believe that our industry requires more transparency, courage, and openness in dealing with this issue."

While it is great that future emissions tests will be evaluated externally and that random on-road testing will be conducted, this only fixes the current emissions test cheating issue. What if the culture of Volkswagen means that cheating is also going on in other areas, such as testing of raw materials, quality assurance of components, or reliability of safety devices?

It is a bit like whack-a-mole. If Volkswagen only focuses on the ugly problem that has currently raised its head, other problems may surface later. Unfortunately, Volkswagen has been very quiet on what it is doing to change a culture that produces liars and cheaters in so many areas of operation.

The few words that have been uttered about a corporate culture change have been "god, mom, and apple pie" statements such as saying there will be an effort to "establish a culture that is open and value-driven." What does this mean in reality? How will this "effort" be implemented? And what are the values that will drive the company into the future?

Mueller told shareholders that, "Our management culture needs to improve. Openness, the courage to make innovations, and speak one's mind, as well as the willingness to cooperate on all essential elements. We need a solid system of values as a compass for our daily work."

Again, a great litany of buzz words. But what do they mean in reality to Volkswagen's 610,000 workers around the world? How will management "walk the talk" with regards to these values? Perhaps Herr Mueller and his leadership colleagues do not yet know.

As Henry Ford said, "You cannot build a reputation on what you are going to do."

Interestingly, in December 2016 Volkswagen announced that it will switch to English as the group's official language. While that makes sense for a multi-national organization with manufacturing operations spread across the globe, it simultaneously puts another significant chasm between the group's corporate culture and senior executives and that of its key subsidiaries and huge native workforce in Germany.

The focus thus far on operational processes and procedures at Volkswagen, which is typical for an engineering-driven organization, worries me. The corporate ethos is a set of core values or operating principles used to provide a framework for an organization's operations and behaviors (both individual behavior and collective behavior). These values have to be defined, agreed upon, inculcated, and exhibited by all employees, most particularly by those at the top. The ethos of the company creates the corporate culture and defines its personality. These are not elements which easily spring or radiate from operational processes and procedures.

The corporate image management process, as articulated in my 1997 book *Corporate Image Management: A Marketing Discipline for the 21st Century*, can be used as a catalyst for change. In fact, it is the very process that CEO Mueller and his leadership team should use to create and define the new Volkswagen going forward.

The corporate image management methodology is a robust and resilient technique for senior executives desiring to infuse change within their organizations as the foundation is built on agreed shared corporate culture and values. The topic of creating a culture based on shared values is discussed in the Leadership Lessons section that follows.

By leveraging the corporate image management process, the entire organization becomes focused on collectively implementing the leadership's desired changes and strategies for future growth, within the framework and structure of a new or revised corporate culture.

This is the direction the leadership team at Volkswagen needs to take.

LEADERSHIP LESSONS:
CREATING A CULTURE OF SHARED VALUES

Good leaders ask good questions. Great leaders ask great questions, especially when something seems to be too good to be true. For instance, a great leader would have asked, "how did we create a solution to one of our industry's most intractable problems (i.e. figuring out how to meet the stringent U.S. NOx emissions standards) at no cost?

Or, "why have we not applied for a patent on our brilliantly engineered technical solution for meeting U.S. NOx emissions standards?"

After all, a company proud of its technical prowess, and led by engineers, would certainly want to showcase its revolutionary and innovative solution via a patent grant. Also, this would be one way to keep competition from copying this revolutionary and innovative solution.

Unfortunately, there is no record of such questions being asked by the Volkswagen leadership team.

Steve Jobs believed that "management is about persuading people to do things they do not want to do, while leadership is about inspiring people to do the things they never thought they could."

By this definition, we could easily say that Volkswagen was headed by a cadre of managers, not leaders.

One of the most important lessons for all leaders to learn from the Volkswagen narrative is the importance of keeping an eye out for the unintended consequences being produced by your corporate culture.

Senior leaders must understand that employees far down the food chain from themselves are fully aware of how to act based on the corporate culture. That's why Daimler AG chairman Dr. Dieter Zetsche can confidently declare, "Daimler employees would have instantly recognized such behavior as VW's as out of bounds."

It is also, no doubt, why Volkswagen recruited Christine Hohmann-Dennhardt from Daimler to be the company's head of integrity and legal affairs. In fact, in announcing this hire, Volkswagen said: "compliance is now firmly entrenched at Daimler and in its corporate culture." Hopefully, Hohmann-Dennhardt can bring some of that Daimler compliance DNA with her and spread it throughout the Volkswagen group.

One of the most important roles of leaders is to create a corporate culture based on shared values. Apparently, the only values shared within Volkswagen were the need to hit sales, revenue, expense, and profit targets. All else seems to have been secondary.

Values, and even ethics and morality for that matter, cannot be driven and inculcated through processes and procedures alone.

It requires a foundation of principles, backed by a collective leadership mindset, that places primary focus on making sure the desired values are living, breathing, tangible concepts used in all future decision making, at all levels of the organization.

They cannot simply be a list of buzz words and desirable traits that adorn the walls in company facilities and are colorfully illustrated in the company's annual report.

Most important, to inculcate and indoctrinate these values with the DNA of the organization will require values-based leadership, a concept I will cover forthwith.

Henry Ford once remarked, "A business that only makes money is a poor business."

Without a doubt, this quote is vastly more true in today's world of Corporate Social Responsibility (CSR), multiple constituencies, more knowledgeable customers, and a highly mobile workforce than it was during the "glorious" Industrial Age of the 1900s.

Likewise, the management philosophies and tools of the 20th century are no longer as useful or effective for leading a 21st-century workforce. In fact, many leadership observers believe the pendulum has currently swung too far in the direction of the management ethos of "what gets measured gets done" and has resulted in too much emphasis on setting specifically measurable criteria for every aspect of business.

While goal setting and measurement tracking are still valid practices, the core leadership philosophy for business owners and managers today is best built on the values of transparency, excellence, and caring for one another. How these core values are expressed through action and behavior differentiate one organization from another.

The best business owners and leaders see their organizations as living and evolving entities driven by shared values.

Every person on a team or in an organization has their own inherent set of personal values. It is an unwise business owner or leader who expects his or her employees to park their individual values at the door upon arrival at work each day. Unfortunately, the dictatorial style of CEO Winterkorn and other senior Volkswagen leaders created an environment where Volkswagen employees felt it necessary to hide and silence their personal values. Such an unwise corporate culture contributed to the wide range of moral, ethical, and legal violations cited above.

The astute business leader will coalesce his or her staff around a set of shared values that set and define the context for individual and collaborative behavior. These values not only drive the decision-making process and collaborative efforts within the global, multi-cultural organization, they are also used as important criteria in the company's recruitment and talent development processes.

Values are the catalyst for behavior. Basing collective and individual action on value goals, rather than stated performance objectives, has three important benefits for the organization:

- It helps to avoid wrong actions that lead to devastating consequences.
- It helps everyone address dilemmas where there is no obvious, clear black and white correct path to take.
- It helps employees respond to the sentiments of others when strongly held opposing views come into play.

A few years ago, the high-powered leadership team at Enron was known as "the smartest guys in the room." But their lack of values-based performance led to the collapse and destruction of Enron and carried the corpse of accounting firm Arthur Anderson with them. It also led to prison sentences for several Enron executives.

Values set the context for behavior. By understanding the values your people bring to the table, and then aligning these with the vital values of the organization, you create teams of people more able to collaborate and work together to produce the results desired.

Great leaders know to monitor and measure the processes and behaviors producing results. They also know that when they modify behaviors that have slipped beyond the edges of the organization's agreed and stated values, their people performance and results return to the desired path and destination.

Values-based leadership is about sometimes taking the hardest path. It is about seeing the company's purpose as more than just a profit-producing machine. It also means putting people and values before profits and short-term "shady" tactics designed to meet quarterly or yearly numbers. As the great investor Warren Buffet said, "*It takes 20 years to build a reputation and five minutes to ruin it.*"

Adds Apple CEO Tim Cook, "My belief is that companies should have values, like people do."

Without a values-based leadership approach, an organization's clock is permanently set at five minutes before disaster.

Likewise, a report a few years ago titled *Reputation Assurance: The Value of a Good Name*, from PriceWaterhouseCoopers, stated, "A single-minded focus that seeks only to satisfy shareholders may ultimately lead to crises and erosion of shareholder value."

When business owners and leaders actively demonstrate strong values, they are better able to:

Create meaningful relationships with diverse stakeholders to drive high performance as they build and develop internal talent.

Inspire and energize their employees and peers, by demonstrating what is expected of the team, and then simultaneously building and developing internal talent.

In fact, values are such an important item on the leadership agenda that astute leaders are now actively seeking new systems and methodologies for cascading critical values throughout their organizations. This is one area where smaller and medium sized businesses will have an advantage over monolithic, huge enterprises as it is much easier to cultivate consistent values-based behaviors across a workforce of 200 than 20,000.

Values are also very important to employees. In fact, the 2012 PWC Annual Global CEO survey reports that 59% of workers say they will seek employers whose corporate responsibility behavior matches their own values. This was higher than the 52% who said they are attracted to employers offering opportunities for career progression.

As Steven Cohen points out in an article in *The Huffington Post* (June 27, 2016), "as the values of fairness, ethics, and environmental sustainability become more widespread, the most sought after employees want to be sure that the organizations they are working for adhere to these standards."

Values are important to employees. Values are important to consumers. Values are important to society.

It is little wonder that incisive and wise business owners and leaders are now deliberately and purposely using shared values as one of the best levers for optimal people performance within their organizations. As a result, they are creating great businesses that deliver significantly more than just money.

Henry Ford would be proud.

Volkswagen Lawsuits and Legal Issues

We live in a litigious world, which is not to say than any of the scores of lawsuits filed against Volkswagen are without merit. But I dare say that the lawsuits in the list below, which contains only the lawsuits that I have become aware of and is by no means a fully comprehensive list, will certainly be keeping Volkswagen's corporate lawyers and outside counsel extremely busy for months and years to come.

These lawsuits have been filed under consumer protection laws, environmental protection and air pollution statutes, and other legal decrees. Some guesstimates of the final cost to Volkswagen for the Dieselgate scandal and its aftermath have soared past the previous record for environmental penalties held by BP with $53.8B for the Deepwater Horizon oil spill. I doubt that this is a record Volkswagen's leadership team looks forward to holding.

And, no doubt, there will be more to come, particularly in Europe. Not to mention, of course, potential criminal investigations and charges for Volkswagen and its executives, managers, and employees in the United States, South Korea, and elsewhere.

144 STEVEN B HOWARD

Here are the lawsuits, potential civil and criminal filings, and other legal matters that Volkswagen has been dealing with, or resolved, since the Dieselgate scandal broke in September 2015.

2015

September 23   Twelve former Volkswagen employees in Brazil file a civil lawsuit accusing the automaker of allowing its workers to be detained and tortured under Brazil's military rule from 1964 to 1985.

October 16   A prosecutor in Verona, Italy leads a raid on Lamborghini's headquarters in Bologna. Lamborghini is owned by Volkswagen AG.

October 17   The U.S. Senate launches an investigation of federal tax credits that Volkswagen customers received for purchasing "environmentally friendly" diesel engines. Depending on the Senate's findings, Volkswagen could be required to pay up to an estimated $50M in Alternative Motor Vehicle credits granted to its customers.

October 28   *The Telegraph* reports that Volkswagen is facing an investigation by the Serious Fraud Office in the U.K., which could lead to actions against the automaker for "corporate criminality."

Additionally, the country's Competition and Market Authority is considering an investigation into the automaker's actions related to the emissions defeat device software installed in up to 1.2 million cars in Britain.

November 2	Volkswagen and Audi are hit with two class-action lawsuits in Australia on behalf of owners of the estimated 100,000 diesel cars from these two brands sold in the country with manipulative emissions test software.
	The Australian Competition and Consumer Commission (ACCC) says it is investigating Volkswagen and warns of possible legal action against the automaker.
December 15	The China Biodiversity Conservation and Green Development Foundation files a public interest suit against Volkswagen in a court in the eastern Chinese port city of Tianjin. The group says it filed the case because Volkswagen "produced the problematic vehicles for the pursuit of higher profits and circumvented Chinese laws, which has worsened the air pollution and affected public health and rights."
December 21	United Auto Workers Local 42 in Chattanooga, TN files charges against Volkswagen Group of America with the National Labor Relations Board for refusing to enter into collective bargaining with a group of skilled trades workers that earlier in the month voted to be represented by the union.

2016

January 12	Sweden's anti-corruption prosecutor opens an aggravated fraud investigation against Volkswagen.

March 14	A whistleblowing former Volkswagen employee in Michigan files a wrongful dismissal suit claiming he was fired for refusing to delete Dieselgate data.
March 15	A $3.6B lawsuit is filed by 278 Volkswagen investors, including California pension fund CalPERS, in a German district court to recover stock market losses incurred due to the Dieselgate affair. Some 70 lawsuits against Volkswagen have now been filed in the Braunschweig regional court.
March 25	The state of Kentucky joins New Jersey, Texas, West Virginia and New Mexico in initiating its own legal action against Volkswagen.
April 4	Over 200 car owners in Ireland have joined in a lawsuit against Volkswagen. The suit asks Volkswagen to take back their cars and seeks exemplary damages for being "misled" on NOx emissions.
April 6	Three family-owned car dealerships file a class-action suit in Illinois federal court, alleging that the automaker intentionally defrauded them when installing the defeat device software in its vehicles. The suit also separately accuses Volkswagen of improperly favoring certain dealers and forcing car dealers into financing arrangements with a company lending affiliate.
April 7	A Chicago-area dealer sues Volkswagen for $5M for selling him a dealership on September 12 last year,

just days before the EPA public announcement of the diesel emissions test cheating scandal.

April 13   The National Labor Relations Board (NRLB) rejects Volkswagen's appeal that skilled trades workers should not be allowed to organize separately from others at its manufacturing facility in Chattanooga, Tennessee.

April 20   Salt Lake County in Utah sues Volkswagen, seeking $5000 per day per car for harming air quality. The suit says 2600 Volkswagen diesel vehicles have been sold in the county.

April 25   The Serious Fraud Office in the U.K. is looking at the issue of compensation for owners of the 1.2 million Volkswagen cars affected by the diesel emissions scandal.

The United Auto Workers (UAW) files unfair labor practices charges against Volkswagen with the National Labor Relations Board for the automaker's continued refusal to bargain with 160 skilled trade workers who voted 71% in December to be represented by the union. Volkswagen has said it would go to the U.S. Federal Appeals Court in an effort to keep UAW from representing a portion of the company's plant workers in Chattanooga, TN.

June 21   Oklahoma's Attorney General sues the Volkswagen Group alleging the company knowingly skirted federal emissions standards to the detriment of

Oklahoma consumers. The lawsuit in Oklahoma County District Court seeks civil penalties of $12,000 per alleged violation of the Oklahoma Consumer Protection Act plus additional compensation for damages as determined by the court.

June 24   Norway's $850B sovereign wealth fund, the world's largest, files a complaint against Volkswagen as part of a joint legal action, in the Braunschweig District Court in Germany.

June 29   Some 30 proposed class-action proceedings have been filed against Volkswagen Canada. There are over 100,000 affected Volkswagen diesel vehicles in Canada.

July 4   A U.S. law firm representing a California teachers' pension fund and other investors files a lawsuit in Braunschweig district court in Germany against Volkswagen for damages.

July 8   The Spanish High Court rules that Volkswagen AG will be liable to answer charges in that country, rather than the group's three Spanish affiliates. The court had opened initial proceedings against Volkswagen in October 2015 with around 700,000 diesel vehicles in Spain (mostly VW and SEAT models) believed to be affected by the defeat device diesel emissions software.

July 11

A Reuters article says that Volkswagen faces millions of dollars in fines in Germany and that what Volkswagen pays in the United States will not mitigate the amount it is fined in Germany. Prosecutors in Braunschweig, near the Volkswagen global headquarters in Wolfsburg, say they will demand that the automaker be fined based on the level of profits it made from selling the 11 million vehicles equipped with the illicit defeat device software.

These punitive damages are in addition to the four criminal investigations being carried out the Braunschweig prosecutor's office: 1) an investigation of 16 people in connection with the decision to enable diesel engines to cheat on emissions tests, 2) an investigation of six Volkswagen employees on suspicion of tax fraud for misstating CO_2 emissions on some of the automaker's vehicles, 3) an investigation into one former member of Volkswagen's legal team for allegedly encouraging employees to destroy files that could be related to the diesel emissions test cheating investigation, and 4) an investigation into former CEO Martin Winterkorn and current VW brand head Herbert Diess for allegedly failing to inform investors in a timely manner about the potential EPA and CARB fines and ramifications from the diesel emissions test cheating.

July 25

The U.S. states of New York, Massachusetts and Maryland file separate, but nearly identical, lawsuits in their respective state courts accusing Volkswagen of violating their environmental laws. The lawsuits could lead to hundreds of millions of dollars, or more, in state fines. The New York suit asks for damages of thousands of dollars per violation per day.

The Law Offices of Thomas L. Young, a plaintiff trial law firm in Florida, releases a statement saying, "We suspect Volkswagen may be forced to pay hundreds of millions, likely billions more, after all the unresolved litigation is better understood and accounted for."

Environmental Protection of Hillsborough County in Florida is seeking penalties up to $5000 a day for each day of Volkswagen's offending vehicle operations in its jurisdiction.

August 3

The German state of Bavaria said it will sue Volkswagen for damages caused by the plunge of Volkswagen's share price following revelation of the diesel emissions test cheating. Bavaria's state pension fund for civil servants lost 700,000 euros ($780,000) when the stock plummeted. The German states of Hesse and Baden-Württemberg are considering joining the Bavarian suite when it is filed in September.

A group of retirement funds across the United States have now filed a class-action suit against Volkswagen in California. The funds claim Volkswagen did not disclose how severe the diesel scandal was and, as a result, the funds lost money they might not have if they had more information. Volkswagen wants the case dismissed claiming the suit would need to be filed in Germany instead of California since its shares are primarily traded on the German stock exchange.

August 4   Law firm Barun Law is bringing more than 4500 civil suits against Volkswagen in South Korea, with many plaintiffs demanding substantially more compensation than U.S. car owners will receive. Some suits are seeking full refunds of the purchase price or lease payments and even for personal damages.

August 8   Volkswagen said it would challenge in an administrative court a 5M euro ($5.54M) fine imposed on it by the Italian anti-trust agency.

Investor lawsuits claiming up to 4B euros ($4.45) in damages against Volkswagen over its diesel emissions scandal are moving ahead in the German courts. The district court in Braunschweig has sent the cases onward to the regional court for selection of a model plaintiff to represent the several hundred private and institutional investors involved in these lawsuits.

August 11	Lawyers representing the plaintiffs in the various lawsuits against Volkswagen bundled together in U.S. District Court, which led to the Proposed Settlement Agreement, say they will seek up to $332.5M in legal fees and costs from Volkswagen.
August 15	A *Wall Street Journal* report says U.S. prosecutors and Volkswagen are negotiating a settlement that could result in significant financial penalties after Justice Department officials found evidence of criminal wrongdoing related to the automaker's diesel emissions test cheating.
August 25	Volkswagen tells a court hearing that it plans to compensate car dealers in the United States. Volkswagen did not specify the amount of compensation, but the Reuters news agency reported it could be close to $1.2B.
August 26	The National Labor Relations Board orders Volkswagen Group of America to recognize and bargain with the United Auto Workers Local 42 as the representatives of a portion of workers at the Volkswagen assembly plant in Chattanooga, Tennessee.
September 1	Volkswagen has filed an appeal of the National Labor Relations Board decision on its dispute with the United Auto Workers (UAW) union in the U.S. Court of Appeals for the District of Columbia. Jörg Hofmann, head of the powerful German union IG

Metall, which has members on the Volkswagen supervisory board, calls for Volkswagen to "no longer act contrary to American labor law and to seek talks with UAW without delay."

Australia's Competition and Consumer Commission (ACCC) is suing Volkswagen's Australian subsidiary for lying about the emission of its diesel vehicles. Volkswagen has sold more than 57,000 diesel engine vehicles in Australia over a five-year period. The ACCC says it wants Volkswagen Group Australia to make public declarations of misconduct, pay unspecified financial penalties, and issue corrective advertising in relation to its actions over a five-year period.

September 6   The former CEO of Bentley and Bugatti, Wolfgang Schreiber, is suing Volkswagen in a Munich court over $100M in royalties, which he believes he deserves for having played a key role in developing Volkswagen's ubiquitous Direct-Shift-Gearbox (DSG) transmission.

September 9   James Liang, a long-time Volkswagen engineer, pleaded guilty to charges of violating the U.S. Clean Air Act, conspiring to defraud the United States, and wire fraud as part of a plea bargain with the U.S. Department of Justice. He faces up to five years in prison and up to a $250,000 fine when sentenced. He is the first individual charged by U.S. authorities for actions relating to the diesel emissions test cheating scam. As part of the plea agreement Liang will cooperate with the Department of Justice in its ongoing criminal investigation.

September 13   A Frankfurt-based law firm has filed 12 lawsuits against Porsche SE, the main shareholder of Volkswagen AG, claiming Porsche did not disclose the financial risks of Volkswagen's emissions test cheating scandal to its shareholders.

September 15   Asset manager Blackrock, the world's largest money manager, is joining a group of institutional investors suing Volkswagen for $2B euros ($2.2B) over the drop in the automaker's stock price after the emissions scandal broke publicly.

September 18   Over 6000 additional investor lawsuits are expected to be filed in the Lower Saxony district court in Braunschweig. This is in addition to the 1400 cases already filed which seek 10.7B euros ($11.9B) in civil redress from Volkswagen for investment losses sustained when the diesel emissions test cheating became public a year ago. The surge in new lawsuit filings is because investors are concerned that the one-year anniversary of the EPA announcement of the first Violation of Notice may be the deadline to file.

September 22   Detlef Stendel, who heads Volkswagen's emissions certification, is questioned by South Korean prosecutors investigating cheating of pollution tests by the carmaker.

September 25   Citing an article in Germany's *BILD Zeitung* newspaper, *Forbes* and Bloomberg report that former Volkswagen CEO Martin Winterkorn was "well aware of the Dieselgate scandal long before it was made public." Documents referenced by *BILD Zeitung* reportedly also "appear to prove that Winterkorn initiated or attempted a cover-up." These documents reportedly include an internal Volkswagen memo dated July 30, 2015 instructing two Volkswagen employees to only "partially disclose" issues with Volkswagen's diesel engines in forthcoming discussions with CARB.

September 30   Volkswagen asks a U.S. federal judge to reject requests from groups representing European investors and customers for documents related to the diesel emissions scandal.

Porsche Automobil Holdings SE, the major shareholder in Volkswagen AG, may face an investor test case over how quickly it informed investors of the implications of the Volkswagen diesel emissions test cheating.

Volkswagen CEO Matthias Mueller tells *Automotive News* at the Paris Motor Show that he is hopeful Volkswagen will reach a settlement with the U.S. Department of Justice before year's end on their criminal investigation with an agreement on the size of a fine.

Volkswagen has agreed to pay $1.21B to its 652 car dealers in the United States. Each dealer will receive an average of $1.85M over an 18-month period.

October 4   *Handelsblatt* reports that some Volkswagen car owners in Germany are planning legal action, believing that the software updates installed to fix diesel emissions are harming vehicle performance.

October 8   Congresswoman Anna Eshoo (D-CA) writes publicly to EPA Administrator Lisa McCarthy saying the proposed $2B settlement with Volkswagen on zero emissions vehicle infrastructure gives the automaker too much authority on how to spend these funds. "A particular concern," she notes allows Volkswagen to make "possible investments in its own proprietary technology and subsidiaries."

October 17   The British government was scathing in its official response to the U.K. Transport Committee Special Report on the emissions test cheating scandal and clearly signals it is willing to pursue legal action against Volkswagen in the future.

Missouri becomes the 17th U.S. state to take legal action against Volkswagen. In filing the state's civil suit, the Missouri attorney general says, "Volkswagen's actions demonstrate a flagrant disregard for Missouri's environmental laws, as well as the health and welfare of Missourians."

October 26   European Union consumer champion Vera Jourova asks for proof that Volkswagen can fulfill its pledge to make vehicles comply with limits on nitrogen oxide (NOx) by the fall of 2017. "We need Volkswagen to guarantee, in a legally binding way and without any time limit, that the repairs will work and do not have any negative impact," she says in a letter to a Volkswagen official.

November 1   Citing substantial progress in talks between the U.S. Department of Justice and Volkswagen, U.S. District Court Judge Charles Breyer sets a December 1 deadline for a report on a resolution fix for the 85,000 3-liter VW, Audi, and Porsche vehicles fitted with the defeat device software.

Two U.S. House of Representative Republicans have requested the EPA provide Congress with more details on the settlement agreement with Volkswagen and to disclose how much excess pollution the automaker's vehicles sold in the U.S. since 2009 have emitted. The Congressmen also expressed concerns that "Volkswagen may be able to obtain substantial competitive benefits, if not a monopoly, on electric vehicle infrastructure," which they write is a "curious outcome for the settlement of a cheating scandal."

158 • STEVEN B HOWARD

November 3	Volkswagen AG chairman Hans Dieter Poetsch is now under investigation by German prosecutors for allegations involving securities law violations for "failing to notify shareholders quickly enough of the financial risks of the diesel emissions test cheating scandal." Poetsch was the Chief Financial Officer of Volkswagen when the automaker was first informed of the EPA Notice of Violation of the U.S. Clean Air Act. He became chairman a few weeks after the emissions test cheating became public knowledge.
	Volkswagen will have a historian investigate the automaker's practices in Brazil during the country's military dictatorship between 1964 and 1985. This follows a civil lawsuit filed by former employees last year claiming 12 Volkswagen workers were arrested and tortured in a Volkswagen factory near Sao Paolo.
November 6	*Bild am Sonntag* reports that the California Air Resources Board (CARB) has discovered several Audi vehicle models running illegal software to bring carbon dioxide (CO_2) emissions within legal limits under laboratory test conditions. The software has apparently been found in both gasoline and diesel Audi models with automatic transmissions produced up until May 2016. The paper also reports that Audi has suspended several engineers after being informed of this matter by CARB earlier this year.
November 8	Volkswagen CEO Matthias Mueller says he hopes "the (U.S.) election results won't have more negative

consequences for Volkswagen." He also said, "I think we're at a point where a consent decree could be reached, but that's the Department of Justice decision, not mine."

A class-action suit on behalf of owners of more than 100,000 Audi vehicles is filed in Chicago federal court. The suit accuses Audi of installing defeat device software into at least six models of 3-liter gasoline powered engines since February 2013 and possibly earlier. The suit also alleges Audi executives encouraged the use of the defeat devices in gas powered vehicles as recently as May, a full eight months after the diesel cheating was publicly revealed by the EPA. This is the first civil suit in the U.S. concerning gasoline engines instead of diesel engines.

November 9   The Illinois Attorney General hits Volkswagen with a lawsuit claiming the automaker violated the state's pollution protection laws. An estimated 19,000 Volkswagen vehicles fitted with the defeat device cheating software are registered in Illinois.

November 11   Reuters reports that the Jones Day law firm conducting the internal investigation at Volkswagen on the diesel emissions test cheating will now question Audi CEO Rupert Stadler regarding the new cheat software device that lowers CO_2 emissions during testing on some Audi diesel and gasoline models.

The U.S. Federal Trade Commission has asked a federal judge to allow the agency to take additional testimony from Volkswagen AG staff over allegations some of the automaker's employees destroyed documents last year related to the diesel emissions test cheating software.

In a court filing, lawyers for the Volkswagen dealer network in the United States seek legal fees up to $36.2M

November 12   Volkswagen AG and Audi AG confirm that both U.S. and European regulators are investigating fresh irregularities related to carbon dioxide (CO_2) emissions levels in a number of Audi models with automatic transmissions. Volkswagen also admits that software in some Audi models can change test behavior in a manner that minimizes CO_2 emissions during testing and return to normal settings when driven on the road.

November 14   Litigation funding company Bentham Europe plans to bankroll a potential 100B euro ($110B) damages claim against Europe's biggest truck makers after they admitted to operating a 14-year price-rigging cartel. The truck manufacturers include Volvo, Daimler, Paccar's DAF, CNH Industrial's Iveco, and Volkswagen's MAN.

December 4   South Korea's Fair Trade Commission fines Volkswagen $31.9M for falsely advertising its diesel-engine vehicles as environmentally friendly. The agency also said criminal complaints may be filed against five current and former executives of the automaker.

December 8   The U.S. Federal Trade Commission (FTC) is seeking more information on whether employees at Volkswagen destroyed cell phones in an effort to hide evidence related to the emissions test cheating defeat device software. It claims some 23 phones are missing in a court filing.

December 9   Swiss prosecutors have opened criminal proceedings and seized evidence from a Swiss automotive importer after an appellate court ruled Swiss investigators must conduct their own investigation of the Volkswagen emissions scandal. Some 2000 criminal complaints have been filed in Switzerland related to the scandal.

December 12   German regulators are now investigating whether Porsche illegally manipulated fuel economy data by installing devices allowing its gasoline engine cars to sense when they are being tested for fuel consumption and carbon dioxide (CO_2) emissions.

December 14   Lab tests conducted by the Joint Research Center of the European Commission reportedly show the latest Audi diesel engine emits double the statutory limits of NOx. The results, which have yet to be publicly revealed, threaten to embroil Audi in another cheat device scandal.

December 19   Volkswagen Canada agrees to pay up to C$2.1B ($1.57B) to settle a class-action lawsuit. About 105,000 Canadian owners of Audi and VW vehicles will receive between C$5,100 and $8,000 each in compensation. They will also be able to sell their cards back to VW and Audi if desired.

December 21   Volkswagen agrees to a $1B settlement in the U.S. that includes buying back or repairing the 85,000 3-liter diesel-powered Audi, Porsche, and VW vehicles fitted with defeat device software used to cheat emissions testing. As part of the agreement, Volkswagen will pay $225M into an environmental trust fund to remediate the excess emissions produced by its vehicles and put $25M into a fund to support the use of zero emission vehicles in California.

2017

January 4   German consumer rights champion myRight has filed the first legal test case in Germany against Volkswagen. The lawsuit asks to force Volkswagen to repurchase vehicles with the emissions test cheating defeat device software at the original price.

January 5   A South Korea court sentenced a Volkswagen executive to 18 months in jail for falsifying documents enabling Volkswagen vehicles to be imported into the country. Two other employees were convicted on related charges.

U.S. District Court Judge Charles Breyer rules that Volkswagen AG and former CEO Martin Winterkorn must face an investor lawsuit filed in California. The suit accuses Volkswagen and a handful of senior executives of not having informed investors in a timely fashion about the emissions test cheating scandal or about potential financial liabilities.

January 8   A British law firm has commenced legal action against Volkswagen, seeking thousands of pounds of compensation for each U.K. driver affected by the Diselgate scandal. The firm says 10,000 drivers have already signed up to the legal action.

January 11   The U.S. Department of Justice (DOJ) and the Environmental Protection Agency (EPA) announce that Volkswagen has agreed to a $4.3B settlement to resolve the U.S. government's civil and criminal investigations. Volkswagen also pleaded guilty to three federal felony charges and has agreed to cooperate with the DOJ's ongoing investigations.

Additionally, the DOJ announced that six Volkswagen executives and employees have been indicted by a federal grand jury on conspiracy and other charges related to the diesel emissions test cheating scandal. This includes Oliver Schmidt, who was taken into custody by FBI agents a few days earlier.

Volkswagen has also agreed to sweeping reforms, new audits, and oversight by an independent monitor for three years as part of its most recent settlement deal with U.S. regulators.

South Korea's Fair Trade Commission, the country's corporate watchdog, fines Volkswagen nearly 37.2B Won ($32M) for false advertising on vehicle emissions. The FTC said it would also file criminal complaints against five current and former VW executives. It is the largest fine ever imposed in South Korea for false advertising.

Simultaneously, Seoul prosecutors indicted seven current and former executives of Volkswagen's Korean operations on charges of fabricating official documents and alleged violation of the Clean Air Conservation Act.

January 18   Volkswagen says it will appeal a German court ruling that the automaker must buy back, at full purchase price, a German customer's diesel car equipped with the emissions test cheating defeat device software. The judges in the rule said Volkswagen had acted "indecently" by installing the software and compared the automaker's deceit to previous cases where winemakers had mixed antifreeze in wine and food manufacturers put horse meat into lasagna.

January 19   The Polish Office of Competition and Consumer Protection initiates legal proceedings against Volkswagen in Poland for misleading customers over emissions. The regulator could fine Volkswagen up to 10 percent of its sales turnover in the country.

January 27   Prosecutors in Germany announce they are expanding their probe into Volkswagen's emissions test cheating scandal and have increased the number of suspects being investigated from 21 to 37 individuals. They also say they now have evidence that former CEO Martin Winterkorn may have known of the cheating earlier than he has publicly acknowledged. They are now investigating Winterkorn for possible charges of fraud, in addition to a suspicion of a securities market violation previously announced. Prosecutors raided 28 locations, including offices and private homes, during the past week in connection with their investigation.

CHAPTER FIVE

Corporate Governance Lessons

Governance of organizations in Germany is unique. All German companies have two boards. One is the management board led by the CEO. This runs the day-to-day activities and operations of the company. Above this is the supervisory board, to which the CEO typically reports. The supervisory board usually has the power to hire and fire management board members and is required to approve all major strategic decisions and investments of the company.

In Volkswagen's case, this structure did not always work so well. For one thing, the 20-person supervisory board at Volkswagen has nine places set aside each for both its workforce and shareholder representatives. The other two places are reserved for the company's home state of Lower Saxony, in itself a significant shareholder as well as home for much of the workforce employed at the Wolfsburg headquarters.

As such, the politicians from Lower Saxony are also keenly concerned with maintaining high employment levels in the state. As are, of course, the representatives from the workforce. Thus, as long as jobs are being protected at one of the state's largest employers these two sets of representatives were willing to give the Volkswagen AG CEO a relatively free hand.

Volkswagen's governance is further complicated by its shareholding structure, where three parties — the Porsche-Piech families, Lower Saxony government and the emirate of Qatar — control 89% of the voting stock. These three sets of stockholders control all nine seats on the Volkswagen supervisory board allocated for shareholders.

With this shareholding in place, there is zero chance for minority shareholders to push for any independent directors to be added to the Volkswagen supervisory board.

You would think that with such a tightly knit shareholding and board governance structure that all would be well in the fiefdom of Volkswagen. Alas, boys will be boys — and powerful men being powerful men — that was not always the case.

In the spring of 2016 the supervisory board discussed shelving the Volkswagen annual dividend for the year, partly as a way to hoard extra cash for the coming diesel emissions scandal payments. That, you might think, was a sensible deliberation worthy of a top-notch board.

In fact, according to numerous media reports, the discussion was also, at least partly if not mainly, a play to diminish the Lower Saxony representation on the supervisory board. Apparently, if no dividend were to be paid, Lower Saxony would lose one of its two seats on the supervisory board. That seat would then be controlled by the other main shareholders, giving them more power and influence on the supervisory board.

The two Lower Saxony representatives, with the voting support of the labor representatives, defeated this ploy and shareholders did receive their annual (albeit reduced) dividend payment.

It is interesting, however, that even in the midst of company-saving negotiations with the EPA and CARB, these powerful men on the Volkswagen supervisory board had the time and energy to engage in some nifty boardroom intrigue.

Around the same time that these boardroom shenanigans were taking place, activist investor TCI Fund Management hammered the Volkswagen supervisory board. TCI complained that the board rewarded itself with excessive pay while allowing bloated costs and poor share market performance to plague the automaker.

TCI founder Chris Hahn wrote a letter to Volkswagen board members saying, "The shares and management (of Volkswagen AG) have been consistent disappointments."

He added, "Excessive top management compensation, unlinked to transparent metrics and paid in cash with no vesting or deferral, has encouraged aggressive management behavior, contributing to the diesel emissions scandal."

Hahn also pointed out that, "Shockingly, in a six-year period, the nine members of the executive board will have been paid around 400M euros ($465M). That is corporate excess on an epic scale; management has been rewarded for failure."

Additionally, Norway's Norgen Bank Investment Management, the world's largest sovereign fund, criticized the ownership structure of Volkswagen AG. Specifically stating that too much power is concentrated with the Porsche-Piech families, the fund's managers said this puts minority shareholders at a disadvantage. NIBM holds a 1.2% stake in Volkswagen.

And while the Volkswagen governance structure provided higher than normal authority and power to the Volkswagen CEO, it did not mean that things were always copacetic between the CEO (Martin Winterkorn) and supervisory board members, particularly the all-powerful Volkswagen Chairman Ferdinand Piech.

For instance, in early 2015 Piech had a falling out with Winterkorn to an extent that he tried (and failed) to replace Herr Winterkorn with Martin Mueller.

Part of this discord between the two reportedly had to do with disagreements over how to handle the queries from CARB and EPA over the irregularities found in diesel engine emission testing. Part of it also had to do with the powerful Piech looking into building a low-cost VW car in China with a new partner, and Winterkorn having to deal with the fallout from Volkswagen's two strategic partners in China when they each caught wind of Piech's moves.

These events led to the strangely, but cryptic, remark by Piech in April 2015 that "I am at a distance to Winterkorn." Winterkorn had been seen as a leading disciple of Piech and many presumed him to be the chairman's eventual heir apparent.

Piech tried to trigger a leadership change before the annual meeting of shareholders on May 5, 2015. However, he was rebuffed by the Volkswagen six-man executive committee. Both the Volkswagen works council and Lower Saxony government representatives backed Winterkorn, as did Piech's cousin Wolfgang Porsche.

In a 5-to-1 vote this steering committee of the supervisory board endorsed Winterkorn as the "best possible CEO at Volkswagen" and agreed to extend his contract when it expired in 2016. Despite this vote, Piech reportedly kept lobbying family members behind the scenes to replace Winterkorn with Matthias Mueller, the chief executive of Porsche.

CEO Winterkorn won the initial battle when Piech was forced to resign as Volkswagen Chairman a few weeks later, with deputy chairman Berthold Huber named as acting chairman until a new chairman could be elected. In a released statement the supervisory board said, "The members of the steering committee came to a consensus that, in light of the past weeks, the mutual trust necessary for successful cooperation was no longer there."

Piech's sudden resignation also put a dent in his own rumored succession plans. He was scheduled to retire at the 2017 annual meeting of shareholders when he turned 80. Industry observers believed he wanted his wife Ursula, who joined the supervisory board in 2012, to replace him as chairman. The Porsche family, however, is believed to have favored Winterkorn as his eventual replacement.

As Jens Meiners wrote in *Car and Driver* (April 27, 2015), the coup against Piech was also:

> *a personal victory for Wolfgang Porsche, who has never forgotten the humiliation of Porsche's botched takeover attempt of VW. It didn't happen, and Porsche ended up under VW's control. The result was a triumph for Piech, who never held the Porsche branch of the family in much esteem. He once derisively described their favorite activities as "knitting, crochet, playing the flute."*

One wonders how big the smile on Piech's face was when Winterkorn subsequently resigned as CEO less than five months later when the diesel emissions test cheating became front-page news. It probably got even larger when Matthias Mueller was chosen as Winterkorn's replacement!

Additionally, two weeks before the diesel emissions test cheating became public knowledge, *Der Spiegel* reported that Piech personally intervened to prevent the Porsche-Piech families from proposing Winterkorn be promoted into the still vacant Volkswagen AG chairman's slot. Instead, CFO Hans Dieter Poetsch was put forward and nominated to become the automaker's next chairman once an extraordinary shareholders meeting could be arranged to vote and confirm the appointment.

Poetsch had won the trust and backing of the Piech and Porsche families when he orchestrated the deal that saw Porsche SE sell its sports car brand to Volkswagen AG in a tax-free transaction that reportedly saved the two families an estimated 1B euros ($1.1B) through a simple loophole in the German tax code that Poetsch exploited. So, in effect, Piech had already extracted his revenge on Winterkorn even before the emissions scandal became headline news by stopping him from rising to the coveted chairmanship position.

Speaking of which, *Bild am Sonntag* reported in August 2016 that Piech informed the Jones Day investigators that he tried unsuccessfully to question Winterkorn about the emissions scandal in March 2015. According to the report, "Winterkorn rebuffed Piech's questioning, responding that he had it all under control." One wonders if part of the battle between these two titans of Volkswagen also had something to do with how the inquiries from the EPA and CARB were being handled.

Power and authority were concentrated in a few key people across the highly interlocked Volkswagen group. For instance, Volkswagen AG CEO Winterkorn was also CEO of Porsche SE, the family-owned holding company that controls a majority stake in Volkswagen. He was also chairman of Volkswagen's flagship luxury brand Audi, the Scania truck division, and the group's Truck & Bus unit.

In many ways the Volkswagen AG supervisory board was a private enclave that acted like an old boy's club and had the aura of a private (almost secretive) society.

Volkswagen may have had the only board in the world where one patriarch figure, Ferdinand Piech, was allowed to bring his wife (and former family nanny) onto it. Mrs. Ursula Piech, a former school teacher and the nanny for a couple of years for Ferdinand's young children before marrying Herr Piech, was made a member of the supervisory board in 2012, despite having no automotive industry experience and never having worked in any large organization of any kind.

Unfortunately, there was nothing that other board members, shareholders, or even regulators could do to prevent this. It was, however, an action that should have raised red flags for professional investors entrusted in investing and managing large pension funds, sovereign wealth funds, and other large pools of money. Why these professional institutional investors remained shareholders in Volkswagen AG, or became shareholders after 2012, is a question their own governance structures should be asking.

TOO MANY INSIDERS

Many observers of Volkswagen were skeptical when Matthias Mueller, who has been with the Volkswagen Group for almost 30 years, was named as CEO Winterkorn's replacement.

At the time of this move Mueller was head of the Porsche brand. Appointing a long-term insider to replace a CEO who has resigned due to a major scandal (despite claiming his personal innocence) is hardly an indicator that a major change in management, governance, or culture is forthcoming. Many thought it would be better if the new CEO came from outside the family group of companies.

Likewise with the decision to name Hans Dieter Poetsch the new Volkswagen AG Chairman. Poetsch had served as the group's Chief Financial Officer (CFO) since 2003.

But that's not the way Volkswagen is governed.

Dirk Toepffer, a member of the Lower Saxony parliament, told AP in October 2015 that an outsider would "fail at the cleanup" Volkswagen needs. "Volkswagen is a different world," he told the news agency. "That means this enterprise functions under different rules than other enterprises. That's why they need someone that knows the structure."

It is a common argument heard both inside and outside the automaker. But is also begs the question: why is it necessary for Volkswagen to "function under different rules than other enterprises"? Isn't this what got the company into this mess in the first place?

Toepffer's other statement to AP is equally troublesome: "Someone who comes completely from the outside and doesn't know how the rules of the game go will fail at the cleanup." Again, why does this member of the state parliament, and so many others with close ties to Volkswagen, feel the automaker should be allowed to play by its own rules?

The one outsider in a key leadership position, other than those newly recruited to the company after the scandal became public, is Herbert Diess the chief for the VW brand. Diess only joined Volkswagen at the start of July 2015, just over two months before the scandal hit. He was formerly BMW's research and development chief.

Unfortunately, Herr Diess may have been too closely involved in the decision not to alert the stock market about the potential penalties from the EPA as soon as they were internally identified. He is currently being investigated, along with former CEO Winterkorn, by German prosecutors on potential stock market manipulation charges.

LEADERSHIP LESSONS
The most obvious leadership lesson from the governance structure of Volkswagen AG is that the lack of independent directors on the

supervisory board stood in the way of a proper scrutiny of Volkswagen executives and managers.

It also prevented a viable option for those with knowledge of the defeat device software to be able to turn to with their information or concerns. Anyone with the inclination to red-flag the use of the cheating software system had no outside channel to alert, other than perhaps the media. With some outside directors on the supervisory board there would have at least been a chance that someone within Volkswagen might have spoken up and reported the wrongdoing.

I would suggest that this governance structure of Volkswagen is another of the root causes leading to the diesel emissions test cheating scandal.

Think about it — if you are part of the leadership team of a company that has three major shareholders owning 89% of the voting stock, and a supervisory board mostly comprising representatives of two of these shareholders plus the union representing your workforce, where would the focus of your decision making be? Who would you be aiming to please day in and day out?

Add to this mixture a corporate climate of stringent goals, aggressive performance management, and a control-and-command leadership style.

Undoubtedly you would be making most of your decisions and taking most of your actions to please your immediate boss and meet short-term metrics.

This does not excuse anyone for taking illegal actions and knowingly creating illegal products, as we will discuss in chapter nine on personal and individual accountability.

However, it does show the need for both the governance structure and the corporate culture to be changed. Changing only the corporate culture, which is all that has been publicly discussed by CEO Mueller and others to date, simply may not be enough to keep Volkswagen from sinning again.

As CEO Mueller said in December 2015, "A company of our size, international reach and complexity cannot be managed with structures from the past." Again, great words from Herr Mueller. But over a year later we have seen no action in changing the governance structure of Volkswagen AG or in any of the entities within the group.

CHAPTER SIX

Branding Lessons

On October 5, 2015, only 17 days after the EPA announcement of the first Notice of Violation, Interbrand released its 16th annual Best Global Brands report. Not surprisingly, since the analytics for this annual ranking of the 100 most valuable global brands was done prior to the revelation of the Dieselgate scandal, Volkswagen, Audi, and Porsche were placed high on this honors list.

Volkswagen was ranked #35 with a $12.5B brand value, down nine percent in value from the previous year, while Audi sat at #44 with a $10.3B brand value, up five percent over the previous year. Porsche was slightly lower, ranked #56 with a brand value of $8.1B which was 12% higher than a year earlier.

Volkswagen was ranked the fifth most valuable German brand, while Audi was next as Germany's sixth most value brand. These two powerful brands were behind only Mercedes-Benz, BMW, Deutsche Telekom, and SAP on the German brand value list by Interbrand. Porsche was a few spots behind, claiming the 12th position in the German branding ranking.

Both the Volkswagen and Audi automotive brands had been moving up in this annual evaluation, which Interbrand says is based on the financial performance of the branded products and services, the role the brand plays in influencing customer choice, and the strength the brand has to command a premium price or secure earnings for the company. In the 2014 report, both Audi (+27%) and Volkswagen (+23%) were in the list of the top five risers for increased brand value over the previous year (2013). Porsche also had a double-digit (11%) brand value gain to $7.2B in 2014 over 2013.

Equally as unsurprising, Volkswagen dropped like a stone thrown in a pond when the 2016 Interbrand Best Global Brands report was released in early October 2016. The report now places the brand value of Volkswagen at just $11.4B, a 9% drop from a year ago. The Volkswagen brand also dropped five places to #40.

Meanwhile, Audi and Porsche escaped from being too tarnished from the Dieselgate scandal. Audi actually leapfrogged the Volkswagen brand with a brand value of $11.8B, moving it up six spots to #38. And Porsche had an 18% increase in brand value to $9.5B and also moved up six places to #50 in this latest Interbrand report.

DESTROYING BRAND EQUITY

Brand equity, of course, is built on the fundamental core component of trust.

Trust takes years to build, minutes to break, and forever to repair.

Volkswagen immediately lost most of its trust equity the moment the EPA went public with is first Notice of Violation. The remainder of any trust equity Volkswagen had with consumers, car owners, dealers, regulators, lawmakers, media, and the general public was slowly eroded as the scope of the cheating scandal expanded, other misdeeds came to light, and as a result of the company's early attempts to protect its leadership team and place the blame for Dieselgate in the hands of a "few rogue engineers."

Michael Horn, President and CEO of Volkswagen of North America at the time the scandal hit, readily admitted the trust issue in his appearance before a Congressional inquiry panel a few weeks after the emissions test cheating became headline news. Volkswagen has "broken the trust of our customers, dealerships, and employees, as well as the public and regulators," he stated bluntly.

IG Metall, Germany's biggest labor union, accused Volkswagen in April 2016 of using the emissions scandal as an excuse and prelude for cutting jobs. In an email to Volkswagen employees the union stated outright that the automaker has "a serious problem of trust."

CEO Matthias Mueller admitted in July 2016 that the trust issue for Volkswagen is far from being resolved. He told reporters, "We have a lot of work to do to earn back trust of the American people." He is absolutely correct. A Harris Poll released around the same time showed that the Volkswagen Group had dropped to dead last in the Reputation Quotient Rankings of America's 100 most visible companies. Volkswagen was rated lower in this survey than some of the most publicly scorned and disliked corporate entities known to the American public, including Halliburton, BP, Comcast, Monsanto, Goldman Sachs, and AIG.

Admitting the problem, and taking appropriate action to restore trust, are two entirely different matters. While Volkswagen's leaders have been good at talking publicly about the trust issue, this huge behemoth of a company has been slow on the action side of the equation.

It is not clearly evident that all the senior leaders at Volkswagen truly understand the gist of its trust problem. For instance, in March *Motor Trend* quoted VW brand chief Herbert Diess saying, "We have to talk more about quality, demonstrate more quality. Perception will change because the product quality is good, but the real question is how fast will it change? Because perception is reality."

Diess is correct that perception is reality. But he is wrong if he thinks consumers in America, and around the world for that matter, think Volkswagen has a problem with perceptions around the quality of its vehicles. Just the opposite is true. Consumer perceptions about Volkswagen's quality are so high they are surprised and shocked to learn that Volkswagen needed to cheat to pass U.S. diesel engine emissions tests.

Volkswagen does not have a quality problem. Focusing future marketing communications and sales pitches on quality will indeed be beneficial. But it will not remove the stigma and negative feelings that many consumers have about Volkswagen's advertising lies and manipulation of diesel engine emissions testing.

Two statements in a June 26, 2016 article in the *New York Times* puts the Volkswagen trust problem into clear perspective:

> *"Volkswagen made such a big and public bet on diesel, and it turns out they were lying to us. The average consumer is going to say 'why should we believe them again?'"* — Brain Clark, associate professor of marketing at the D'Amore-McKim School of Business at Northeastern University.

> *"I thought it was a clean diesel. I couldn't continue to drive the car and think of myself as an environmentalist."* — Marjorie Hodges Shaw, assistant professor, law and bioethics at the University of Rochester Medical School of Medicine and Dentistry.

As Wharton management professor John Paul MacDuffie said, "The green consumer feels betrayed."

These feelings are shared by many Volkswagen car owners, including even its most loyal customers. As one long-term customer said, "VW will not get a single penny extra from me. I have been a VW fan for the last 20 years, and now they have probably just lost one of their most valuable customers."

Adds another highly disgruntled and irate Volkswagen customer, "I would walk before I bought another VW, Audi, or Porsche. They committed intentional fraud. That takes them off my list."

And, in an analogy I wish I had thought of myself, a constituent wrote to Congressman Peter Welch (D-VT) saying in part, "Volkswagen is the Lance Armstrong of the (auto) industry." Ouch! Not exactly a brand association that will help to build equity in the Volkswagen brand.

"This was one of the most egregious examples of a company deceiving the public," said Bill Nelson, U.S. Senator from Florida upon hearing the news that the U.S. Federal Trade Commission had filed a false advertising suit against Volkswagen. "Hopefully the court will provide adequate redress to consumers and send a strong message that this type of corporate behavior won't be tolerated."

With this substantial dent in its trust equity, Volkswagen's brand equity has subsequently eroded as well. This is borne out by several research studies, a few of which we will cite here.

The Reputation Institute measures companies in over 15 countries on a continuous basis. In their 2015 reputation research study, conducted in the first three months of 2015, Volkswagen was ranked 14th. It was also ranked 11th in the 2015 Global Corporate Social Responsibility (CSR) RepTrak 100 study, which ranks organizations based on the general public's perceptions of three dimensions of reputation — workplace, governance, and citizenship.

According to a case study of the Volkswagen saga produced by the Reputation Institution, damage to the automaker's reputation was immediate. Just one month after the EPA announcement of the First Notice of Violation, Volkswagen dropped 22 points in Germany and 11 points in the U.S. in these ongoing studies. By the end of the year, Volkswagen's reputation scores had also dropped by 23 to 30 points in France, Italy, Spain, and the United Kingdom.

In a fascinating finding in this research, consumers in this research were significantly less willing to "give Volkswagen the benefit of doubt in a time of crisis." Scores for this foundational trust question dropped 28 to 34 percentage points in France, Italy, and the U.K. between the first quarter and the last quarter of 2015. In addition, willingness to purchase Volkswagen products dropped 21 to 38 percentage points across all five European markets surveyed from the start of the year (pre-scandal) to the end of the year (post-scandal).

Not surprisingly, a strong correlation was seen between the declines in trust and the deterioration in the scores on the willingness to buy Volkswagen products.

Additionally, a survey by the German Marshall Fund, a nonpartisan American think tank dedicated to promoting cooperation and understanding between North America and Europe, found 46% of U.S. citizens no longer trust the Volkswagen brand.

In May 2016, the annual Customer Loyalty Engagement Index showed Volkswagen to have the lowest emotional engagement strength in the United States. This study from Brand Keys surveyed 42,792 American consumers to measure how brands disappoint their own customers. Volkswagen was the most disappointing and unsatisfying brand of the 635 brands surveyed, with an emotional engagement score of just 29%.

That was lower than Blackberry (30%), American Apparel (38%), and Sears (42%).

Fortunately for Volkswagen and its brand image, most of the murky details surrounding the emissions test cheating scandal have not fully registered with consumers.

For instance, in November 2016 a report in the *New York Times* shows the extent to which some employees at Volkswagen went to hide the truth about the defeat device software:

> *Volkswagen engineers went so far as to concoct fake engineering data to try to explain a huge discrepancy between the readings in official laboratories and how much the cars polluted on the road, said Alberto Ayala, deputy executive officer of the California Air Resources Board, which did much of the detective work that led to Volkswagen's exposure.*
>
> *"They lied through their teeth," Mr. Ayala said in an interview in California last month.*

Research over the years has shown that consumers are more willing to forgive, and eventually trust again, companies that make mistakes of competency than the ones who are caught in errors of character. After all, the underlying value system in organizations caught cheating or violating the law is much harder to change and fix than mistakes resulting from incompetence or poor decisions.

The question that only time will eventually answer is "can Volkswagen ever be trusted again after this blatant deception we now call Dieselgate?"

ADVERTISING LIES AND PR OBFUSCATION
Why is so much customer and public enmity for Volkswagen so hostile?

I think there are two underlying causes. First, as an organization they blatantly lied to us and to the regulators we entrust with keeping our air clean and ensuring that polluting vehicles are not allowed onto our roads. Second, and perhaps more important, their advertising and marketing communications through the years played to both our emotional and rational sides (as all good advertising should).

So now both consumers and non-consumers of Volkswagen products feel like suckers; like they have been roped in and swindled by the kin of carnival shills.

Volkswagen had been building trust equity with consumers and the public in America dating back to the award-winning classic advertisements by advertising agency Doyle Dane Bernbach. For those of us old enough to remember, the television commercial showing "how the man who drives the snow plow drives to the snow plow" (spoiler alert: in a Volkswagen Beetle) and the one showing the 7000 quality control technicians in white coats "a mile long" who have to improve every new Volkswagen vehicle made are two of their all-time classic television commercials.

Who wouldn't trust the company building these products?

So naturally when that same company decades later tells us that it is now building "clean diesel" engines that are "environmentally friendly," who would question the veracity of these claims?

Fortunately, the folks at ICCT eventually did. And now many of us will likely scrutinize and question all forthcoming claims from Volkswagen, Porsche, and Audi, at least for the near to medium term future.

In a move that was, at best, a cosmetic one, Volkswagen dropped its "Das Auto" tagline in December 2015. Yes, it reduced the proliferation of negative spinoff idioms and memes like Das Cheaters and Das Emissions, but it had no impact on the continued erosion of the Volkswagen brand in subsequent months. That erosion was caused by management actions and the continuous flow of leaks and bad news surrounding the company and its ever growing scandal.

Plus, in an unbelievable incident that goes into the "what the f*ck were they thinking?" category, Volkswagen actually released a new television and advertising campaign in February 2016 in the United Kingdom with the tagline for the print ads reading, "It's more than just a car. It's keeping your promises."

While the tagline in the 60-second televisions spot was slightly less egregious ("It's more than just a car. It's a lifelong companion."), neither should have ever been considered, much less actually used, by a company whose trust issues result from corporate malfeasance and illicit behavior on a grand scale. Volkswagen is perhaps the last company in the world which should be talking about "keeping promises" in its advertising materials.

Volkswagen's communications with car owners, or the lack thereof, during the past year has also impacted the brand's reputation and customer loyalty scores.

A survey released in early July 2016 by car shopping website CarGurus of more than 400 Volkswagen diesel vehicle owners revealed that a whopping 63% were not satisfied with the way the Volkswagen Settlement options were communicated to them. In addition, less than half (48%) believed Volkswagen was taking appropriate measures to rectify the Dieselgate situation.

"The Volkswagen situation has introduced challenges on a new level for both VW and car owners who have been loyal to the brand," noted Sarah Welch, SVP Consumer Marketing at CarGurus in the release announcement of the survey results. "Our survey shows that owners are still processing the information they've received, and VW has a lot of work to do to remain in their good graces."

The survey also showed that 40% of Volkswagen diesel vehicle owners had already decided to take the buyback option from Volkswagen and about 47% were undecided at the time. Only 13% of the respondents indicated they would definitely keep their current Volkswagen vehicles.

These sentiments are being echoed in the actions of Volkswagen car owners. By early September, about six weeks after the Proposed Settlement Agreement was made public, roughly half of the 475,000 affected car owners had signed up to participate in the settlement agreement. According to Elizabeth Cabraser, the lead plaintiff attorney in the case, the majority of the 210,000 owners and lessors who had enrolled elected to take the buyback option from Volkswagen. Cabraser did not provide specific figures.

When asked about future car purchase in the CarGurus survey, 21% of the respondents said they would definitely not buy another Volkswagen vehicle and 36% said they had not decided if they would purchase another Volkswagen branded car in the future. However, in a glimmer of hope for Volkswagen's future prospects in the United States, 43% did say they would consider buying another Volkswagen vehicle despite the emissions test cheating scandal. It will be interesting to track how many in this 43% bucket willing to at least consider Volkswagen in future car purchases actually do so.

In the Autolist survey cited earlier in chapter three, willingness to buy a Volkswagen model among over 2300 U.S. car owners surveyed was down 28% in the December 2015 through January 2016 timeframe as compared to the levels recorded only months earlier before the cheating scandal became publicly known.

EUROPEAN INEQUALITY

While all of the trust issues above apply equally outside the United States, there is one additional element of trust applicable in Europe and other markets.

This is the element of equal treatment for Volkswagen car owners in other parts of the world, most particularly in Europe and Australia.

While Volkswagen car owners in the United States (and potentially in Canada as well) are being given buyback options and settlement payments of $5100 to $10,000 each, no such compensation is being offered to Volkswagen car owners outside North America.

The reasons behind this, particularly in Europe, are two-fold: a) doing so for the 8.5 million vehicle owners in Europe could bankrupt Volkswagen, and b) the diesel emissions rules and testing procedures are not as stringent as in the United States and Canada.

That being said, it still hasn't stopped the issue of equal treatment being raised, particularly by opportunistic European parliamentarians.

"Treating customers in Europe differently than U.S. customers is no way to win back trust," according to Elzbieta Bienkowska, European Industry Commissioner. She has also reportedly written to Volkswagen AG CEO Matthias Mueller "demanding" that U.S. and European customers be compensated in the same way. Fortunately for Volkswagen her office does not have the power or authority to enforce her demands.

With a similar sentiment, the German Justice Ministry spokesperson has publicly said that "unequal treatment cannot be in the best interest of Volkswagen."

Shortly after Judge Breyer accepted the Proposed Settlement Agreement in the United States for review, Commissioner Bienkowska said it would be unfair for European customers to be treated differently than U.S. customers just because of a different legal system. "Volkswagen should voluntarily pay European car owners compensation that is comparable with that which they will pay U.S. consumers," the commissioner stated.

From the Volkswagen viewpoint, however, this simply is not practical. For one thing, the tougher NOx emissions standards in the U.S. makes it more difficult to fix the non-compliant diesel engines in Volkswagen vehicles. In fact, a technical fix may not even be feasible, which is one reason the automaker may be forced to buy back all of the offending vehicles in the United States.

Additionally, as Herr Mueller pointed out in an interview with the German newspaper *Welt am Sonntag*, "Volkswagen is solid financially, but you do not have to be a mathematician to see that damage payments in some arbitrary amount would even be too much for Volkswagen to cope with." He was referring, of course, to the fact that the automaker simply does not have the financial wherewithal to make compensatory payments to 8.5 million customers with affected vehicles across Europe.

While that may be true from Volkswagen's perspective, it is not a satisfactory situation for many European Volkswagen car owners. As such, Burford Capital, the world's largest provider of finance for litigation and arbitration, is supplying funding to the Hausfeld & Co. law firm to sign European car owners onto a class-action lawsuit. "VW cannot cheat European consumers and escape accountability," claims Michael Hausfeld, chairman of the U.S. based law firm.

He added, in a refrain likely to be repeated for months or years to come, "Europeans are no less worthy of justice than their American counterparts."

LEADERSHIP LESSONS

One last lesson that the Volkswagen leadership team (and all organizational leaders) needs to take to heart now that Judge Breyer has ruled on the acceptance of the Settlement Agreement:

> a damaged corporate image is never repaired from a legal settlement.

It will be natural for the Volkswagen leadership team to breathe a collective sigh of relief now that once Judge Breyer has accepted the Settlement Agreement. But it will be foolhardy for them to think that this legal settlement is putting Dieselgate "behind them" or that the impact of the scandal is over.

In fact, all the legal settlements Volkswagen makes down the road will merely be more baby steps in its corporate image and reputation recovery process. It will be years before Dieselgate is behind them. It will be years until the last of the civil suits and class-action suits are settled. And, most important, it will be years before the car buying public and regulators stop associating the words liars, cheaters, fraudsters, and similar descriptors with the brands Volkswagen, VW, SEAT, Skoda, Audi, and Porsche.

CHAPTER SEVEN

Crisis Communications Lessons

In most corporate scandals, the attempt to cover up the wrongdoing, and the wrong-footed attempts to publicly minimize its impact, are often more costly than the original misdeed.

This is certainly true in the Volkswagen saga case, even in spite of the enormity of the original sin.

Saying this does not minimize the severity of the Dieselgate legal breaches and health impact from creating, installing, and hiding the defeat device emissions test cheating software. But one wonders if an immediate admission of guilt, and a quicker pace in reaching the settlement agreements, might have resulted in lower penalties and less brand equity damage. In terms of penalties and future criminal charges, perhaps only the folks at EPA and CARB know the answer to this.

VOLKSWAGEN'S COMMUNICATIONS MISCUES

A ceaseless series of communications errors has plagued Volkswagen from the start of the diesel emissions test cheating scandal, impacting its brand reputation and brand equity while no doubt angering many key constituents.

We saw earlier how its public and private communications led to frayed relationships with key regulators at both the EPA and CARB. We also saw research evidence of the high levels of dissatisfaction by affected diesel vehicle owners with how Volkswagen communicated with them in the months between the public unveiling of the cheating scandal and the filing of the Proposed Settlement Agreement in U.S. Federal District Court.

This has not gone unnoticed by observers of the Volkswagen saga. As Professor Erik Gordon at University of Michigan Ross School of Business said in one *Financial Times* article, "VW is taking every opportunity to compound its troubles with U.S. regulators and the damage to its image with U.S. consumers."

Among the litany of communications miscues and mistakes the automaker and its leaders have made, here are a few worth highlighting:

- CEO Matthias Mueller's statement to National Public Radio denying that Volkswagen employees had lied to the EPA. In fact, Volkswagen had already admitted to the EPA that it had been deceiving the agency (and CARB) for years when Mueller made his statements in an NPR interview in January 2016.

- Volkswagen AG refusing to turn over internal emails or executive communications to state attorneys general in the U.S., citing Germany's strict privacy laws. This led the New York Attorney General to publicly declare, "Our patience with Volkswagen wears thin." He also stated that Volkswagen's "spotty" cooperation was "more of the kind one expects from a company in denial than one seeking to leave behind a culture of admitted deception."

- The initial and continued corporate response to blame a handful of "rogue engineers" for creating and propagating the emissions scandal all on their very own without management knowledge or approval.

- Initially denying the allegations in the EPA's second Notice of Violation, only to have to admit a week later that not only were the allegations true, but the scope of the violations far surpassed what the EPA originally believed.

- Believing it could buy goodwill from impacted car owners in the U.S. by giving them $1000 in gift cards and vouchers, half of which could only be used at Volkswagen dealerships.

- Submitting rushed, incomplete and insufficient proposals on diesel engine fixes to both EPA and CARB, only to have these soundly and vehemently rejected.

- Continuously referring to the emissions test cheating as "the diesel issue" in speeches and corporate communications releases. This has continued right through to January 2017 in the company's formal response to the $4.3B penalty and criminal charges it agreed to with the U.S. Department of Justice.

RESPONDING TO THE CRISIS

The whole notion that a couple of "rogue engineers" were responsible for creating and installing the defeat software never passed the smell test from day one.

Did Volkswagen really expect us to believe that a few engineers acted altruistically and independently on behalf of the company to single-handedly solve the automaker's most significant diesel engine conundrum?

And, if this indeed was the act of only a few misguided engineers working without any management or supervisory approval, why did Volkswagen spend 14 months stonewalling the EPA inquiry and trying to place the blame on faulty third-party tests?

The first branding related leadership lesson from the Volkswagen saga is about how to respond to a crisis. Well, actually it is really the second lesson. The first lesson is: do not engage in deliberate illegal and illicit activities in the first place.

There are numerous books, articles, and guides on how to communicate during a crisis situation. There are also hundreds of experts available at a moment's notice to advise leaders on crisis communication and assist them through any situation.

Unfortunately, it appears that the leadership team at Volkswagen never read any of these books, articles, or guides before the diesel emissions test cheating scandal erupted. Equally as unfortunate, it also appears that in typical Volkswagen style these leaders allowed their "we know best" attitudes to convince themselves that they could handle this crisis without outside assistance.

And thus the EPA announcement of the defeat device software turned into a scandal and continues on as a saga of growing proportions.

The first thing leaders should understand is that journalists can smell a developing scandal like sharks smell blood in the ocean currents. And, the bigger the organization, the longer and longer a scandal can brew and the bigger it will seem. Both of which keeps journalists, editors, and their media bosses happy. Longevity of a scandal is a leader's worst nightmare.

Think about it. For over 18 months — for more than 500 consecutive days — the leaders of Volkswagen have awakened with thoughts of "what new piece of scandal related bad news will we have to deal with today?" and "where is the next hit going to come from?"

To get an idea of what these leaders have been through, read the comprehensive timeline of the Volkswagen saga in chapter 11. You will see that almost every day for the past 17 months there was a new lawsuit to review, or a new issue to contend with, or a new public threat from a regulator or politician. Day after day after day. Without let up. A constant barrage of new allegations, rumors, legal issues, and other challenges that needed to be faced.

For over 500 consecutive days they have had conversations with each other, and sometimes just with themselves, asking "how do we handle this?" and "where do we go from here?"

It is exhausting. Frustrating. Agonizing. And maddening to be facing new elements of the same crisis over and over again for such a long period of time. Especially when there remains no end in sight and no finality to what now seems like an everlasting situation.

It is additionally tiring trying to handle the ongoing situation for leaders like CEO Mueller and VW brand chief Diess who were not part of the leadership team when the cheating software was created and implemented. Nor were they part of the leadership team when the initial year-long discussions with EPA and CARB were taking place (except for the last two months when Diess joined the management board after being recruited from BMW). Cleaning up someone else's mess is definitely more tiring and mental energy sapping than fixing a problem you are responsible for creating.

However, that is only part of the story. For the more important other part of the story — and the ongoing leadership lesson — is how these new leaders responded to the crisis and why their actions, words, and messages were key factors in turning this scandal into today's multidimensional saga.

One of the worst techniques for trying to manage the perceptions of stakeholders during a crisis is through calculated word and message spinning. By that I mean the considered use of words or phrases with the intention to either reduce the perceived severity of the situation or in an attempt to cast it in a better light (i.e. highlighting the silver lining in the dark clouds).

This is a ruse that is easy to fall into, especially when leaders are being coached by internal counsel, external lawyers, or their own communication specialists to "keep the message positive" or to "not play into the media's hands."

It is a trap Volkswagen's leaders and the company's huge internal communication team easily fell into. For instance, at the end of October 2015, about six weeks after the EPA public announcement of the first Notice of Violation, the company referred to the emissions test cheating scandal as "the diesel issue" and the newly found CO_2 emissions problems as the emissions "irregularities" when reporting its third quarter loss.

This language automatically looks like the company is hiding something. For weeks headlines around the world have linked Volkswagen with such words as cheating, scandal, Dieselgate, air pollution related deaths, and environmental risks. And yet the communications folks holed up in the Wolfsburg headquarters think they can downplay this rapidly escalating crisis by referring to it as "the diesel issue," almost as if the fault lies in the diesel fuel running their cars and not the cheating defeat device software controlling noxious emissions during laboratory tests.

Likewise, when the EPA issued is second Notice of Violation concerning defeat device software in various 3-liter engines, Volkswagen's official first response was a denial that any emissions related software installed in these engines had been used "in a forbidden manner." This non-denial denial of the EPA allegations did not set well with the federal regulator. Especially when Volkswagen later admitted that it had failed to declare three specific auxiliary engine control devices in their 3-liter engines to the EPA as required by U.S. law.

In another example of trying to put a positive spin on the scandal, Volkswagen's head of electrical and electrical development publicly declared at the Mobile World Congress in Shanghai in July 2016 that Dieselgate forced the automaker to speed up its digitization efforts faster than planned. While that may be particularly good news for his department at Volkswagen, I seriously doubt it was comforting to the hundreds of thousands of Volkswagen car owners across the United States who were still anxiously waiting for news of a proposed settlement agreement at the time. Nor was it likely to be comforting words to hear for the millions of Volkswagen car owners in Europe, Asia, Africa, Africa, and South America still waiting for their diesel vehicles to be fixed.

We witnessed such word spinning from Volkswagen throughout this saga. For instance, when the German prosecutors announced they were launching an investigation into former CEO Martin Winterkorn regarding why Volkswagen did not inform investors earlier of the potential financial fines and penalties from the EPA, Volkswagen's official reaction was "there is no new information in the prosecutor's announcement." Of course there wasn't. The new formal investigation was just getting started.

Likewise, in announcing preliminary findings from the Jones Day internal investigation, Volkswagen said "no serious violations by senior board members" had been uncovered. This immediately opens the questions, "so what about the non-serious violations? What are these?" And were there any serious violations by non-senior board members?

If there were violations, then admit what these are, show that the organization is learning from whatever mistakes were made, and move on. That's transparency. Hiding behind the phrase "no serious violations" is neither transparent nor trust building.

The last thing an organization should do during a crisis (or at any time for that matter) is hide behind legal speak, word spinning, and strategically placed adjectives. If there were no violations, then say so. If there were some "non-serious" violations, say so. And then say what the organization has learned and what changes are being made to prevent repetition or replication of the wrongdoing.

I am reminded of the way Singapore Airlines CEO Dr. Cheong Choong Kong handled the tragic crash of one its flights during takeoff in rough weather in Taipei in October 2006. Disastrously the SIA pilots were attempting to take off on a runway that was undergoing construction. The plane catastrophically plowed into a concrete barrier and construction equipment on the closed runway.

Within hours of the crash he had flown from Singapore to Taipei to take personal charge of the media conferences and liaison with local Taiwanese officials.

In one of the most memorable press conferences I have ever witnessed, Dr. Cheong made it clear to everyone what SIA stood for as a company, what its priorities would be, and how the airline would fulfill its obligations to its many stakeholders.

Much to the chagrin, displeasure and mortification of the airline's lawyers and insurers, Dr. Cheong flatly said, in response to a reporter's question if the SIA pilots had been misled onto the wrong runway by those in the control tower, "They are our pilots, it was our aircraft, and the aircraft should not have been on that runway. We accept full responsibility."

Boom. Bing. In one statement the SIA CEO took full responsibility for the situation and full control of the story line.

It (the plane crash) happened. Errors in judgment and processes were made. SIA will fix these. SIA is deeply sorry for the tragic loss of lives and the injuries suffered. SIA will continue to be one of the top airline companies in the world. That's the story line that emanated from Dr. Cheong's press conference statement.

No corporate speak. No corporate word spinning. And thus no long-term scandal or saga.

The second communication crisis lesson is not to let your organization's second-line leaders or spokespeople around the world make claims and statements that will later prove to be false. When this happens the reputation for integrity and veracity of both the individuals and the organization are damaged.

For example, Paul Willis, the head of Volkswagen in the United Kingdom, told lawmakers in a parliamentary transport committee inquiry into the diesel emissions test cheating impact on U.K. car owners that it was "implausible that senior people in the company would have known of these issues with regard to the testing regime."

He also said in his testimony in October 2015, "I don't think there's more to come out," and that he found it inconceivable "that this is a deliberate attempt to mislead people."

These are the kinds of statements that, if later proven to be untrue (as they were), backfires on both the individual and the company. Sure, Mr. Willis can always claim that his statements were "based on what he knew at the time," but that just falls squarely into the corporate speak and word spinning category discussed above.

Another poor tactic to use in crisis communications is any attempt to change the story line. Volkswagen tried this with a bombardment of new product announcements and a whole host of press announcements on new initiatives — 30 battery-powered vehicles to be incorporated into its fleet by 2025, a $300M investment in ride-hailing Gett, and planned developments of self-driving cars before the end of the decade. There was also news releases and planted stories on new SUV models, the possible building of a large battery production manufacturing plant in Germany, and even an investment in a cyber security venture.

All of these futuristic announcements were obviously intended to show that Volkswagen is investing for the future and that the automaker would resiliently move past today's awkward emissions scandal and return to great industry prowess again. That's all well and good, but the constant flurry of press announcements did little to allay the concerns and interests of car owners, media outlets, regulators, and the general public in how the emissions scandal was unfolding.

Additionally, all of these massive investments undoubtedly hurt Volkswagen in its negotiations with the lawyers for the U.S. government, CARB, and state attorneys general. After all, if Volkswagen has so much money sitting around for these major investments, how can it possibly plead "poor boy" with the plaintiff lawyers negotiating the Proposed Settlement Agreement?

The third lesson from the Volkswagen saga in terms of crisis communications is that leaders should not be overly optimistic in their comments regarding the timetable for fixing an issue or in winning back trust and confidence from customers.

Time and again during the past year we have seen Volkswagen miss publicly declared deadline after deadline, on everything from how quickly it will have technical fixes for its vehicles to when the results of the Jones Day internal investigation will be released to how speedily the company will bounce back from this scandal.

While it is good to be positive in one's outlook during a crisis, for this provides confidence to both customers and employees, overly optimistic statements that include stipulated dates or timelines only serve to set leaders up as deluders and prevaricators whose statements cannot be trusted.

For instance, at the German car show in March 2015 Volkswagen brand chief Herbert Diess told an audience, "We know Volkswagen has some making up to do. And we are confident we can win back the trust of our customers quickly." Really? Based on what premise? All of the research at the time, and since, tells a very different story and indicate that customer trust will not return quickly.

Up until that last word Herr Diess's comment was probably fine. But that last word establishes expectations that have an extremely high probability of failure.

A month later, in a letter to German car dealers, Thomas Zahn, head of sales and marketing for passenger cards, wrote, "VW has not won back trust as quickly as expected."

Under what illusions were their expectations made? Less than seven months after a major seven-year cheating scandal is made public, with no proposed settlement agreement and no verifiable technical fix in sight, how could anyone at Volkswagen have believed customer trust would have been won back by now?

Why did Volkswagen apparently constantly underestimate the impact its cheating scandal was having? Is the leadership team so insular that it could not understand that this was never going to be a short-term problem lasting roughly the length of a European soccer season?

This again drives home the point about the lack of diversity and the absence of outside directors on the Volkswagen supervisory board. It also drives home the point of running a global enterprise across numerous cultures and countries with a leadership team comprising exactly one culture.

CRISIS COMMUNICATIONS PLAYBOOK

As mentioned at the beginning of this chapter, there are numerous books, articles, and guides on how to communicate publicly and internally when faced with a corporate crisis.

Here are the key steps that I have used when advising my own clients over the years when dealing with any significant event that could turn into a public relations disaster:

1. Select one to three people to be the official spokesperson(s) for the organization on all matters related to the crisis situation. Instruct all employees that no other person is to speak to the media or make any public pronouncements, even in response to questions, on any matter related to the crisis. Note: one person is ideal, but in a global organization like Volkswagen it may be necessary to have one per region (i.e. one for Europe, one for Asia and one for North America and South America) due to varied time zones and media cycles.

2. Be as transparent and forthright as possible on all issues. If legal impediments (such as a nation's privacy laws) prevent you from revealing information or answering questions, be very specific as to what legal restrictions are being applied.

3. Decide, in as far advance as possible, what information will not be revealed and then prepare to take media and public hits when these issues or topics arise.

4. Use real-world language, not corporate speak or unnecessary technical terminology, in all communications.

5. Promise to correct problems and fix errors. If it is a human mistake, admit this and explain how the company will cascade learning from this mistake throughout the organization to prevent repeating or replication of the error.

6. Focus on problem solving, not blame. This will at times be difficult, as the media tends to look for blame. But constant repetition of the mantra "we are focusing on fixing the problem and preventing any reoccurrence over finding and allocating blame" will eventually win out.

7. Minimize defensive tonality and posture.

8. Reveal more information sooner (as long as it is factual and not speculation) rather than waiting until all information and details are available. Be sure to specify when only partial information is being presented and why.

9. Avoid references to timelines and deadlines as much as possible (again usually a key focus of media and regulators). Be 110% sure that any timelines or deadlines mentioned are achievable.

10. Unless employee safety or employment is the main issue, focus priority of communications in this order: customers, employees, government or regulatory officials, business partners, impacted public, the general public, shareholders. The exception to this is if stock market rules or national legislation dictates how shareholders and potential investors should be informed.

CHAPTER EIGHT

Corporate Responsibility Lessons

L et's start with a basic premise: every organization, and in fact every individual, has the obligation to make the world a better place for our children and grandchildren to inherit.

It is that simple.

It is also a huge responsibility.

From a corporate perspective, this is augmented by responsibilities to four specific sets of stakeholders: customers, employees, shareholders, and the communities in which the organization operates.

Much like the racial segregation and marriage equality laws that have evolved in recent decades, the moral compass on corporate responsibility continues to evolve.

This progression has been created by a combination of societal pressures, changing social values and mores, and an increasingly more knowledgeable and frustrated global population. Added to this combustible mix is a more frequently active citizenry that does not hesitate to punish or correct organizations deemed to be outside the boundaries of proper corporate citizenship.

We even see organizations themselves now taking stands against other organizations or situations negatively impacting the world, for instance:

- Starbucks committing to 100% ethically sourced coffee and tea in a global program that aims to positively impact the lives and livelihoods of farmers and their communities.

- Intel committing to use minerals from conflict-free sources in the Congo so that their purchases of such minerals for their microchips do not fund the militant violence and human-rights atrocities in the Democratic Republic of the Congo.

- Grocery chain NTUC FairPrice in Singapore removing products from its shelves made by the company suspected of being involved in the burning of forests in Indonesia which annually causes an unhealthy smoke haze to descend upon Singapore for weeks.

In society, when people do not live up to their collective and individual responsibilities to the community, they are usually jailed, ostracized, or outcast.

In the corporate world, such failure to meet the duties of corporate responsibility result in massive loss of value, reputation, market share, and, of course, sustainable success.

There can be little doubt, therefore, Corporate Responsibility is one of the pillars of sustainable success for any organization or corporate entity.

The key word here is sustainable.

PUBLIC HEALTH IMPACT
OF THE DIESEL EMISSIONS TEST CHEATING

Let's add a second premise: corporations should not knowingly manufacture and sell products that cause deaths or harm the environment more than legal statutes allow.

In the case of Volkswagen, they did both.

It has long been established that nitrogen oxides (NOx) contribute to respiratory and cardiovascular diseases which can lead to disability and death. This is why such NOx emissions are tightly regulated by the EPA and other regulatory bodies around the world.

An analysis reported in the *International Journal of Environmental Research and Public Policy* (September 8, 2016) quantifies the health and economic impacts of the additional NOx emissions attributed over the course of a single year by the non-compliant Volkswagen diesel vehicles across the United States. The analysis for the article was led by scientists and researchers at the Northwestern University Feinberg School of Medicine and the Columbia University Mailman School of Public Health using the EPA's Co-Benefits Risk Assessment (COBRA) screening model.

The COBRA model is a peer-reviewed tool that derives changes of ambient fine particulate matter (PM) concentrations related to NOx emissions. Analysts use the PM levels determined by the model to estimate health and economic costs. It is an approach similar to what EPA uses for its own regulatory impact analyses.

Using the COBRA model, the authors calculated that a single year of extra NOx emissions would be responsible for 5 to 50 premature deaths, up to 17,526 employee work days with restricted activity due to respiratory and cardiovascular health-related issues, and a cost to the economy between $43M and $423M. The ranges were based on low, medium and high impact estimates using the COBRA algorithm.

Those figures are for one year. The emissions test cheating by Volkswagen has now been going on for eight years. Multiply those numbers by eight years and the impact is phenomenal: 40 to 400 premature deaths, as many as 140,000 work days with restricted employee activity, and an economic cost between $348M and $3.4B.

Plus, almost all of these high-emitting vehicles are still on our roads today, causing continued public health harm and economic costs.

Despite these frightening numbers, the authors of the study believe the actual effect of non-compliant Volkswagen vehicle emissions is almost certainly substantially worse than indicated. For one thing, the analysis is based only on the 485,000 Volkswagen diesel vehicles with 2-liter engines. It does not take into account the extra emissions being spewed from the 85,000 vehicles with larger 3-liter diesel engines.

"Emissions of nitrogen oxides from these vehicles were as much as 40 times higher than the EPA standard, adding up to 15,000 metric tons of these chemicals into the air we breathe every year," stated Andrea Baccarelli, chair of the department of environmental health sciences at the Columbia University Mailman School of Public Health. "It is crucial that Americans and their government officials know the extent of the damage done to public health and the economy."

So the Volkswagen diesel emissions test cheating is much more than just dishonesty and deceitfulness for competitive advantage. It is also duplicitous and unscrupulous conduct with serious public health and economic cost impacts.

As Louise Ellman, chairman of the U.K. Transport Select Committee pointed out, "Volkswagen has acted cynically to cheat emissions tests which exist solely to protect human health."

Again, this analysis of the public health and economic costs of the non-compliant diesel emissions is just for the 475,000 Volkswagen vehicles sold in the United States. It does not take into account the 11M other non-compliant Volkswagen vehicles in Europe, Asia, Latin America, Australia, Canada, and elsewhere also spewing out dangerous NOx emissions.

VOLKSWAGEN'S CORPORATE RESPONSIBILITIES

Despite Milton Friedman's famed dictum on return on investment, corporate leaders today have a responsibility to all stakeholders, not just shareholders. These other stakeholders include employees, customers, suppliers, distributors, the communities in which they operate, and this planet we call home.

When I look at the Volkswagen saga, it is apparent to me that the Volkswagen leadership team failed all of these key stakeholder constituents.

First, employees. Volkswagen employs over 610,000 people worldwide. Let's assume that its diesel engine cars would not have met EPA emission standards in the USA without the company resorting to the cheating it engaged in. That obviously would have resulted in reduced sales, and possibly led to a reduced workforce.

On the other hand, the lost sales might not have been so significant. After all, Volkswagen's cheating diesel vehicles only numbered 475,000 through seven years, or roughly 68,000 cars per annum. That is merely a drop in the bucket for an automaker with annual sales in excess of 10 million vehicles.

So can cheating be condoned when it is perceived to be in the best interest of employees and shareholders?

Such a mentality treats the concept of "best interest" on a short-term thinking basis. And all it does is postpone the inevitable. Job losses that would have occurred if car sales declined are now likely to happen over the next few years as the impact of this scandal cascades.

The same goes for shareholders. Short-term holders of shares in Volkswagen benefitted over the seven years while this cheating was being perpetuated. Now, of course, the share price is down 40% from its pre-scandal levels. So while one set of shareholders may have benefitted (temporarily), the entire shareholder base is now negatively and massively impacted. One can only hope that this latter group includes all those involved in executing and covering up this duplicitous scandal.

Organizational leaders, of course, must still exhibit responsibilities to the company's shareholders. But here's the rub: should all shareholders be treated equally?

This certainly was not the case at Volkswagen. The leadership team appears to be most concerned with its responsibilities to, and relationships with, the three major shareholders —the Porsche-Piech families, Lower Saxony government, and the Qatar emirate — as the three combined to own 89% of the voting stock and 57% of the overall shares.

At times Volkswagen even appears to be fairly callous and dismissive in its treatment of minority shareholders, as we saw with the company's haughty response to the call by many shareholders for an external and independent inquiry into the Volkswagen diesel emissions test cheating scandal.

German investors' association DSW and Brussels-based Deminor, which represents shareholders, were the most publicly vocal in calling for such an independent investigation.

Instead, Volkswagen created a Special Committee on Diesel engines, headed by Wolfgang Porsche, to investigate the scandal and hired law firm Jones Day to find those responsible. Porsche is the head of the family clan that controls Volkswagen.

This led DSW spokesman Juergen Kunz to publicly express the doubts surrounding thoroughness and fairness being felt by the minority shareholders. "When you have an independent investigation you can be sure that the findings will be published," stated Kunz. He then added, "With internal investigations you do not know whether everything has been made transparent."

I will share with you in a few pages how important Corporate Responsibility is to consumers. It is pretty obvious that Volkswagen has collectively failed in its responsibilities to its customers.

Buyers of the Volkswagen, SEAT, Skoda, Audi, and Porsche cars that have the dishonest software installed now own vehicles with greatly reduced resale value. They also face the inconvenience of eventually having to bring their cars into a dealership to have the corrected software installed. Or, if they live in the United States, having to go through the process of arranging a buy back of their vehicles and then researching and purchasing a replacement car.

Potential customers of Volkswagen are undoubtedly looking elsewhere for their next vehicle purchase. Reduced sales will impact the VW labor force, its car dealership network, and even its suppliers of materials and parts. Hence, in failing in its responsibilities to its customers, Volkswagen has also impacted both its sales channels and its supply chain network.

Volkswagen as a corporate entity — which means both its leadership team as well as every employee with knowledge of these shenanigans — had a responsibility to their customers, fellow employees (and their families), the dealer network owners and employees (and their families), and the owners and employees of all its materials and parts suppliers (and their families).

Volkswagen — meaning its leadership team and the employees with knowledge of this deliberate subterfuge — failed to live up to their collective and individual responsibilities to these stakeholders and their families.

A WORLD OF CORPORATE MISCREANTS

Volkswagen, of course, is not the only corporate miscreant in the world. In the following sidebar section, over 40 other instances of illegal, immoral, and unethical corporate behaviors and actions are listed.

In fact, hardly a day goes by without a headline reporting corporate malfeasance and wrongdoing. Sadly, many of these acts are by big-name global icons that should be setting the standards for good conduct, such as Citibank, Wells Fargo, HSBC, BP, Goldman Sachs, Tesco, Dow Chemicals, and Deloitte.

It is not too great a stretch to ask if ethical conduct is even a core value in the business world today. Or have corporate leaders become so enamored with, and driven by, revenue and profit figures that all else has become secondary?

As Edward L. Queen, director of the Emory University Program in Ethics and Servant Leadership, points out in his by-lined article in the *New Republic* (September 28, 2015), "Far too much of the world's corporate leadership is driven by moral midgets who have been educated far beyond their capacities for good judgment." He also blames devotion to Milton Friedman's assertion that "the only duty of a corporation is return on investment," and the habit of leaders to "regularly ignore his (Friedman's) caveat of doing so within the law and social norms."

This wrong-hearted and solitary focus and devotion to return on investment needs to stop, just like the segregationist views of 20th-century political leaders had to be tossed away. It is doing more harm than good.

VALUES AND RESPONSIBILITY

It is time for corporations, particularly the large, heavily funded behemoths that control most of the business world (and a great part of the political and legislative world), to enter an Era of Responsibility (which I will discuss below).

I am not the only one who thinks so. Even major institutional investors are starting to voice their concerns. In October 2016 the Institutional Investors Group on Climate Change (IIGCC) published a reported titled Investor Expectations of Automotive Companies.

In this report, IIGCC stated that vehicle makers must put climate change specialists on their boards, better engage with policymakers, and invest more heavily in low emission cars. IIGCC, a network of over 250 global investors with assets more than $24 trillion, also said the auto industry must accelerate its readiness for a low-carbon world or face a sell-off of their shares.

"Long-term investors want to ensure that automotive companies are prepared for the challenges stemming from climate change, new technologies, changing policies, and shifts in demand caused by global trends," explained Dr. Hans-Christoph Hirt, co-head of investment house Hermes EOS and a member of the IIGCC.

He added, "Investors expect the industry to embark upon a smoother route to future prosperity by developing and implementing long-term business strategies that are resilient to climate change and resulting regulatory shifts."

Making sure the automotive industry closes the gap between real world emissions levels and laboratory emissions testing was also highlighted in the IIGCC report as one of the key issues needing urgent attention and fixing by carmakers. These investors also called on automotive manufacturers to reduce greenhouse gasses across their respective supply chains.

In other words, these major global investors want the automotive industry to collectively exhibit more responsibility for correcting and lowering its impact on climate change and public health.

Most leaders know that values matter to both customers and employees. We now see that values also matter to major institutional investors as well.

Organizational leaders can no longer treat the so-called soft issues — those not directly related to revenues, costs, and profits — as secondary luxuries or superfluities. We live and operate today in a transparent and open world, where corporate, political, and governmental secrets can easily be exposed and virally communicated around the world via the Internet. How leaders tackle increasingly important issues like employee safety, diversity, fairness in hiring and promotions, creating non-confrontational workplace climates, equality across genders and cultures, and rigorous adherence to legal and moral standards will directly and indirectly impact revenues, costs, profits, and the corporate brand image.

Steven Cohen, the executive director at the Earth Institute, provides a strong recipe for sustainable success in his *Huffington Post* (June 27, 2016) article:

Management must explicitly add the costs of energy, water, raw materials, and waste to the organization's financial control system.

They must also add the risks of damage to the environment into the organization's strategic and operational planning process.

Senior management must ask if the potential cost of environmental impact has been considered and, if not calculated, at least estimated.

ERA OF RESPONSIBILITY

We live in a world today where the trust levels for businesses, corporations, governments, politicians, business leaders, and just about every other formal institution is at or near all-time lows.

Refresh your mind with some of the headlines and key stories of recent years: financial institutions going bankrupt, Toyota mishandling a global recall of vehicles, the BP oil spill in the Gulf of Mexico; trust in politicians around the globe going down the drain, brand endorsing sports stars caught cheating on their spouses, impacting not only their personal lives but the employees and corporations associated with their endorsed brands.

Fortunately, in the world of commerce, as in science, for every action there is almost always an equal and opposite reaction.

For the past few years I have been observing media trends, researching numerous topics and industries, and discussing the state of today's society with a highly diverse mix of professionals and lay people. The reaction to today's state of affairs I see coming is a segue into an Era of Responsibility.

Those organizations which take the initiative to help solve the problems of society, including the environment, will be the ones rewarded with loyal customers. This is particularly true for the millennial generation that is approaching its peak years of discretionary spending power.

Those organizations which take immediate, clear, and transparent responsibility for fixing any problems they cause — including immediate acknowledgment of their errors, sincere apologies for their mistakes, rapid action to fix their messes, and the required investment to prevent a repeat of the problem — will be forgiven by customers and go relatively unpunished.

Those which do not will quickly lose customers, loyalty, sales, and profits as their misdeeds will promptly and swiftly be broadcast through all social media and Internet channels.

For the past two decades, it seems that fear, greed, and egos have been the most established drivers of successful businesses and their leaders. The backlash to this will be consumers demanding ethics, morality, fairness, mutual respect, and social contribution in their dealings with business and government entities.

This conclusion is supported by the findings of the Edelman goodpurpose® Consumer Study of 6,000 people in 10 countries, which showed that an increasing number of people are spending on brands that have a social purpose, despite the prolonged stagnant or slow growth in global economies.

In this study, 57% of respondents globally said a company or brand has earned their business because it has been doing its part to support good causes. Most interestingly, the countries reporting the highest level of such consumer support were China (85%) and India (84%). Two-thirds (67%) globally also reported they would switch brands if another brand of similar quality supported a good cause, which means that a corporation's or brand's identification with supporting social causes would be a key differentiator between brands with similar features and attributes.

As Mitchell Markson, Edelman's Chief Executive Officer, stated when these survey results were released, "People are demanding social purpose, and brands are recognizing it as an area where they can differentiate themselves, not only to meet government compliance requirements, but also to build brand equity."

In a sign of hope for the world that our children will inherit, the vast majority (87%) of respondents to this survey globally agreed it was their duty to contribute to a better society and environment and 82% feel they can personally make a difference. But here is the number most important to marketers: 83% are willing to change their own consumption habits to help make tomorrow's world a better place.

Also, as the survey notes, 66% of the respondents in these 10 countries no longer believe it is good enough for corporations and brands to merely give money away to charitable causes. The belief now is that to be truly authentic corporations and brands must fully integrate good causes into their day-to-day business activities, as well as into their internal processes and procedures.

This takes the concept of social purpose and corporate responsibility to an entirely new level.

Authenticity and trust will be two of the key cornerstones for corporate reputations in this forthcoming Era of Responsibility. This will come not only from your policies and public pronouncements, but also from the actions and beliefs of your employees.

Dov Seidman, author of *HOW: Why HOW We Do Anything Means Everything...in Business (and in Life)* believes there is a link between enlightened corporate behavior and performance. He argues that the most successful businesses of the future will also be the most moral ones, not as a result of formal Corporate Social Responsibility (CSR) initiatives and programs, but from what he labels sustainable values. Unlike situational values, sustainable values are ones with sustaining human relationships built into their day-to-day practices and behaviors. In Seidman's view, how an organization is led, governed and operates is equally as important to its future success as the products and services it produces.

I highly recommend to you a four-minute video on YouTube featuring Corporate Philosopher Roger Steare, Professor of Ethics at London's Cass

Business School, in which he says, "Money is simply a promissory trust. When we break promises and we break trust, we destroy money, which is what we have seen in the past two years on a global scale."

The Era of Responsibility is not a fad that will pass and be quickly forgotten once economies return to substantial growth levels.

It is a trend that is going to impact elections, market share, social institutions, and the composition of the various stock market indices around the world. Like most trends, those who get in front at the beginning will be the ones who remain ahead as the tide carries others along.

I read with great interest a few years ago that La Trobe University's Graduate School of Management in Melbourne will present Australia's first Master's Degree wholly focused on corporate responsibility — the Masters of Corporate Responsibility. I, for one, cannot wait for the day when MCR degrees out number MBA degrees.

Hopefully this initiative by La Trobe University will catch on like wildfire at universities across the world. Until then, enter the Era of Responsibility with due caution and with the principles of morality, humanity, and doing the right thing in business as espoused by Corporate Philosopher Roger Steare in the above video clip and in his book *Ethicability*.

And remember, authenticity is required when engaging customers and stakeholders in the Era of Responsibility.

More important, every organization — including yours — has a responsibility to ensure that our children and grandchildren inherit a better world.

LEADERSHIP LESSONS

One of the most obvious leadership lessons from the Volkswagen saga is the need for leaders to ensure a safe, non-confrontational working environment for all employees.

This starts with ensuring respect in the workplace, at all levels (and between all levels) of the organization.

One cornerstone of Values Based Leadership is respect. Everyone in the organization, but particularly those in leadership positions, should foster respect for everyone (both within and external to the organization).

Unfortunately, this is not always the case. A University of Michigan study of 1100 workers reported that 71% experienced incidents of incivility or disrespect in the workplace. In another report, over half of 14,000 workers around the world said they had felt disrespected in the workplace during the prior week. And a British Workplace Behavior Survey estimated that nearly 2 million workers in Britain had experienced some form of violence at work over a two-year period.

Christine Porath, an associate professor at the McDonough School of Business at Georgetown University, wrote in the McKinsey Quarterly (December 2016) that "research shows that hurtful workplace behavior can depress performance, increase employee turnover, and even mar customer relationships." According to her research incivility in the workplace is "rampant and on the rise," with 62% of the thousands of workers she surveyed in 2016 saying they were treated rudely at work at least once a month.

This is another huge leadership lesson. And another area where leaders at all levels of organizations need to be seen "walking the talk." Leaders do this by showing respect for everyone they come into contact with, including indirect contact such as phone calls and email. This is essential for developing productive relationships and managing conflict in the workplace. There should be no tolerance for especially damaging and degrading forms of disrespect in the work environment such as bullying, harassment, backstabbing, sabotage, harmful comments, or denigrating gossip.

Former Egyptian President Anwar al-Sadat once said, "There can be hope only for a society which acts as one big family, and not as many separate ones."

The same can be said for all organizations, whether large or small. One of the best ways for leaders to break down the silos found in an organization is by establishing firm ground rules that promote respect amongst all co-workers, as well as by the organization's employees to its customers, suppliers, vendors, partners, regulators, and all other external parties.

In a respectful work environment the following traits can be found:

- Personal differences are put aside to focus on solving problems and creating solutions.

- Everyone treats all others with respect at all times.

- Open and honest constructive communication takes place.

- Differences in opinions and ideas are tolerated and respected.

- There is no talking behind another person's back.

- When problems between individuals arise they are handled forthrightly, constructively, and openly.

- It is assumed that everyone is doing the best they can with the resources at hand and that everyone's heart is in the right place for the good of the organization and its workers.

The main benefit of a respectful working environment is that less time and energy is spent handling conflicts (particularly personality conflicts and people issues), resulting in more time available for productive work and getting the right things done.

A respectful working environment is also less stressful, which results in higher employee motivation, fewer sick days and absenteeism, and overall higher levels of productivity.

Although not mentioned specifically above, corporations and their leaders also have the responsibility to ensure that trust in the capitalist system is not eroded.

As Robert Reich, former Secretary of Labor and currently professor of public policy at the University of California, wrote in the *New York Times* (July 26, 2016):

The real threat to capitalism is no longer communism or fascism but a steady undermining of the trust modern economies need for growth and stability.

The corporate executives who knowingly violate the law, or intentionally look the other way when those below them do, erode the moral foundation on which capitalism is built.

His thoughts echo those of Don Arsely, professor of psychology and behavioral economics at Duke University, who wrote in the *New York Times* almost a year earlier (September 15, 2015):

When an individual or company acts dishonestly, they pollute the trust pool — they erode the social trust we have in one another — and we are all worse for it.

Other Corporate Scandals and Misdeeds

The list of corporate scandals and misdeeds in this section is not meant to be comprehensive. However, it is indicative of the many corporate scandals, wrongdoing, errors, and misdeeds being perpetrated upon customers, society, and the planet. These are the ones I compiled during my research and tracking of the Volkswagen saga. I am sure there are many, many more of which I am unaware.

Of course, the settlements listed below do not necessarily imply guilt or culpability. Some corporate leaders may decide it is easier to pay a settlement fee or even a fine than suffer through the process of a lengthy court battle. A cynic might believe such decisions as relatively easy to make since such leaders are usually playing and paying with other people's money.

2013   HSBC pays a $1.92B settlement for violating U.S. sanctions by conducting business for customers in Iran, Libya, Sudan, Myanmar, and Cuba. The bank also allowed the Sinaloa drug cartel in Mexico and the Norte del Valle cartel in Colombia to launder $881M.

Toyota will pay $1.6B to settle a class-action lawsuit to compensate vehicle owners who suffered financial losses after widespread reports of sudden, unintended acceleration in its vehicles in 2009 and 2010.

2015

September 17 — General Motors will pay $900M to settle criminal charges related to its flawed ignition switch that has been tied to at least 124 deaths.

November 2 — Honda was fined a record $70M in January 2015 for failing to report more than 1700 claims of death or injury to the database of the U.S. National Highway Traffic Safety Administration.

November 4 — Deutsche Bank is paying $258M to settle charges by the U.S. Federal Reserve and the New York Department of Financial Services over wiring a collective $11B in transactions on behalf of countries and entities subject to U.S. sanctions, including Iran, Iraq, Libya, Myanmar, Syria, and Sudan between 1999 and 2006.

November 18 — The New York State Department of Financial Services announces a $150M fine against British bank Barclays over "misconduct" in foreign exchange services offered to its clients.

November 26

Tesco, Britain's largest supermarket group, agrees to a $12M payout to U.S. shareholders to settle one of two class-action suits over its accounting scandal. Tesco had previously admitted it had overstated its profits because it had incorrectly booked payments from suppliers.

The U.K. Financial Conduct Authority fines Barclays £72M ($109M) for disregarding its own rules on making background checks on clients and the origins of their cash.

December 24

Toshiba is fined 7.4B yen ($73M) by Japan's Financial Services Agency for a $1.3B accounting scandal. An investigation earlier in the year discovered widespread accounting errors throughout Toshiba and blamed a corporate culture in which employees found it difficult to question their superiors.

December 28

JP Morgan Chase will pay $307M for steering investors toward its own products.

December 30

Barclays investment bank will pay $10M in compensation and a $3.75M fine to settle accusations by the U.S. Financial Resolution Authority that it allowed U.S. customers to make unsuitable mutual fund deals between January 2010 and June 2015.

December 30	Swiss Bank Julius Baer has set aside $547M after reaching a deal with the U.S. Attorney's office to settle accusations it helped U.S. clients avoid taxes.

2016

January 1	Two additional Swiss banks agree to pay a total of $107M to the U.S. Department of Justice to avoid possible prosecution for helping Americans evade taxes.
January 31	Barclays and Credit Suisse settle federal and state charges they misled investors in their "dark pools" by agreeing to pay a total of $154.3M in fines and disgorgement. Barclays also admitted to breaking the law.
February 5	HSBC is fined $470M for "abusive mortgage practices" during the 2008 financial crisis. The fine is a settlement with the U.S. Department of Justice, 49 states, and the District of Columbia.
February 24	Citibank will pay $8M in fines and penalties imposed by the Consumer Finance Protection Bureau for illegal debt collection practices.
February 26	Dow Chemicals settles a class-action lawsuit which alleged that Dow and other companies intentionally colluded to inflate polyurethane prices in the late 1990s and early 2000s.

March 30   Pest control company Terminix is fined $10M for use of a dangerous pesticide at a U.S. Virgin Islands resort.

Two phony cancer charities that swindled donors out of more than $75M get shut down by Georgia's Attorney General. Working with the Federal Trade Commission and agencies from all 50 states Attorney General Sam Olens brought to a close Cancer Fund of America (CFA) and Cancer Support Services (CSS) that allegedly spent the overwhelming majority of donations on their operations, families, friends, and fundraisers.

April 4   A federal judge approves BP's $20.8B settlement with the U.S. Department of Justice and five U.S. Gulf States over its 2010 oil spill.

April 8   Uber agrees to pay $10M to settle a lawsuit over driver background checks. The company could be forced to pay up to a total of $25M. The $10M is due in the next two months and the remainder can be waived if Uber complies with the terms of the lawsuit.

April 11   Goldman Sachs agrees to pay $5.1B to settle allegations it failed to properly vet mortgage-backed securities before selling them to investors as high-quality debt. The settlement includes a $2.39B civil penalty, $875M in cash payments to the working group that negotiated the settlement, and $1.8B in consumer relief to homeowners and borrowers hurt by the financial crisis.

April 29   CalFire seeks $90M from PG&E after investigators determine the utility's power line sparked a deadly fire last year. The fire killed two people, injured one, and destroyed 965 structures.

May 11   Mitsubishi Motors used wrong mileage tests on almost all its vehicles sold in Japan since 1991 — a 25-year period — according to a report in the *Asahi* newspaper. The Japanese Transport Ministry is now investigating Mitsubishi Motors over the use of non-compliant and incorrect mileage data.

May 25   Citibank agrees to pay $425M in fines to settle civil charges it attempted to manipulate financial benchmarks between 2007 and 2012.

May 31   Deloitte agrees to pay $114M to resolve allegations it submitted false claims under a U.S. government contract.

Suzuki Motor Corp discloses it has been using improper methods to test fuel economy on more than 2.1 million vehicles.

June 17   HSBC pays $1.6B to settle a long-running securities fraud case involving the credit card and mortgage company Household International it purchased in 2002.

June 23   Bank of America pays $415M to settle a Securities and Exchange Commission (SEC) inquiry that found its Merrill Lynch unit misused billions of dollars of client money to finance its own trades. Merrill Lynch will pay $50M in restitution for profits made on these trades from 2009 to 2012, $7M in interest, and a $358M penalty.

UBS agrees to pay $19.5M to settle SEC charges that it made false or misleading statements and omissions in the sale of structured note products to investors.

June 29   Toyota recalls 1.43 million vehicles for defective airbags. These are not related to the massive recalls of Takata air bags by Toyota and other car manufacturers.

July 7   Volkswagen is one of six automotive manufacturers whose offices were raided by the German antitrust regulator as part of a probe into steel price-fixing allegations. Reports suggest the six may have formed a cartel to keep the price of steel used to make car parts low. The investigation could last anywhere from a few months to several years. Fines of up to 10% of a guilty party's annual sales turnover can be imposed by the antitrust regulator authority.

July 14   BP will pay an additional $2.5B for the Deepwater Horizon oil spill of 2010, bringing its total pretax fines to $61.6B ($44B post tax).

July 18   Fiat Chrysler is under federal fraud investigation of allegations that the maker of Dodge and Jeep vehicles inflated sales figures. The investigations by the U.S. Department of Justice and the Securities and Exchange Commission (SEC) include both civil and criminal allegations. According to the *Wall Street Journal* (July 18, 2016), these investigations "mark the latest legal headache for Fiat Chrysler, which last year faced financial penalties for safety problems that included lapses with recalls covering millions of vehicles and regulatory reporting failures." In addition, the company was recently sued by owners of newer Jeeps who say the vehicles have a joystick like gear-shift difficult to use.

Two oil refiners agree to pay $425M to reduce air pollution in a settlement with U.S. Government. The agreement with subsidiaries of Tesoro Corp of San Antonio and Par Hawaii Refining resolves accusations of Clean Air Act violations against the two oil refiners and is also expected to reduce pollution emissions in six states by almost 43,000 tons per year.

August 9   Pacific Gas and Electric is found guilty by a federal jury on five felony counts of failing to adequately inspect its gas pipeline. The California utility was also found guilty of one count of misleading federal investigators about the standards it used to identify high-risk pipelines. An internal company memo used as evidence by federal prosecutors reportedly described the PG&E database of aging pipelines of containing "a ton of errors." The utility faces up to $3 million in fines. A blast from one of its pipelines in San Bruno, CA killed eight people, injured 38, and destroyed over 50 homes in this suburb south of San Francisco. California regulators previously fined the company $1.6B for the blast.

August 10   A June 2016 Harris Poll shows that over 75% of consumers in the United States are concerned about food safety. This comes on the back of three major food scares and recalls in the last two years — from Blue Bell Creameries, Chipotle Mexican Grill, and General Mills.

Goldman Sachs is fined $36.3M for the use and disclosure of confidential materials that the United States regulators use in the supervision of banks.

September 21   Independent tests in the United States have found that the energy consumption of Samsung and LG television sets decreases dramatically under test conditions, but can rise by as much as 45% in real world use, according to the Natural Resources Defense Council.

Additionally, if consumers make changes to their main picture menu settings, energy use in televisions from Samsung, LG and Vizio can actually double, costing over $1B in energy charges for consumers and adding an extra 5 million tons of CO_2 into the air over 10 years.

September 30   Wells Fargo will pay $24M to settle allegations it illegally repossessed 413 cars between 2008 and 2015 from U.S. armed services members without a court order, in violation of federal law. The bank was fined an additional $20M by the Office of the Comptroller of the Currency for denying members of the military certain banking protections beginning in 2006.

October 11   Comcast is fined $2.3M by the U.S. Federal Communications Commission for charging customers for services and equipment they had not authorized.

October 18   Deutsche Bank agrees to pay $38M to settle U.S. litigation over allegations it illegally conspired with banks to fix the price of silver at the expense of investors.

October 19   T-Mobile will pay $48M to resolve a Federal Communications Commission (FCC) probe into whether it adequately disclosed speed and data restrictions to its "unlimited" data plan subscribers.

The settlement includes a $7.5M fine, $35.5M in consumer benefits for T-Mobile and Metro PCS customers with the "unlimited" plans, and at least $5M in services and equipment to U.S. schools.

October 26   Vodafone is fined a record £4.6M ($5.6M) in Britain for "serious and sustained" customer failures, including not updating accounts when mobile phone users topped up their credit to make calls.

October 31   Wells Fargo has agreed to pay $50M to settle a class-action lawsuit that accused the beleaguered bank of overcharging hundreds of thousands of homeowners for appraisals ordered after they had defaulted on their mortgage loans.

November 9   Deutsche Bank is reportedly in the midst of negotiations with the U.S. Department of Justice over a settlement for its alleged misselling of toxic mortgage securities in the run-up to the financial crisis.

November 13   Toyota Motor Corp reportedly agrees to a settlement of up to $3.4B to resolve a federal class-action suit brought by U.S. owners of pickup trucks and sport utility vehicles (SUVs) whose frames could rust through. The proposed settlement covers about 1.5 million Tacoma compact pickups, Tundra full-size pickups, and Sequoia SUVs alleged to have received inadequate rust protection that could lead to serious corrosion impacting the structural integrity of the vehicles.

November 17   JP Morgan's systemic bribery in China was so blatant, according to media reports, that the bank had an internal spreadsheet to track it. JP Morgan will pay $130M ($264M) to settle charges it corruptly influenced government officials in China by hiring their relatives to win business.

U.S. Federal prosecutors file wire fraud and conspiracy charges against former executives of Valeant Pharmaceuticals and a mail-order pharmacy it helped to establish. Valeant is now the target of more than 10 different government probes and multiple shareholder lawsuits.

November 21   A U.S. Appeals Court rules that Bank of America must face a fraud lawsuit by construction company Tutor Perini. The lawsuit accuses Bank of America of defrauding the construction company by selling it millions of dollars of auction-rate securities the bank knew were on the brink of collapse.

November 25   Two of Australia's largest banks offer to pay fines of A$15M ($11M) for "cartel conduct" related to trading of foreign exchange contracts on the Malaysian Ringgit. Investment bank Macquarie Group and banking behemoth Australia and New Zealand Banking Group (ANZ) will also likely face prosecution in Australia and other jurisdictions as well.

The U.K. Serious Fraud Office has expanded its inquiry into Rolls-Royce over suspicions the company was involved in bribery activities in Iraq since 2005.

December 2

Two banks have been fined a total of $5.3M for breaching Singapore's money laundering rules. Standard Chartered Bank was fined S$5.7M ($3.6M) for "significant lapses" in customer due diligence measures and controls, while private bank Coutts was fined S$2.4M ($1.7M) for inadequate customer due diligence on "politically exposed persons." The action results from the findings of an international probe into allegations that individuals close to Malaysia's Prime Minister stole more than $1B from a Malaysia government development fund.

United Airlines (UAL) will pay $2.4M to settle civil charges with the Securities and Exchange Commission (SEC) over the airline reinstating a direct flight from New Jersey to South Carolina as a personal favor to David Samson, the Chairman of the Port Authority of New York and New Jersey. The SEC claimed UAL added the flight to win Port Authority approval of a hanger project at Newark Airport. It also claimed Samson lobbied for the flight so he could travel non-stop to a home in South Carolina.

December 7

The European Commission fines Credit Agricole, HSBC, and JPMorgan Chase a total of $520M for involvement in a 7-bank cartel to fix prices of financial benchmarks linked to the euro between September 2005 and May 2008. Deutsche Bank, RBS, and Societe Generale admitted guilt in December 2013 and were fined a collective 824.6M euros ($886M), the sixth largest cartel fine imposed by the European Commission. Barclays avoided a fine because it alerted the EU Commissioner.

Pfizer is fined $106M by Britain's Competition and Markets Authority for "charging excessive and unfair prices" in the U.K. on its epilepsy drugs. Pfizer had raised pricing on its anti-epilepsy medicine by 2600% in 2012.

December 9

The U.S. Federal Trade Commission says AT&T will soon start refunding more than $88M to customers affected by unauthorized charges on their monthly bills. Around 2.7M current and former AT&T subscribers will receive an average of approximately $31.

GNC, the largest retailer of supplements in the U.S., agrees to pay $2.25M to settle a complaint filed by the Department of Justice related to ensuring the legality of the products it sells.

December 14   ConAgra Grocery Products is given an $8M fine and forced to forfeit $3.2M in cash after pleading guilty to selling peanut butter contaminated with salmonella.

The owner of the hacked infidelity website Ashley Madison will pay a $1.6M penalty to settle an investigation by the U.S. Federal Trade Commission and several states into lax data security and deceptive practices.

December 15   Attorneys General in 20 U.S. states have charged six generic pharmaceutical companies, including industry behemoths Teva and Mylan, of scheming to artificially inflate the prices of an antibiotic and a diabetes drug.

The parent company of DeVry University says it has agreed to settle a lawsuit with the U.S. Federal Trade Commission for $100M. The FTC has accused the school of false advertising.

December 16   An Australian court has fined Reckitt Benckiser, the U.K. manufacturer of pain reliever Nurofen, A$6M ($4.4M) for misleading consumers by saying its Nurofen Specific Pain products were formulated to treat a specific type of pain. This is the largest corporate penalty awarded by an Australian court for misleading conduct under the Australian Consumer Law.

December 20   Morgan Stanley will pay $7.5M to settle civil charges that it violated customer protection rules when it conducted trades using customer cash to lower its borrowing costs.

December 21   The Swiss Competition Commission has fined several European and U.S. banks over $97M over interest rate cartels.

Two Brazilian companies accused of a massive bribery scheme will pay over $3.5B in fines to U.S. and Brazilian authorities. The huge construction giant Odebrecht will pay $2.6B and its petroleum subsidiary Braskem will pay roughly $957M for their dealings with Petrobras, the state-controlled Brazilian oil company. The U.S. Department of Justice said this was the agency's largest corporate bribery resolution to date.

December 22   Barclays Bank is being sued by the U.S. Department of Justice over alleged fraud in the sale of mortgage securities in the run-up to the 2008 financial crisis.

December 23   Deutsche Bank and Credit Suisse have agreed to tentative settlements with the U.S. Department of Justice over their dealings in mortgage-backed bonds. Deutsche Bank will pay $3.1B in fines and

$4.1B in consumer relief, while Credit Suisse will pay $2.5B in fines and $2.8B in consumer relief.

December 29

General Cable will pay over $75M to settle allegations that it had bribed officials in Angola, Bangladesh, and China to win business. The settlement was announced by the U.S. Department of Justice and the Securities and Exchange Commission.

2017

January 3

Media reports say Toshiba Corp will be accused by Japan's Securities and Exchange Surveillance Commission of misreporting profits by 40B Yen ($340M) over three years.

Credit bureaus Equifax and TransUnion are fined $23.1M as part of a settlement with the U.S. Consumer Financial Protection Bureau, which said the firms misled consumers into paying for credit scores that might be dramatically different from the scores used by lenders.

January 4

The former head of Reckitt Benckiser's South Korean business unit is given a seven-year jail sentence for criminal negligence following the deaths of almost 100 people related to a humidifier disinfectant manufactured by the company.

January 13

Japanese airbag manufacturer Takata will pay $1B to settle charges related to a deadly defect in its airbags that led to a massive recall and has been linked to 16 deaths, including 11 in the U.S. Three high-level executives have been indicted on wire fraud and conspiracy charges and the company has pleaded to a felony account of wire fraud.

MedStar Ambulance, which operates in Massachusetts, will pay a $12.7M penalty to settle claims that it fraudulently billed Medicare.

January 14   Moody's Corp has agreed to pay $864M to settle with the U.S. Department of Justice, 21 state attorneys, and the District of Columbia over its ratings of risky mortgage securities prior to the 2008 financial crisis. DOJ will be paid a $437.5M penalty and the remaining $426.3M will be split between the states and Washington, D.C.

January 19   Citigroup Inc. pays $25M to settle allegations from the Commodity Futures Trading Commission that one of its units entered U.S. Treasury futures market orders with the intent of canceling them, a practice known as "spoofing."

A federal lawsuit by the Consumer Financial Protection Bureau accuses Navient, the largest student loan server in the U.S., of deceiving borrowers to the tune of $4B. The suit alleges that customers who took out student loans were hit with unnecessary interest payments, denied options to reduce their debt, and suffered damage to their credit scores.

January 20   Uber will pay $20M to settle with the Federal Trade Commission allegations that it duped people into driving for its ride-hailing service with false promises about how much they would earn and how much they would have to pay to finance a car.

Thousands of HSBC credit card customers will share £4M ($5M) in compensation for having to pay unreasonable debt collection charges imposed by two subsidiaries of the bank.

January 21   The Consumer Financial Protection Bureau orders CitiFinancial Servicing and CitiMortgage, two subsidiaries of banking giant Citigroup, to pay $28.8M for giving "the runaround" to cash-strapped homeowners who were facing mortgage foreclosures. Some 41,000 customers will receive approximately $400 each in refunds from CitiMortgage.

January 25   BT Group PLC was hit with a pair of investor lawsuits in the U.S. after the telecommunication's company's stock market value dropped over 20% in a single day over an accounting scandal in Italy.

January 31   Deutsche Bank is fined nearly $630M over alleged money laundering in Russia reportedly worth $10B. The fines were levied by New York State's

Department of Financial Services ($425M) and Britain's Financial Conduct Authority ($204M). The matter is also currently being investigated by the U.S. Department of Justice.

CHAPTER NINE

Individual Accountability Lessons

In the very first discussion I had regarding the shocking news of the Volkswagen diesel emissions test cheating, in a phone conversation with my good friend Alex Chan in Singapore, I raised the question that still bothers me most today: why did not one single Volkswagen employee speak up and make management, or regulators, or even the media, aware of this deliberate scheme to cheat and commit fraud?

The silence surrounding this subterfuge from the entire Volkswagen employee base is a moral and ethical question with ramifications for organizational leaders around the world.

Ironically, in the Volkswagen Group Code of Conduct issued during the CEO tenure of Martin Winterkorn, the opening section titled General Conduct Requirements is quite prophetic:

> *The reputation of the Volkswagen Group is determined in large part by the demeanor, actions and behavior of each individual employee. Inappropriate behavior by just one employee can cause serious damage to the organization.*

Wonderful words. But apparently not wonderful enough to spur anyone to go against an entrenched code of silence culture prevalent throughout the organization.

I wonder if this would have been any different had the above paragraph included one additional sentence:

> Appropriate behavior by any one employee can prevent serious damage to the organization.

WORKPLACE CLIMATE IMPACTS ACCOUNTABILITY

When leaders create a performance culture in which specific performance targets and metrics are the main yardsticks of evaluation, they often unintentionally create a climate where mistrust, non-cooperation between workgroups and individuals, and a code of silence reign supreme.

Command-and-control leadership is often exemplified as leadership by fear. Usually taking the forms of both aggressive interactions and passive-aggressive behavior, this leadership style often creates a culture of foreboding silence. It also cultivates a fear of stepping out too far and raising one's head too high. This in turn leads to a dearth of innovation, employee engagement, acceptance for change, and personal accountability.

Such performance driven cultures can also be unsafe workplaces for supervisory and frontline staff. The unwritten rules of self-preservation in such corporate cultures create an unwillingness to speak up, question directions, or even proffer innovative thoughts.

Thus, not only are innovation and new ideas lost, but the risk of cutting corners or engaging in illicit activities in order to meet performance targets is unquestionably high. We have seen such cheating and rule breaking being rampant in the financial services industry for numerous years (with the falsification of customer accounts at Wells Fargo being the latest example). Now we are witnessing it in the automotive, pharmaceutical, cable television, and even the sports management industries.

Performance cultures often come with autocratic management styles that are dismissive of employee questions and rooted in real or imagined fear. They also have rigid hierarchies with excessive respect being given to seniority and job titles. Such corporate cultures tend to eliminate constructive conflict and disallow any refusal to follow orders, even when such directives may have harmful consequences of which upper management are unaware.

These are neither safe nor smart workplace environments.

BATTLING A CULTURE OF SILENCE

There are over 610,000 employees at Volkswagen. Of course, most of them were not privy to the defeat device software. But certainly a significant number were. And others would have heard whispers or rumors about the clever and innovative way Volkswagen's engineers had gotten around those cumbersome and troubling U.S. diesel emissions regulations.

In fact, news reports in April 2016 cite the existence of a PowerPoint presentation that specifically details how to cheat NOx emissions testing in laboratory environments. The presentation was reportedly prepared by a top technology executive in 2006. How many employees had seen, or were aware of, this presentation deck?

Also in April 2016 Volkswagen released a statement on the status of Jones Day internal investigation, saying that 65 million documents had been submitted for electronic review and around 450 interviews had been conducted. Media reports that month add that Jones Day investigators were also reviewing over 1500 laptops and computers.

246 • STEVEN B HOWARD

In an October 2016 filing in U.S. District Court, Volkswagen states it has turned over more than 20 million documents to the U.S. Department of Justice. Certainly all these documents were not generated by a few "rogue engineers." And certainly all these laptops and computers being studied and examined were being used by more than just a handful of engineers.

Speaking of the Department of Justice, in their charges against U.S. based Volkswagen engineer Robert Liang the agency refers to several group email exchanges. While the number of recipients included in these group emails at Volkswagen is not specified by the DOJ it is again evidence that more than just two or three people have been involved in perpetuating this scandal.

At this point in time we can surmise that dozens, and perhaps hundreds, of employees were knowledgeable about the defeat device software creation, implementation, and concealment.

Remember, this deliberate cheating went on for over seven years before it was exposed by ICCT. One would presume it is pretty dumb to think that dozens or hundreds of employees could keep the cheating software quiet, especially over a seven year period. But that is exactly what they did.

What kind of a corporate culture and workplace climate creates such a fortitude of silence? One might argue that this is truly a testament to a very strong (albeit immoral and unethical) corporate culture.

Maybe some reports were made internally. Perhaps one or more employees raised their concerns in meetings, or even in writing but were shot down or ignored. We do not know yet for sure. Hopefully, the Jones Day investigation report will provide greater clarity on these issues.

There were some media reports in February 2015 that a veteran Volkswagen AG quality control executive, Bernd Gottweis, had written to then CEO Martin Winterkorn in May 2014 raising a red flag about emissions tests from U.S. environmental authorities. Volkswagen subsequently confirmed the existence, but not the details, of the memorandum and would only say that it was included in a stack of papers Winterkorn had taken home to read over a weekend. The Volkswagen statement also noted that "whether and to what extent Mr. Winterkorn took notice of this memo is not documented."

Gottweis had been recalled from retirement to help deal with the emissions problem after Volkswagen had been notified by U.S. regulators of the ICCT on-road emissions test results. But, from what we currently know from media reports, Gottweis was only concerned about not having a "plausible explanation" to give to authorities explaining the higher NOx emissions found in the on-road testing by ICCT. He was also concerned that U.S. officials were likely to investigate whether Volkswagen cars were equipped with a "so-called defeat device." Apparently, however, he did not express concerns about the illegality of the company's actions nor about the potential damage to the Volkswagen brand and corporate reputation.

This may be one example of other reports we will learn about when the results of the Jones Day internal investigation are released, if indeed they are.

However, the fact that not a single staff member of Volkswagen came forward publicly is of great concern. How was this corporate code of silence able to trump individual accountability and individual moral and ethical values?

A story in the *New York Times* (December 15, 2015) illustrates how this might happen, particularly if the story was widely shared throughout the company and all its automotive divisions. The story tells of Volkswagen CEO Martin Winterkorn severely chastising a pair of technicians for correcting him when he mistakenly thought a push-button console was a touch-screen display.

A story like this will likely spread throughout the company, conveying and reinforcing the message that employees should contradict or correct supervisors at their own personal risk. Likewise, employees should refrain from delivering bad news to supervisors or raising doubts about actions believed to have been approved by supervisors.

Even senior staff at Volkswagen were not spared Winterkorn's brusqueness, in private or in public. A video on YouTube shows Winterkorn inspecting a new model from Hyundai at the Frankfurt Motor Show in 2011. When seated in the driver's seat, he adjusts the steering column, only to discover that it makes no noise. "Bischoff!" he barks out, summoning the automaker's design chief Klaus Bischoff. Pointing at the steering wheel he angrily growls to this senior executive in front of other Volkswagen staff, "Nothing makes a clonking sound here!"

Stories such as these, when repeated and cascaded throughout a company led by control-and-command managers, easily create and reinforce a corporate-wide code of silence. Add to this the insular governance structure of the Volkswagen Group and its subsidiaries and the lack of any outside directors on any of the company's supervisory boards. It is little wonder, however disappointing and disheartening, that not a single Volkswagen employee throughout the seven years of deliberate emissions test cheating came forward or went public with their knowledge or concerns.

One wonders how many of the engineers and others involved in creating, installing, updating, and hiding the defeat device software from regulators and customers belong to professional associations that have codes of conduct for their members? How many of these have values emanating from strong political or religious views? How many are parents educating their own children about morals and about doing what is right instead of keeping silent about what is wrong?

Yet they all parked their personal values and moral ethical codes at the front gate when entering Volkswagen factories and premises. All allowed a culture of silence to infuse them with a callous disregard for the health (and probable premature deaths) of others and for the direct impact on the planet's environment.

Employees utilize a culture of silence when there is a belief that supervisors or leaders "shoot the messenger here." It becomes an internal cultural norm to keep one's head down and mouth closed, as well as a keenly instinctive methodology of employment survivability. In such workplace climates individuals feel a greater responsibility to themselves and to their own survival within the organization than to the collective good of the organization or to their fellow workers.

In this culture of silence it becomes easy for any individual to rationalize their silence. After all, no single employee was individually causing more NOx emissions to be emitted from the automaker's engines. These emissions were simply the result of the engine's design and management's disapproval of a $330 piece of equipment for budgetary reasons.

Those employees in the know could rationalize their complicity by simply telling themselves that all they were doing with their silence was not allowing the actual levels of emissions to be found out and reported during laboratory emissions tests. No harm. No foul.

Unfortunately, there was harm, to both individuals exposed to increased NOx emissions and to the environment. And the result of this culture of silence now impacts:

- Hundreds, perhaps thousands of jobs at Volkswagen.

- Hundreds of thousands of Volkswagen customers around the world, many of whom reportedly will no longer be loyal to the Volkswagen, Audi, or Porsche brands.

- The retirement and pension funds of millions of individuals around the world.

- The corporate and brand reputation of Volkswagen.

- Thousands of people living near Volkswagen factories whose local councils now have to charge for services previously paid by Volkswagen's local tax contributions, as the carmaker's profits decline due to Dieselgate related costs and reserves.

How can outsiders impact an entrenched culture of silence, one that is not endemic solely to Volkswagen? It is an issue that many legal authorities and academics have grappled with in recent years, particularly with the rise in corporate malfeasance we partially highlighted in the previous sidebar.

John C. Coffee, Jr., the Adolf A. Berle Professor of Law at Columbia University Law School and Director of its Center on Corporate Governance, has two interesting ideas on how the corporate code of silence can be minimized in the future. Writing in the Columbia Law School *Blue Sky Blog* (May 23, 2016), his two policy ideas are well worth consideration by lawmakers around the world:

> *First, the law could impose a collective penalty on all corporate managers regardless of their individual culpability. For example, a corporate conviction on a non-trivial charge could result automatically in the suspension of all stock option, stock bonus and similar incentive*

compensation plans for a period of years. This threat of a collective responsibility should deter corporate executives at all levels and give them a common interest in corporate law compliance. Indeed, under such a legal regime, the individual corporate executive who did cause the corporation to commit a crime would be seen as disloyal to his fellow executives (because he was subjecting them to serious financial loss). The key attraction of this approach is that it uses peer pressure (both to cause the individual executive not to violate the law and to motivate all executives to monitor for conduct that could result in a law violation).

A second proposal starts from the premise that Volkswagen was protected by a culture of silence.....the real issue here is how to break down this culture of silence.

The most direct means to this end is to reward officers, employees and other agents to reveal corporate law violations. The strategy here is to bribe employees to reveal what their company wants to hide. This approach requires an expanded system of bounties for whistle-blowers.

The superior alternative then is a defendant-funded system for rewarding the whistle-blower that does not depend on a specific violation. Consider this alternative: if as little as 5% of the total penalty that Volkswagen eventually pays to U.S. agencies were contributed instead to a trust fund set up by the settlement agreement to reward whistle blowers, this fund could be administered by trustees selected by the regulators and used to reward whistleblowers at either Volkswagen or any other auto manufacturer. Not only *would Volkswagen be deterred, but so might Takata, Toyota, and GM (just to mention only recent cases).*

INDIVIDUAL ACCOUNTABILITY

Too much of the literature on individual accountability in the workplace focuses on being accountable for results achieved and mistakes made. But there is a higher level of individual accountability, especially for leaders.

Individual accountability also means being morally responsible and accountable for stopping illegal, illicit, and immoral actions, and for reporting these as soon as one learns of them or suspects such.

However, once a leaders allows individual accountability to drift or become an intermittent action, rather than a core value, results suffer and problematic events inevitably arise.

Increasing the right kind of individual accountability in an organization does not going happen through a set of corporate guidelines and some posters displayed around company premises. After all, Volkswagen had a well written and detailed 24-page Corporate Conduct Guidelines book that did nothing to prevent or stop deliberate cheating and fraudulent actions.

Individual accountability will happen when the actions of leaders change. It will only start to happen after leaders are first seen exhibiting high standards of accountability, ethical excellence and moral fortitude in place of executive excess.

Here's another Volkswagen story that highlights how far the automaker has to move in this regard. In August 2016 Audi chairman Rupert Stadler was forced to reimburse $12,500 euros ($14,000) to the company for the cost of a beer drinking competition he reportedly organized in May for about 30 top executives. At this time Volkswagen was still in the midst of negotiations with lawyers representing the U.S. Department of Justice, EPA, CARB, and the Federal Trade Commission.

According to media reports the party featured plenty of beer as well as a Bavarian brass band flown in to perform. It is hard for lower level employees to break a culture of silence, or to start accepting and exhibiting individual accountability, when they see or hear about such excessive executive entertainment, even if the cost to the company was only temporary. Apparently Herr Stadler thought it was morally and ethically permissible to charge the cost of this party to the company. That alone sends a huge message to Audi's management ranks and employee workforce.

As mentioned before, actions speak louder than words and corporate guide books.

Individual accountability goes beyond post-action reward, retribution, and punishment.

After all, every corporate criminal act involves individual wrongdoing and illegal action. Individuals commit the crimes for which corporate offenders pay. So individual lawbreakers need to be held legally accountable for their actions and punished appropriately, either by the relevant legal system or by their corporate paymasters.

Often, though, this is not the case as leaders of corporations willingly (and sometimes unwillingly) pay huge fines in exchange for speedy settlements with regulators that include clauses not to prosecute individuals.

Apparently, however, Volkswagen and its employees may not be so lucky this time around. The U.S. Department of Justice continues to pursue a criminal investigation with both the automaker and individuals as targets. It looks like at least one of the six Volkswagen executives indicted on federal felony charges (and already arrested by FBI agents) in the U.S. will either be tried or plead guilty via some sort of plea deal arrangement. Additionally, there is likely to be more criminal charges laid against individuals in South Korea, where one Volkswagen employee is already serving jail time. And criminal charges against the company or employees are still possible in Germany, Britain, and other European markets.

ADVOCATING FOR WHAT IS RIGHT

A core component of individual accountability is the need for individuals at all levels of an organization to speak up and be heard.

Even in the most stringent control-and-command organizations, individuals need to assert their right to speak out and voice their concerns over actions that may be illegal or immoral.

This, of course, takes courage. But in an Era of Responsibility such courage needs to become the norm, and it needs to be rewarded. Or leaders will eventually have to face the unintended consequences brought about by a culture of silence, as Volkswagen's leaders have.

This may be the most important leadership lesson stemming from the Volkswagen saga.

Individual accountability applies at all levels of all organizations, albeit in different shapes and forms.

For instance, for mid-level leaders and supervisors there is often a need to advocate for what is right with upper management and more senior leaders.

Likewise, individuals also need to demonstrate confidence and courage when providing feedback to their own bosses and other senior leaders. They also need to assert their right to express their viewpoints, concerns, and questions in a professional manner.

This is particularly important for mid-level leaders tasked with implementing strategies handed down or pushed upon them from above. Mid-level leaders need to be stronger advocates for advising senior leaders what is required to successfully implement a strategic plan. Otherwise, as seen in chapter four on Corporate Leadership Lessons, strategic plans are more likely to fail to meet stated objectives and results.

Admittedly, advocating for what is right is not always easy. This is especially true when trust, openness, and honesty have not been mutually established between leaders and managers operating at different levels within an organization. However, it is not impossible to do so, particularly if the following seven-step model for advocating for what is right is followed:

1) Base your argument or position on facts.

2) Name your sources (unless these are strictly confidential).

3) Challenge information presented to you, especially if such information is unsourced or undocumented. If it is documented or sourced, be sure to challenge the information, not the source.

4) Control your boiling point by exercising self-control. You know what angers you, so prepare yourself not to be agitated. The next step also helps with this.

5) Ignore statements without merit. Examples are "you guys in marketing always back the customer over operations," or "people in R&D never understand the many manufacturing challenges we face."

6) Focus on the big picture and shared outcomes.

7) Incorporate the best points from others and restate your position (revised or not).

LEADERSHIP ACCOUNTABILITY

When leaders talk about ensuring accountability they are usually referring to concepts such as holding people accountable for results.

Good leaders take this a step further by emphasizing that accountability is about more than just results. They hold both themselves and others accountable for the decisions made and the options generated that are producing the results, as well as for the actual outcomes. A good leader will also hold herself or himself accountable for utilizing the right level of delegation when appropriately empowering team members.

Good leaders also have a bigger organizational perspective, thus holding themselves and others accountable for how their decisions and actions impact other departments and business units as well as customers and business partners.

Great leaders go even further by holding themselves and other leaders accountable for their leadership behaviors, actions, and for making ethical decisions. I call this Leadership Accountability.

Senior leaders and executives who understand and utilize Leadership Accountability often realize that they are not in the best position to identify and know all the challenges involved in strategy execution. Unfortunately, too many leaders have leadership mindsets and personal fears of inadequacies that prevent them readily admitting this. As such they do not solicit ideas and inputs from others, nor do they appear willingly receptive of unsolicited ideas and inputs.

As a result, in far too many organizations there is a culture of reluctance within the lower leadership ranks to raise concerns and red flags with more senior colleagues or more experienced team members.

This is even more prevalent when team members are from hierarchical cultures such as those found in North Asia, China, parts of Latin America, and Eastern Europe.

Leaders can only change this culture of reluctance by being seen as open to suggestions, questions, and even push-back by their followers and peers. Only a "walk the talk" solution will result in the desired culture change, and it will not happen overnight.

As I often counsel the leaders I coach and develop, "Leaders who don't listen will eventually be surrounded by people who refuse to speak." Listening is one of the most important leadership skills.

In fact, I always tell my leadership development participants that since they each have two ears and one mouth, they should use these proportionately in communicating as a leader. In other words, they will benefit most from listening twice as much as they speak.

I firmly believe that listening is the number one communication skill a leader must have. This is particularly true for new leaders, as the tendency is to think that once one is put into a leadership position it is a requirement to have all the answers and to bark out all the orders. Nothing could be further from the truth.

There is more to listening than simply hearing the words others are saying. Rather, leaders need to develop their active listening skills, which means observing the emotions, feelings, expressions, and body language behind what is being said. It also means acutely listening for what is not being said and for what is intentionally being left out.

Stephen Covey, author of the book *The 7 Habits of Highly Effective People*, identified a key problem in communicating, both professionally and personally. He noted that too many of us "listen with the intent to respond, not with the intent to understand."

Listening with the intent to understand is a crucial skill for leaders. Fortunately, it is also one that can be developed and enhanced, through practice and reflection.

Great leaders devote a significant amount of energy and time to clarifying and understanding the perspectives, ideas, concerns, and questions of others (particularly of those they lead). Additionally, great leaders do not see clarification questions from team members, peers, or others as a sign of push-back or dissension. In fact, they appreciate such questions and inputs, knowing full well that open and honest dialogues are a key builder of trust.

I introduced the concept of Leadership Accountability in the summer of 2016 in my book *8 Keys To Becoming A Great Leader: With Leadership Lessons from Gibbs, Yoda and Capt'n Jack Sparrow*. Here's an excerpt from that book on building and maintaining Leadership Accountability:

> *At the heart of Leadership Accountability is trust.*
>
> *Trust is more than the leader being held accountable for doing what they say they will do. Trust also means the leader will make decisions based on what is best for the entire organization, its customers, and the world we live in.*
>
> *Such trust means that personal and departmental agendas are put aside for the greater good and sustainable health of the organization.*
>
> *Great leaders build trust through transparency and honesty. They are willing to explain the reasons behind decisions. They are also willing to acknowledge when they do not know the answer or solution to a problem.*

Long gone are the days when leaders should never exhibit weakness or vulnerability in front of their team members. Doing so does not cause staff and direct reports to question or doubt your leadership skills. It causes them to see you as human, and as someone struggling with some of the same issues and concerns they are. It is archaic and utter nonsense to think otherwise.

Despite his control and command leadership style, even Special Agent Gibbs is not afraid to admit when he doesn't know something, is unsure of a situation, or even when he is wrong. Not surprisingly, this leadership teacher has rules for all such situations:

When you need help, ask. (Gibbs Rule 28)

Sometimes you're wrong. (Gibbs Rule 51)

Gibbs also holds himself as accountable for his own actions as he does for his team members. Rule 45, which he invokes upon both himself and various team members, is very clear about this: "Clean up the mess that you make."

Without a doubt leaders need to be strong and exhibit resilience, especially during a crisis situation or in particularly difficult and trying times. Such exhibition of strength and displays of resilience will be appreciated and admired by your team members when you and your team are facing enormous challenges and demanding situations.

However, there are appropriate situations and times when, in a positive and forthcoming way, and with the right audience, leaders can admit their vulnerabilities, blind spots, uncertainties, and weaknesses.

In doing so, great leaders become trusted by their followers. Such trust enables followers and other team members to be more willing to raise problems and concerns with their leaders, allowing problems to be dealt with sooner when they are more manageable.

Without trust, no aspect of your leadership philosophy or leadership mindset matters. Without trust your leadership philosophy, mindset, and beliefs are simply invalid and unlikely to be accepted by others.

Every leader makes mistakes. Great leaders readily acknowledge their errors and mistakes. And not just to themselves! They own up and admit slipups, blunders, incorrect decisions, miscalculations, and poor leadership behavior to their colleagues, peers, and direct reports. Average leaders tend to ignore, brush over, or cover up their occasional mistakes, often in the hopes that nobody has noticed. Believe me, they have!

Here are the types of mistakes that leaders make that break the bonds of trust:

- *Showing favoritism to one or more team members.*

- *Withholding information on purpose to keep others, particularly peers, out of the loop or misinformed.*

- *Showing up unannounced at a meeting being led by a direct report.*

- *Taking credit for the work of your team without sharing the credit.*

- *Giving feedback in anger.*

- *Gossiping or spreading knowingly false stories about colleagues.*

- *Demanding someone do something simply because you're the boss.*

- *Not recognizing efforts of team members and considering extra efforts to merely be "part of the job requirement."*

- *Frequently missing or being late to meetings with team members simply because you're the (very busy) boss, thus not respecting their time, their workloads, and their commitments to others.*

- *Not keeping promises and commitments.*

- *Making vague, general promises and commitments that you know team members perceive as more rock solid, especially when it concerns their career advancement opportunities.*

All of these are easy mistakes to make in the hustle and bustle of the day. But while they may seem like minor infractions, each is a trust buster; especially when they become frequent leadership behaviors.

Leadership Accountability is a mixture of vulnerability, humility, self-confidence, forgiveness, ethical judgment, and a personal code upon which to based leadership behaviors and actions.

It takes all this, and more, to consistently hold yourself and others accountable for all leadership behaviors, actions, and decisions.

When Leadership Accountability is absent, as we have seen at Volkswagen, Enron, HSBC, Wells Fargo, the U.S. Veterans Administration, and other organizations, devastating disasters and ethical crises often arise. In some instances, neither the brand nor the organization recovers from Leadership Accountability lapses.

LEADERSHIP LESSONS

It has often been said that "managers do things right while leaders do the right things." There's a great deal of truth in this pithy observation. Especially as our concept of Leadership Accountability is applied.

Managers should be responsible for ensuring appropriate implementation of policies, procedures, and processes. Leaders, in addition to determining and communicating direction, are responsible for people leadership and people development. This includes leadership and development of themselves.

Know Thyself, the words inscribed in gold letters on the temple of Apollo at Delphi, is probably the most important two-word phrase ever chiseled or written.

The most important part of knowing yourself, particularly for a leader, is knowing what your values are. For the concept of values-based leadership, which we highlighted in chapter four (Corporate Leadership Lessons), also applies to self-leadership and the notion of Leadership Accountability described above.

Your values define your character. Living your values means having character.

At the end of the day, what you are — your character — is vastly more important than what you do, especially in terms of your vocation, career, or chosen lifestyle. What you do for a living is not truly who you are, although this concept has been greatly misplaced in the materialistic, economy-driven focus of the past few decades.

J. C. Watts, an American football player and politician, has one of the best definitions of character: *"Character is doing the right thing when nobody is looking. There are too many people who think that the only thing that is right is to get by, and the only thing that is wrong is to get caught."*

Principles form your personal and professional values and should not be situational in nature. They are the rocks upon which your decisions for action should be made. As Edward R. Lyman wrote:

> *Principle — particularly moral principle —can never be a weathervane, spinning around this way and that with the shifting winds of expediency. Moral principle is a compass forever fixed and forever true.*

Living your values is not always easy. As the old saying goes, temptation is always just around the corner. It is often far too easy to pursue short-term amusement or glee that is in conflict with your true values. When you do not live your values, however, trouble inevitably crops up.

One of the causes of such problems is that too many people do not give enough thought to their values. They know they have values, deep down, but they fail to take the time to reflect upon them and use these to guide their decision-making processes.

Those who are in close touch with their own personal values tend not to have major catastrophes and calamities in their lives, unless of course they engage in actions or activities that are not congruent with their personal values.

As Stephen R. Covey wrote in *First Things First*, "The essence of principle-centered living is to create an open channel with that deep inner knowing, and acting with integrity to it. It is having the character and competence to listen to and live by our conscience."

The bottom line is that the actions and decisions of people in tune with their core personal values fall within their own comfort zones because of the alignment with those personal values. Such people tend to be very comfortable with their own actions, even when others around them get enraged when they cannot understand the decisions made or actions taken.

Core values unconsciously, and sometimes even consciously, guide and govern our decisions, particularly our major decisions. Hence, they help determine and steer us toward our futures.

When we know what is important to us — when we know what our values are — making decisions and taking action is so much easier and comfortable. When decisions and actions are taken with the perspective of your values in mind, your confidence in these decisions and actions is increased and you are more readily able to put self-doubt aside and cast off the criticisms of others. As Roy Disney, brother of Walt, points out, "It's not hard to make decisions when you know what your values are."

Adds novelist William Faulkner, "I have found that the greatest help in meeting any problem with decency and self-respect and whatever courage is demanded is to know where you yourself stand. That is, to have in words what you believe and are acting from."

Likewise, when you take action or make decisions that are not in alignment with your values, three things happen almost automatically:

1) Your self-doubt escalates.

2) Your confidence level drops.

3) The criticisms of others have an air of truth about them.

In fact, the criticisms of others will sting sharply, because deep inside you will be pinged by the error of your ways. Even though the "mental you" and the "emotional you" may not admit or accept that you are out of alignment with your values, your body will send strong signals that something is not right (often a gut feeling, clammy hands, or a sense of anxiety).

Unfortunately, due to ego-led stubbornness or a false sense of self-confidence created by talking to yourself, you may attempt to override these physical sensations by trying to rationalize or justify your misguided action or decision. Trying to convince yourself to ignore these signals is most assuredly a sign that your actions or decisions are not in alignment with your core values.

Consciously living your values will result in a more rewarding life. As author Ayn Rand said, "Happiness is that state of consciousness which proceeds from the achievement of one's values."

Research shows that those whose working lives mirror or encapsulate their personal values are generally more productive and happiest with their professional lives. This makes sense. After all, when people go to work they should not be required to leave their values at home.

If the values of your working environment clash with your personal values, removing yourself as quickly as feasible from that working environment is mandatory for your spiritual, physical, and emotional health (and growth). You are not likely to find enjoyment, be productive, or consider your work to be meaningful in an environment where the workplace values are not in sync with your personal values. This is equally true for the team members you lead as it is for you.

CREATE A CULTURE OF VOICE

The art of great leadership mandates a positive and future-focus mindset. You will not find many successful leaders who are pessimistic. Nor are those focused solely on short-term results, such as quarterly revenues and unit sales, likely to be successful over the long term (a result we have seen in the Volkswagen saga).

This does not mean leadership requires wearing rose-colored glasses or having an unrealistic view that all will become right soon.

Rather, the art of great leadership requires a solid grounding in both understanding the reality of any situation, while simultaneously being able to integrate various viewpoints of reality that you and others hold. This means both understanding the status quo and being able to question the underlining nature of the status quo, and how this is perceived and believed by others.

Part of questioning the status quo requires creating what Rob Bogosian, author of the book *Breaking Corporate Silence*, calls a culture of voice.

It can also be labeled a culture of inclusion, a workplace climate characterized by leaders who listen, ask open-ended questions, seek input from others, know the difference between clarifying questions and push-back questions from team members, and who acknowledge the worthiness of subordinate contributions and concerns.

It is also a corporate culture underpinned by values-based leadership (see chapter four on Corporate Leadership Lessons).

Some leaders are born to lead. Most leaders are created by circumstances, aptitude, and an internal willingness or drive to lead others.

The thing is: anyone at any level of an organization can be a great leader.

Great leadership is not something reserved for senior management, business owners, and entrepreneurs. Anyone can be a great leader, if only of themselves. One does not need direct reports or to head a multi-functional team to be a great leader. As such, anyone can implement the art of great leadership and the skills of great leadership.

The Financial Costs of the Scandal Scorecard

What has been the financial cost of the Volkswagen scandal? We have kept a list of the fines, penalties, and legal fees that have been publicized over the past 17 months. Again, this is by no means a comprehensive and definitive list, but the current scorecard shows an approximate total of US$23.5B.

Of course, Volkswagen may appeal some of these fines. And additional fines and penalties are undoubtedly still forthcoming. And there are additional fees to the lawyers of the plaintiffs in a couple of the settlement agreements that still need to be negotiated and agreed to.

Also this list does not take into account all of the internal costs for managing the scandal, nor does it include the fees paid to Jones Day for their internal investigation.

But we can safely say that the financial cost for Volkswagen to date is well over $24 billion.

2015		
November 26	14.1B won fine imposed by South Korea Environment Ministry.	$12.3M

2016		
January 9	Fines in Brazil over the emissions scandal.	$13M
February 18	168M peso fine by Mexico's Profepa environmental protection agency for importing and selling 2016 models without the mandatory environmental certification.	$8.9M
March 10	Rs460M penalty imposed by excise department of Pune, India for allegedly evading taxes by undervaluing cars sold in India between 2010 and 2014.	$7.4M
May 26	Audi Volkswagen Taiwan Co. fined NT$55M for false advertising concerning the emission levels of certain vehicles.	$154,000
July 8	Civil penalties paid to California to resolve claims made by the state's Attorney General's office against Volkswagen under the state's unfair competition law.	$86M
July 29	Washington State Department of Ecology fines Volkswagen for the 21,000 Volkswagen diesel vehicles registered in the state putting people's health at risk.	$176M

August 4	17.8B won fine imposed by South Korea for forging documents on emissions and noise-level tests.	$16.1M
August 8	5 million euro fine by Italy's anti-trust agency for allegedly misinforming car buyers about diesel emissions results. This is the highest fine in its power.	$5.54M
October 3	Volkswagen agrees to compensate it U.S. dealer network an average of $1.85M over an 18-month period.	$1.21B
October 14	Volkswagen agrees to pay the lawyers for the plaintiffs for legal fees and costs related to the U.S. Settlement Agreement.	$175M
October 26	The U.S. Settlement Agreement includes $10B to fix or buy back 465,000 diesel vehicles plus $4.7B paid into two environmental remediation funds.	$14.7B
December 19	C$2.1B settlement in Canada to buy back and pay restitution to 105,000 Canadian owners of the 2-liter vehicles fitted with diesel engine emissions test cheating software.	$1.57B
December 19	C$15M ($11.2M) fine paid to the Canadian Competition Bureau.	$11.2M
December 30	The U.K. Transport Minister reveals that Volkswagen has agreed to reimburse the British government £1.1M for the cost of	$1.4M

	vehicle emissions tests on other automotive manufacturers conducted by the U.K. government earlier in the year.	
2017		
January 11	$4.3B criminal and civil fines	$4.3B
January 11	A fine of 37.2B won is levied against Volkswagen in South Korea for false advertising on vehicle emissions.	$32M
January 31	Volkswagen agrees to a Proposed Settlement on the 85,000 3-liter Audi, Porsche, and VW vehicles in the U.S. equipped with the emissions test cheating defeat device.	$1.2B

CHAPTER TEN

It Is Still Not Over

As this book goes into production the first week of February 2017, the Volkswagen Saga is far from over.

In fact, it is likely to heat up on the criminal front, and in Europe, now that almost all the civil issues with the U.S. government have been settled.

Additionally, there are dozens of investor lawsuits in various jurisdictions around the world waiting for court dates. And though a $1.2B settlement agreement on the class-action lawsuit on behalf of car owners of the 3-liter diesel Audi, Porsche, and VW vehicles has been agreed to, it will not receive final approval from U.S. District Court Judge Breyer until May 2017.

Here is where the saga stands at the moment:

Volkswagen has agreed to over $23B in fines, penalties, and potential compensatory payments to vehicle owners in the U.S. and Canada.

Volkswagen has been fined over $100M by statutory bodies and government regulators in other countries, including Brazil, India, Italy, Mexico, South Korea, and Taiwan.

One Volkswagen executive in South Korea has been sentenced to 18 months in jail. Two of his colleagues have been convicted of crimes but not yet sentenced.

A long-time Volkswagen engineer in the U.S. has pleaded guilty to three federal felony charges and is scheduled for sentencing in May.

Six Volkswagen executives and employees in Germany have been indicted by a U.S. federal grand jury on a variety of felony charges. One of them has been arrested by the FBI and is currently in jail, having been denied bail.

Only a handful of the 11 million Volkswagen vehicles with emissions testing defeat device software have been fixed or bought back by Volkswagen and taken off the road. Almost all of them continue to spew dangerous nitrogen oxide (NOx) pollutants into the air a full 17 months after this cheating scandal was publicly raised by the EPA and nearly three full years after West Virginia University first published its test results.

Here is a list of the key outstanding issues that Volkswagen's leadership team and its employees will have to grapple with in the coming months and years:

Defeat Device Repairs

Fixing the bulk of the 8.5 million vehicles in Europe fitted with the defeat device software.

Finish buying back or repairing the 475,000 2-liter vehicles in the U.S. and the 105,000 such vehicles in Canada.

Buying back or repairing the 85,000 3-liter vehicles in the U.S.

Financial

Settlement arrangement on the legal fees with the lawyers for the plaintiffs in the 3-liter class-action suit in the U.S.

Settlement arrangement on the legal fees for the lawyers representing the U.S. dealer network

Settlement arrangement on the legal fees with the lawyers for the plaintiffs in the Canadian class-action suit.

Investor Lawsuits

Settlement of the class-action lawsuit by investors filed in the U.S.

Settlement of the 1700+ investor lawsuits filed in Germany.

Settlement of the $110B class-action lawsuit against Volkswagen's MAN truck division and other truck manufacturers.

Car Owner Lawsuits

Approval by U.S. District Court Judge Charles Breyer of the compensatory payments for car owners of the 3-liter vehicles fitted with the defeat device software in the U.S.

Settlement of the class-action lawsuit on behalf of 100,000 Audi car owners related to the CO_2 emissions issue.

Settlement of vehicle owner class-action suits in Ireland and South Korea.

Volkswagen's appeal of a German court ruling that the automaker must buy back a German customer's diesel car equipped with the emissions test cheating defeat device software at "full purchase price."

Miscellaneous Suits

Settlement of the 20+ lawsuits filed by U.S. states alleging violations of their respective environmental, clean air, and consumer protection laws.

Settlement of the lawsuit by the Chicago-area dealer who bought a Volkswagen dealership just days before the EPA announced the first Notice of Violation.

Settlement of the patent lawsuit by the former CEO of Bentley and Bugatti.

Settlement of the legal action undertaken by the Australian Competition and Consumer Commission (ACCC).

Settlement of legal actions and investigations undertaken by regulatory agencies in Britain, Canada, China, Germany, Poland, Spain, Sweden, Switzerland, and other nations.

Settlement of the patent infringement complaint filed by Paice LLC with the U.S. International Trade Commission.

Resolution of Volkswagen's appeal of the National Labor Relations Board rulings on the unionization of part of its workforce in Chattanooga, Tennessee.

Criminal

Potential criminal charges for Volkswagen employees in South Korea for submitting false documentation to authorities and for false advertising.

The sentencing of Volkswagen engineer James Liang in the U.S.

Resolution of the felony charges against the six Volkswagen executives and employees indicted in the U.S.

Potential additional criminal charges as the U.S. Department of Justice investigation continues.

Possible criminal charges in Germany for violation of the country's stock market disclosure rules (currently under investigation by the Braunschweig prosecutor's office).

Other potential criminal charges in Germany against the 37 individuals being investigated by the Braunschweig prosecutor's office, including a possible fraud charge against former CEO Martin Winterkorn.

Legal / Regulatory

Resolution of the CO_2 emissions problems on the Audi vehicles with standard transmissions.

Resolution of the NOx emissions problems reportedly found by the European Commission's Joint Research Center on the new Audi EA-288 diesel engine.

Resolution of inquiry into whether Porsche has used a defeat device that detects emissions testing by monitoring steering wheel movement.

And, of course, the biggest and most significant outstanding issue is the release of the Jones Day internal investigation report, something that has been promised but continuously delayed for almost a year.

In addition, Volkswagen and the rest of the automotive industry will likely face new rules and regulations after the European Union parliamentary committee completes its investigation and recommends new legislation. This will most likely include laws on real-world, on-road emissions testing and tighter restrictions on how automakers manipulate, laboratory emissions tests.

Additionally, Volkswagen and the rest of the automotive industry need to start preparing for real-world, on-road emissions testing. The 42% gap found in the International Council on Clean Transportation (ICCT) study between the amount of CO_2 an average car emits during a lab test and when actually driven on the road is unacceptable.

This is not just a European problem, either. In Australia, testing by the Australian Automobile Association (AAA) in late 2016 showed an across-the-board difference of 20% in fuel efficiency between laboratory tests and on-road tests. In some case the cars examined by AAA had a 35% discrepancy between what the mileage claims on the manufacturer's sticker and what the vehicles actually achieve when driven in real-world conditions. Significantly higher greenhouse gas emissions were also found in the AAA tests.

LEADERSHIP LESSONS

One significant lesson for all leaders, particularly those in the U.S. is that individual criminal activity is more likely to result in individual charges and penalties than ever before. The U.S. Department of Justice has thus far taken baby steps to implementing its relatively new policy of enforcing individual accountability for corporate wrongdoing.

This policy was set out in September 2015 by Deputy Attorney General Sally Quillian Yates, just nine days before the EPA's public announcement of the first Notice of Violation issued to Volkswagen. In her memo Yates writes, "One of the most effective ways to combat corporate misconduct is by seeking accountability from the individuals who perpetrated the wrongdoing. Such accountability is important for several reasons: it deters future illegal activity, it incentivizes changes in corporate behavior, it ensures that the proper parties are held responsible for their actions, and it promotes the public's confidence in our justice system."

The Yates Memo goes on to describe the various steps that DOJ investigators should take in any investigation of corporate misconduct, stipulating that "civil attorneys investigating corporate wrongdoing should maintain a focus on the responsible individuals, recognizing that holding them to account is an important part of protecting the public in the long term." It also states that future criminal and civil corporate investigations should focus on individuals from the inception of any investigation.

As the first line of the Yates Memo states, "Fighting corporate fraud and other misconduct is a top priority of the Department of Justice." Based on the DOJ actions and results with Volkswagen and other corporate miscreants in recent months, this has become obviously true.

As U.S. Attorney Barbara McQuade told a news conference in January 2017, "Corporations and individuals who cheat will be held accountable. Cheaters will not be allowed to gain an advantage over those who play by the rules." She was speaking at a press conference announcing the DOJ's $1B settlement with Takata.

Indications are that the new Trump administration will maintain the policies outlined in the Yates Memo. As the new administration takes over there are several corporate investigations underway started during the Obama administration, and these are not likely to be dropped before they are completed.

Additionally, in his confirmation hearings before the U.S. Senate, newly appointed Attorney General Jeff Sessions showed support for disciplining executives and employees for corporate crimes. In his testimony Sessions, who served for 12 years as a U.S. Attorney and for two years as Attorney General of Alabama before becoming a U.S. Senator stated that, "sometimes it seems to me that the corporate officers who caused a problem should be subjected to more severe punishment than the stockholders of the company who didn't know anything about it."

CHAPTER ELEVEN

Detailed Timeline
of the
Volkswagen Saga

The Volkswagen saga unraveled daily for over 500 consecutive days in a drip-drip-drip fashion resembling a leaky garden hose. As you will see in the detailed timeline below, hardly a day has gone by since September 18, 2015 where there wasn't some news about Volkswagen, or some new aspect of the saga, appearing in the press.

The dates below attempt to represent the dates on which events happened, though this has not always been possible. In such cases the dates below represent the dates on which media articles have appeared.

2009	Volkswagen AG engineers begin to install defeat device software into vehicles to dupe U.S. diesel emissions laboratory tests and bypass tougher U.S. Environmental Protection Agency (EPA) rules capping nitrogen oxide (NOx) emissions.
2013	Researchers from the International Council on Clean Transportation and West Virginia University find significant abnormalities when conducting on-road

testing of emission levels on Volkswagen cars with diesel engines compared to reported laboratory testing results.

2014

April ICCT publicizes its testing findings and simultaneously notifies EPA and the California Air Resources Board (CARB) of the irregularities and deviations found during their tests.

May EPA and CARB notify Volkswagen of the ICCT test results and request clarification and explanation from the automaker. The two regulators also begin their own investigations.

Volkswagen initially argues that the tests by WVU and ICCT are flawed. They also blame the problem on technical issues which they claim to be fixing. Back-and-forth discussions and correspondence ensue between the automaker and regulators for well over a year.

December Officials at CARB and EPA agree to allow a voluntary recall of Volkswagen's diesel cars to fix what the automaker insisted was an easily fixable technical glitch that had caused the aberrations between the laboratory and on-road emissions test results.

2015

April Recall letters sent to car owners by Volkswagen of America to California owners of diesel-powered Audis and VWs informing them of an "emissions service action" affecting their vehicles. The software update was described in the letter as "the vehicle's engine management software has been improved to assure your vehicle's tailpipe emissions are optimized and operating efficiently."

July 8
After CARB tested vehicles that had undergone the software "fix" it found that the NOx levels were still above allowable limits. CARB shares its findings with Volkswagen and the EPA and threatens to withhold certificates allowing future Volkswagen diesel sales in California. The EPA agrees and also says it will not approve Volkswagen diesel cars in the upcoming 2016 model year for sale without an explanation for the "real world" discrepancies.

September 3
Faced with the threat of not being able to import or sell any 2016 model year diesel vehicles, Volkswagen tells U.S. regulators it had installed defeat devices in some diesel engines.

September 9
RobecoSAM crowns Volkswagen as the world's most sustainable car company. Volkswagen issues a press release celebrating the title.

September 18
The Environmental Protection Agency (EPA) in the U.S. publicly announces Volkswagen's wrongdoing and the issuance of a Notice of Violation of the U.S. Clean Air Act. The EPA says that Volkswagen has installed a "defeat device" on more than 475,000 cars with 2-liter, four-cylinder diesel engines that

enabled them to cheat on U.S. emissions tests. This software reduced nitrogen oxide (NOx) emissions when the cars were placed on laboratory test machines, but then allowed higher (and illegal) emissions and improved performance during on-road driving. The affected cars are from the VW, Audi, and Porsche brands.

September 22   Volkswagen admits that about 11 million vehicles around the world with various configurations of its diesel engines have been fitted with the defeat device software. It sets aside 6.5B euros ($7.2B) to deal with expected costs, including anticipated recalls to fix or replace the cheating software.

September 23   Volkswagen Group CEO Martin Winterkorn resigns, taking full responsibility for the "irregularities" found by U.S. regulators while simultaneously insisting he personally did nothing wrong.

September 25   EPA says it will toughen tests for all carmakers and will scrutinize at least 28 diesel models made by BMW, Chrysler, General Motors, Land Rover, and Mercedes-Benz.

Volkswagen names Matthias Mueller as the new CEO. Mueller is head of Volkswagen's Porsche sports car division.

September 27   Citing two German newspaper articles, *Business Insider* reports that Volkswagen ignored warnings from staff and a supplier that the emissions test rigging software was illegal.

The German Federal Motor Transport Authority (KBA) gives Volkswagen a deadline of October 7 to submit a plan laying out whether and when its vehicles will meet emissions standards. Failure to comply could result in KBA withdrawing the approval for the affected vehicles, meaning they could not be legally sold or moved in Germany.

September 28   Audi spokesman admits to *Car & Driver* that roughly 2.1 million Audi cars are fitted with the emissions-cheating device.

Several media reports state that Volkswagen has suspended three top engineers as a direct result of investigations into the scandal.

Porsche SE buys an additional 1.5% stake of ordinary shares in Volkswagen AG from Suzuki.

An article in the *Financial Times* argues that the Volkswagen scandal is worse than Enron, writing "most corporate scandals stem from negligence or the failure to come clean about corporate wrongdoing. Far fewer involve deliberate fraud and criminal intent."

September 29   Volkswagen confirms that commercial vehicles and cars from its Spanish unit SEAT are included in the 11 million vehicles fitted with diesel engines that can cheat emission tests.

Volkswagen announces it has commissioned the U.S. law firm Jones Day to conduct an internal investigation into the cheating scandal.

RobecoSAM and SAP Dow Jones Indices announced that Volkswagen will be dropped from the Dow Jones Top Sustainability Index as of October 6.

September 30 30 U.S. State Attorneys General have banded together to launch a probe into Volkswagen separate from the U.S. federal government investigation.

Volkswagen rolls out a website page that tells owners who input data about their vehicles whether they have been affected by the cheating diesel emissions test.

Martin Winterkorn steps down from his remaining senior roles within the Volkswagen Group. Despite resigning as Volkswagen AG CEO the previous week, he had remained as CEO of Porsche SE (the holding company that has a majority stake in Volkswagen AG), chairman of Audi, chairman of the Scania truck division, and chairman of the group's truck and bus division.

October 1 Volkswagen names Hans Dieter Poetsch, the group's Chief Financial Officer, as its new supervisory board chairman. This fills a vacancy created when previous chairman Ferdinand Piech resigned in April.

October 4   Volkswagen takes out full-page ads in Germany's Sunday newspapers to say: "We will do everything possible to win back your trust."

October 5   Volkswagen suspends sales of some vehicles in Australia.

October 6   CEO Mueller warns of "massive cutbacks" and that the process will "not be painless."

October 7   Volkswagen withdraws its application to the EPA to certify its 2016 lineup of diesel-powered vehicles for sale in the U.S.

    Volkswagen sales increased by just 1% in September, compared to double-digit growth for General Motors, Fiat Chrysler, and Ford.

October 8   German prosecutors raid the Volkswagen company headquarters in Wolfsburg in search of evidence related to the emissions test cheating software.

    Michael Horn, CEO and President of Volkswagen of America, admits in written testimony to a Congressional oversight committee that he learned 18 months ago about the cheating software when the West Virginia University emissions tests results were first published.

    In his testimony during a two-hour congressional hearing Horn was asked to answer two basic questions: 1) who fitted the cheat device into Volkswagen vehicles, and 2) what are Volkswagen's plans to fix the affected cars? Horn apologizes for the scandal and recites the company line that blames "a couple of software engineers" for the emissions test cheating scandal. He says fixing the affected cars could take 1-2 years.

One Congressman states during the hearing that "Volkswagen is either incompetent or guilty of a massive cover-up."

October 9   EPA is reportedly investigating a **second** emissions-control software that Volkswagen may have failed to disclose.

California gives Volkswagen until November 20 to come up with a plan to fix diesel cars sold and/or registered in the state.

Angry Volkswagen customers start a website called VWShame.com to sell anti-VW bumper stickers. These bumper stickers tout slogans such as "VW took me for a ride" and "VW. German for FU." The website promises to send 5% of sales proceeds as donations to the International Council for Clean Transportation, the nonprofit which notified EPA of Volkswagen's emissions test cheating.

October 10   *Car and Driver* reports that Bosch wrote to Volkswagen in 2007 to warn that using the diesel engine management software it supplied to Volkswagen in publicly sold vehicles was illegal.

Bosh claims to have supplied the software under the impression it would only be used in vehicle testing.

Car and Driver also cites a report in the *Frankfurter Allgemeine Zeitung* newspaper that one of Volkswagen's engineers tried to blow the whistle on the illegal emissions test cheating program in 2011.

October 11   U.S. Senator Charles Schumer says the federal government should seek maximum fines against Volkswagen (estimated at $18 billion) and demand that the automaker also gives rebates to customers.

October 12   S+P lowers the credit rating for Volkswagen AG, citing "VW's internal controls have been shown to be inadequate in preventing or identifying alleged illegal behavior." The credit rating agency also said the potential for other violations "represents a significant reputational and financial risk."

The European Investment Bank (EIB) is investigating how Volkswagen has used $5.2 billion in loans it has received from it. EIB President Werner Hoyer said EIB, a nonprofit public lending institution, may have to demand the loans be paid back immediately based on the outcome of the investigation. An unspecified percentage of the loans by EIB to Volkswagen were reportedly intended for the development of low-emission engines. "The EIB could take a hit," said Hoyer as the bank "has to fulfill certain climate targets with our loans."

Kelly Blue Book – the bible in the USA for pricing of used cars – said the Volkswagen models affected by the emission cheating scandal had lost 13% of their resale value from September 1 to October 2. VW diesel cars were selling at a premium before the scandal hit since they were some of the few diesel passenger vehicles available in the U.S.

The Texas Attorney General files a lawsuit against Volkswagen and Audi of America citing breaches of the state's consumer protection laws. A separate suit is also filed alleging that Volkswagen broke Texas clean air laws.

The Environmental Protection Ministry in China announces an investigation into Volkswagen's imported and locally produced vehicles in the country to ascertain if they are in compliance with the country's emissions standards.

October 13	Volkswagen plans to recover from the diesel saga by focusing on electronic vehicles instead of diesel engines.
October 14	Volkswagen advises the U.S. Environmental Protection Agency (EPA) that its 2016 diesel cars contain a new and different emissions software that "would probably help their exhaust systems run cleaner during government tests."
October 15	Germany's automotive regulator KBA orders a nationwide recall all 2.6 million Volkswagen cars in

the country fitted with emissions test cheating software. As part of the European Union, Germany's recall is automatically applied across the EU.

German media reports that a fourth manager in Volkswagen has been suspended.

October 16   A prosecutor in Verona, Italy leads a raid on Lamborghini's headquarters in Bologna. Lamborghini is owned by Volkswagen AG.

Volkswagen AG announces that Christina Hohmann-Dennhardt, the compliance chief at rival Daimler AG, will join Volkswagen in a management and board position to focus on integrity and legal affairs, effective January 1st. Hohmann-Dennhardt will also become the first female executive board member at Volkswagen AG.

The Federal Trade Commission in the U.S. begins reviewing Volkswagen's "Clean Diesel" television commercials for fraudulent claims.

October 17   Volkswagen CEO Mueller says he expects a recall to begin in January 2016 and all affected cars to be fixed by end of 2016.

Mueller also says Volkswagen will be able to recover from the emissions scandal in as little as two years. "We have a chance to be shining again in two to three years," Mueller reportedly told Volkswagen managers according to the *Telegraph* newspaper.

S+P downgrades Volkswagen's credit rating, citing deficiencies in management and governance in the wake of the emissions scandal. Long-term and short-term corporate credit ratings are both cut from A to A-minus.

New Zealand owners of 8800 vehicles caught up in the Volkswagen global emissions scandal are being invited to join a class-action lawsuit organized by a Wellington law firm.

Germany's environment minister urges tougher emission testing throughout the European Union, saying Germany and the rest of the EU need to act quickly to implement real-world testing and calling carmakers to account.

The law firm Quinn Emanuel has been retained by claim funding group Bentham to prepare a 49B euro (US$44B) lawsuit for Volkswagen AG shareholders. Bentham expects to recover around 20% of any damages won in return for covering the legal fees of the lawsuits.

The U.S. Senate launches an investigation of federal tax credits that Volkswagen customers received for purchasing "environmentally friendly" diesel engines. Depending on the Senate's findings, Volkswagen could be required to pay up to an estimated $50M in Alternative Motor Vehicle credits granted to its customers.

China's General Administration of Quality Supervision, Inspection and Quarantine (AQSIQ) says it is "highly concerned" about the methodology used by Volkswagen to trick emissions tests and that it would take appropriate follow-up measures. The Chinese environment ministry also said it would launch an investigation into Volkswagen vehicles.

Two film studios have acquired the rights to a book about Volkswagen's emissions scandal. Paramount Pictures and Appian Way Productions, which is run by activist actor Leonardo DiCaprio, have agreed to the rights to a forthcoming book by *New York Times* journalist Jack Ewing.

October 18   Police raid Volkswagen's headquarters in France.

October 20   Dyson accuses Bosch of being "like Volkswagen."

Der Spiegel reports at least 30 Volkswagen managers played a role in using the software program to cheat emissions tests.

Volkswagen's newly chosen head of North America, Winfried Vahland, is leaving just three weeks after being designated due to differences with the Volkswagen board on the group's restructuring plans for the region. These plans have now been placed on hold.

Volkswagen employee representatives and the main employee union demand greater transparency at the automaker.

The *Financial Times* reports that the European Union's top environmental officer, EU environment commissioner Janez Potočnik, warned his EU colleagues in 2013 that automakers were rigging European emissions tests.

Investigations have commenced in at least five countries – France, Germany, Italy, Spain and the USA – over emissions test rigging by Volkswagen.

45 states and the District of Columbia have joined a multistate investigation led by attorneys general determining how Volkswagen was able to game emissions tests and hide that its "Clean Diesel" cars omitted up to 40 times allowable emissions of nitrogen oxide (NOx). In addition, Harris County in Texas is suing Volkswagen for more than $100M, while California and Texas are each conducting their own investigations.

Newly appointed CEO Mueller tells a press conference that profits, not sales, will be the new focus for the automaker's management. "A lot has become secondary to going higher, faster, further, especially return on sales," he said. "It's not about selling 100,000 cars more or less than a big competitor. It is rather about qualitative growth."

October 21   A Norwegian shipowner seeks $50 million in compensation from a marine unit of Volkswagen for rigging performance tests of ship engines.

The German state of Lower Saxony files a criminal complaint after discovering that a file on scandal-hit Volkswagen had disappeared. The file is said to include internal government memos on the emissions scandal.

October 23   Complaints against Volkswagen in the U.S. are reportedly including violations of the Racketeer Influenced and Corrupt Organizations Act (RICO) alleging the carmaker knowingly committed fraud across state lines.

October 26   NPR reports that the emissions scandal is hurting VW owners in the U.S. trying to sell their diesel engine cars.

October 28   Volkswagen suspends the head of the company's powertrain electronics over an alleged role in the diesel scandal.

An article in *The Telegraph* says Volkswagen is facing an investigation by the Serious Fraud Office in the U.K., which could lead to action against the automaker for "corporate criminality."

Additionally, the U.K. Competition and Market Authority is considering starting an investigation into the automaker's actions related to the emissions defeat device software installed in up to 1.2 million cars in Britain.

Volkswagen reveals its first quarterly loss in 15 years, after taking a $7.4B charge to cover costs related to the emissions test cheating scandal. The company reports a $1.83B pretax loss for the third quarter of the year.

October 29   Volkswagen hires Thomas Sedron, interim CEO at Opel in 2012-2013 and former head of GM's Chevrolet and Cadillac brands in Europe, to run group strategy. It is the second prominent hire Volkswagen has made from outside the company in the past two weeks.

Bloomberg reports that Volkswagen failed to report at least one death and three injuries involving its vehicles to the U.S. National Highway Traffic Safety Administration's database designed to save lives by spotting possible vehicle defects. Volkswagen said the previous week that it was commissioning an outside audit of its compliance with U.S. safety reporting laws.

November 2   The Environmental Protection Agency (EPA) in the U.S. issues a new Notice of Violation saying the Volkswagen Group violated the U.S. Clean Air Act in using illegal software in some 3-liter, six-cylinder diesel engines to circumvent U.S. emissions laws. The notice cites models from Audi, Porsche, and VW brands and impacts roughly 10,000 vehicles. Volkswagen denies the validity and accuracy of the EPA notice.

German Chancellor Angela Merkel says Volkswagen needs to deal with the diesel emissions test cheating scandal in a transparent manner.

China's top quality watchdog announces a recall of 5906 Volkswagen luxury brand Bentley cars due to battery defects that could lead to overheating.

Around 600 people have filed criminal complaints in Switzerland connected to the emissions test cheating scandal.

Volkswagen and Audi are hit with two class-action lawsuits in Australia on behalf of 100,000 owners of diesel cars in the country equipped with the defeat device emissions test cheating software.

The Australia Competition and Consumer Commission (ACCC) says it is investigating Volkswagen and warns of possible legal action against the automaker.

November 4   Volkswagen announces that an internal investigation has revealed "unexplained irregularities" in the carbon dioxide (CO_2) emissions in 800,000 of its vehicles, a development it said could cost the company another two billion euros ($2.2B). The company also said these 800,000 vehicles were "predominately diesel engines," which thus raises the possibility for the first time that some Volkswagen vehicles with gasoline-powered engines may also have previously unidentified emissions problems.

Volkswagen shares fall to their lowest level in five years after the announcement that "irregularities" in how the carmaker has presented the fuel consumption data of various models during their certification process. This brings the drop to Volkswagen shares to over one-third since the public revealing six weeks ago of the diesel engine emission testing scandal.

Volkswagen says there are 98,000 petrol cars affected by their CO_2 underreporting issues in the U.K. — part of the 800,000 affected worldwide.

Daimler AG CEO Dr. Dieter Zetsche calls Volkswagen's use of emissions-cheating devices "a blow to our industry" and damaging to the Made in Germany brand.

Moody's downgrades Volkswagen's credit rating from A3 to A2 and includes a negative outlook, saying the downgrading reflects mounting risks to Volkswagen's reputation and future earnings following the company's announcement the previous day regarding irregularities in CO_2 and fuel consumption levels and the fresh allegations two days ago from the EPA that defeat devices were also installed in certain Audi, Porsche, and Volkswagen Touareg models in the U.S.

November 5

According to the EPA, Bosch's popular diesel engine software program is not preprogrammed to cheat emissions laboratory tests. Both Mercedes-Benz and BMW use the same engine management software system made by Bosch as Volkswagen.

Der Spiegel magazine in Germany reports that "at least 30" managers at Volkswagen were involved in the company's emission test cheating. This comes just weeks after Michael Horn, Volkswagen's head in the United States, told a congressional panel that only "a couple of software engineers" were responsible for installing the emission test defeat software.

Volkswagen reportedly suspends the head of its main transmission plant in Kassel after he is investigated as part of the emission cheating scandal. He had previously overseen the development of diesel engines at Volkswagen between 2006 and 2010.

In a column in *Road and Track* magazine, former General Motors CEO Robert Schultz blames a tyrannical leadership style and culture at Volkswagen under Chairman Ferdinand Piech as being responsible for the Volkswagen emissions test cheating scandal.

The *New York Times* reports that former CEO Martin Winterkorn knew of potential emissions problems in 2014.

November 6

Volkswagen asks European finance ministers to charge the company, and not car owners, for any additional taxes related to fuel usage or CO2 emissions due as a result of the automaker underreporting these figures for 800,000 cars in Europe.

The head of the powerful California Air Resources Board (CARB) says, "Volkswagen is so far not handling the scandal correctly. Every additional gram of nitrogen oxide increases the health risks for our citizens. Volkswagen has not acknowledged that in any way or made any effort to really solve the problem."

November 9

Volkswagen admits that the 3-liter engines identified in the second EPA Notice of Violation on November 2nd do in fact have the illegal defeat device software installed. It also reveals that this software has been installed in over 85,000 vehicles sold in the U.S.A. since 2009, a figure that is over eight times what EPA indicated a week ago.

Nordeo Asset Management, the Scandinavian fund manager, becomes the first major investor to signal an intention to sue Volkswagen over the company's manipulation of emissions tests. The $210 billion fund manager tells reporters it plans to join several different class-action suits against Volkswagen.

Environmental activists from Greenpeace protest outside the main entrance to Volkswagen's headquarters in Wolfsburg, Germany, unfurling a banner that reads "Das Problem."

Volkswagen plans to offer $1000 in gift cards and vouchers to owners of diesel cars in the U.S. in an attempt to win back the trust of drivers and car buyers. Car owners of vehicles containing the emissions test cheat software will get a $500 Visa debit card for use anywhere and a $500 voucher for services or merchandise at Volkswagen Group car dealers.

November 11   German authorities will begin investigating the diesel emissions of every car sold in the country, which amounts to over 50 models from 24 automakers. The German Federal Motor Transport Authority (KBA) also says it has "verified indications from third parties regarding unusual pollutants emission."

November 12   Volkswagen gives its employees until November 30 to come clean with any knowledge related to the automaker's emissions test cheating scandal to designated company representatives in order to receive immunity. Those who reveal what they know by the deadline will not be fired and will not have damage claims brought against them.

November 14   The head of Corporate Communications at Volkswagen leaves the company, just weeks after the departure of his former boss late last month.

Brazil fines Volkswagen $13M over the emissions scandal.

November 15   Volkswagen runs full-page ads in over 30 newspapers across the U.S. asking for "continued patience" and announcing its goodwill package for affected car owners with copy that reads, "We sincerely hope you see this as a first step toward restoring your invaluable trust."

November 16   Volkswagen appoints Michael Steiner, head of vehicle development and quality, as its compliance commissioner working with regulatory and compliance authorities globally. He will report to new CEO Matthias Mueller.

November 20   The supervisory board of Volkswagen says it will cap spending on property, plant, and equipment at around 12B euros ($13.2B), an 8% reduction on its previous plan of around $13B euros in capital spending for 2016.

November 22   Volkswagen CEO Matthias Mueller tells the automaker's workers in a "town hall" speech in the Wolfsburg headquarters that the current emissions scandal is "technically and financially manageable."

November 24

German prosecutors launch a tax evasion probe at Volkswagen, in connection with the emission test cheating scandal. In Germany, vehicles are taxed according to fuel consumption. The prosecutors will investigate whether owners of affected Volkswagen vehicles underpaid on taxes, a matter which the prosecutor's spokesman said was "not small."

German technical inspectors say policymakers are partly to blame for the scope of Volkswagen's emissions scandal and say inspectors have never been allowed to check the engine control software used by automakers.

November 26

The South Korean government tells Volkswagen to recall 125,500 diesel vehicles over faked emission tests. The South Korean Environment Ministry also fines Volkswagen 14.1B won ($12.3M).

Audi suspends two engineers as an internal investigation into the emissions scandal continues.

The California Air Resources Board (CARB) orders Volkswagen to come up with a plan for repairing 15,000 3-litre diesel engines sold in the state since 2005.

November 27

The Volkswagen Works Council Chief says the fresh CO_2 emissions crisis has hit new car orders. Would-be buyers are growing cautious about VW cars after the automaker admitted to understating fuel consumption and CO_2 output.

November 29   Reuters reports that Volkswagen knew fuel usage and CO_2 output in some cars was too high a year ago.

November 30   Over 500,000 Europeans a year may be dying from conditions related to air pollution, according to a report from the European Union environmental watchdog.

December 2   The Porsche family signals support for Volkswagen despite the emissions scandal.

The *Telegraph* newspaper reports that around 50 Volkswagen employees have testified in the internal probe being conducted over the emissions scandal.

December 3   Volkswagen secures a $30B bridging loan to cover potential Dieselgate costs.

December 4   Volkswagen car sales in the U.K. plunged 20% in November compared to a year ago. This follows a nearly 10% drop in October over the corresponding period in 2014. Britain is the automaker's fourth largest market.

Workers who repair and maintain machinery and robots at the Volkswagen plant in Chattanooga, TN vote 108-44 in favor of representation by the United Auto Workers union. Volkswagen said it plans to appeal a ruling that allowed the vote to the full National Labor Relations Board.

December 7   Volkswagen understated carbon dioxide (CO_2) emissions on far fewer vehicles that initially feared the company said. Internal investigations found the company had understated fuel consumption, and thus CO_2 emissions, on only 36,000 vehicles compared to the preliminary estimate of 800,000.

The Reuters news agency reports that German prosecutors are now investigating Volkswagen's former CEO Martin Winterkorn over fraud allegations.

Volkswagen's Bentley unit recalls 37,640 cars for battery cable problems.

December 8   Volkswagen is suspended from the FTSE4Good Index and banned from re-entry for at least two years. This is known as the FTSE Ethical Index by investors.

December 10   Volkswagen's CEO Mueller tells reporters the scandal is "not a one-off error, but an unbroken chain of mistakes." He also asks for patience as the company pursues those responsible.

December 11   Volkswagen says only a small group of individuals within the company are to blame for the diesel emissions test cheating scandal and the utilization of the software defeat device in its cars.

In a less-than-apologetic comment, new CEO says he "will not get down on his knees" when making any apologies during his trip to the U.S. in January, his first since taking over as CEO a few days after the scandal broke nearly three months ago.

December 12	*CNN Money* reports that Volkswagen has suspended nine managers over the diesel emissions scandal.
December 16	The European Parliament plans to set up a committee to investigate Volkswagen's emissions scandal and whether regulatory oversight of the car industry in Europe is too lax. In typical bureaucratic fashion, some 45 members will sit on the committee. The inquiry could last up to a year and will investigate alleged contraventions of European Union law and alleged "maladministration" in the application of the law, according to a proposal approved by various political group leaders prior to a formal vote by parliamentarians.

DW reports that Volkswagen now faces new fraud charges by the European Commission's Anti-Fraud Office. |
| December 17 | Volkswagen announces major structural organization changes to streamline reporting and its internal decision-making process. As part of the restructuring, the number of managers reporting directly to the CEO will be reduced almost in half. |
| December 19 | Volkswagen retains attorney Kenneth Feinberg to help administer a program that will handle settlement claims with U.S. car owners impacted by the emissions test scandal, reportedly in the hopes of attaining quick settlements that prevent future lawsuits. |

December 21   The business daily *Handelsblatt* and German public television's investigative news program *Frontal 21* report that former Volkswagen CEO Martin Winterkorn will receive his basic annual salary of $1.8M, plus a range of generous bonuses, through the end of 2016 when his contract expires. The company reportedly replies that it saw "no reason not to continue paying him."

December 23   After almost 10 years, Volkswagen is dropping its "Das Auto" global advertising slogan. Replacing the "People's Car" slogan beneath the automaker's famous badge-shaped logo will be just the word "Volkswagen."

December 25   The *Globe and Mail* newspaper reports that the Canadian federal government plans to increase the number of vehicles it runs through safety tests in light of the ongoing diesel emissions scandal.

2016

January 4   The U.S. Justice Department, acting on behalf of the EPA, files a $48B lawsuit against Volkswagen, Audi, and Porsche for allegedly violating U.S environmental laws, including the Clean Air Act.

January 6   VW brand head Herbert Diess apologizes on behalf of the company to several hundred industry professionals and journalists attending the Consumer Electronics Show in Las Vegas. Diess says, "We disappointed our customers and the

American people, for which I am truly sorry and for which I apologize."

January 8   U.S. state attorneys general claim Volkswagen is not cooperating enough with their investigations into the diesel emissions test cheating scandal. They also accuse the company of withholding evidence. New York Attorney General Eric T. Schneiderman says "Our patience with Volkswagen is wearing thin. Volkswagen's cooperation with the states' investigation has been spotty, and frankly more of the kind one expects from a company in denial than one seeking to leave behind a culture of admitted deception."

German newspaper *Sueddeutsche Zeitung* reports that 50 Volkswagen employees, including several division heads, have stepped forward as part of an internal amnesty program to help the company clear up the scandal.

January 10   Volkswagen CEO Mueller apologizes for the automaker's emissions test cheating scandal at a media reception on the eve of the Detroit Auto Show. He also announces that Volkswagen will invest $900M to produce a new mid-size SUV at its Chattanooga, TN assembly plant, creating approximately 2000 jobs.

January 11   Volkswagen announces a "goodwill" program comprising two $500 prepaid gift cards to U.S.

owners of the 3-litre TDI diesel engines impacted by the emissions test cheating scandal. One gift card can be used anywhere, whereas the second is redeemable only at Volkswagen dealerships.

January 12

The California Air Resources Board (CARB) rejects Volkswagen's plan to fix the 2-liter diesel engines impacted by the original emissions test cheating software with scathing language. *Fortune* magazine described the CARB communication to Volkswagen as "raw and verging on contemptuous," and as a "reflection of how strained relations between CARB and Volkswagen have become."

CARB said it was rejecting the proposed repairs because they lacked enough information for a technical evaluation and do not adequately address overall impacts on vehicle performance, emissions, and safety.

"Volkswagen made a decision to cheat on emissions tests and then tried to cover it up," stated CARB Chair Mary D. Nichols. "They continued and compounded the lie and when they were caught they tried to deny it. The result is thousands of tons of nitrogen oxide that has harmed the health of Californians. They need to make it right."

In a separate letter to top executives of Volkswagen of America, CARB's head of emissions compliance and automotive regulations Annette Herbert wrote that Volkswagen's proposals were "incomplete, substantially deficient and fall far short of meeting the legal requirements to return these vehicles to the claimed certified configuration."

A media report says a Volkswagen engineer told his bosses about CO_2 manipulation problems in October, but Volkswagen only admitted to the CO_2 problem in 800,000 vehicles in November. The article states that tampering began in 2013 and continued until the end of 2015.

Sweden's anti-corruption prosecutor opens an aggravated fraud investigation against Volkswagen.

January 19   Volkswagen names Hinrich Woebcken to its new position as head of North America, encompassing Canada, Mexico, and the USA. The position initially went to long-time Volkswagen executive Winfried Vahland, but he quit in October after less than three weeks in the position.

Europe's Industry Commissioner writes to Volkswagen CEO Matthias Mueller requesting detailed information on cars affected by the emissions scandal, including the number of vehicles per member state and per year affected. She also asks for technical details on the company's "corrective measures" plans.

January 20   The New Mexico Attorney General files a suit in state district court alleging Volkswagen, Audi, and

Porsche, and their U.S. subsidiaries violated the state's air quality standards and engaged in deceptive marketing in passing off certain diesel models as clean and efficient.

January 21   In a case that could have broader ramifications, a Florida lemon law board declares an emissions test cheating Volkswagen vehicle to be a "lemon" and orders VW to buy it back.

South Korea's antitrust regulator is probing Volkswagen over its advertising claims on emissions from its cars. The Yonhap news agency reports that the Korea Fair Trade Commission is investigating if the carmaker ran false ads by claiming its cars met the European Union's strict Euro 5 emissions standards.

January 22   European Industry Commissioner Elzbieta Bienkowska reportedly writes to Volkswagen CEO Mueller demanding that European and U.S. customers be compensated in the same way in response to the company's emissions scandal.

January 24   The CEO of Robert Bosch says Volkswagen bears the blame for the diesel cheating scandal that uses its engine management software.

January 25   Volkswagen's labor leader rejects the company's push for a big rise in productivity, saying the planned changes by management were causing "unease" among workers.

January 27   The European Union reportedly will seek more power over national car regulations.

Volkswagen recalls 67,000 caddy light commercial vans globally because faulty bolting of the main power supply unit could switch on the ignition.

January 28   Volkswagen starts its recall of diesel cars in Europe.

January 30   Volkswagen continues to maintain that the software used to cheat U.S. emissions tests "is not a forbidden defeat device" under European rules.

February 6   The world's largest sovereign fund — Norway's Norgen Bank Investment Management — criticizes Volkswagen AG's ownership structure, saying too much power is concentrated with the Porsche-Piech family and that this puts minority shareholders at a disadvantage. NBIM holds a 1.2% stake in Volkswagen.

Volkswagen replaces its top U.S. lawyer with an outsider.

February 8   Volkswagen's Quality Control Chief Frank Tuch is leaving the automaker "at his own request," and will be replaced by Hans-Joachim Rothenpieler, head of technical development. Tuch was one of nine top-level managers put on leave shortly after the diesel emissions scandal broke.

Volkswagen announces delays in publication of its 2015 financial results (due on March 10) and its annual meeting of shareholders (scheduled for April 21) by 4-6 weeks as the company struggles to estimate the escalating costs of the diesel emissions scandal.

February 10   A Dutch foundation, the Volkswagen Investor Settlement Foundation, says it has won the support of dozens of institutional shareholders for its efforts to seek a deal with Volkswagen and have this applied worldwide based on a Dutch law covering global collective settlements.

February 15   An article in *Fortune* has two startling revelations that, if true, could have significant legal implications for Volkswagen. The article says that Volkswagen was aware of the defeat device software in 2014 and details a memo sent to then CEO Martin Winterkorn by Bernd Gottweis. The article also cites sources saying that Herbert Diess, global VW brand head held meetings on August 24th and 25th to make preparations for how to react to the impending scandal.

February 16   The *New York Times* editorial board publishes an opinion piece saying Volkswagen AG should have reacted differently following the emissions scandal and that the company seems unable "to understand that, from the public's point of view, the scandal is not so much about cheating on tests as it is about concealing the threat its cars pose to the health of the public."

U.S. District Court Judge Charles Breyer said, "time was running out" and gave Volkswagen a March 24 deadline to have a suitable fix in place for the emissions-cheating diesel cars on American roads.

February 18   Germany's Vice Chancellor and Economy Minister says Volkswagen risks damaging the Made in Germany brand.

The European Automobile Manufacturers' Association (ACEA) says "tougher European emissions testing regime could mean small diesel car models are withdrawn." It claims that implementing real driving emissions laws would mean new technology to curb pollution and that this could add weight and costs to vehicles.

South Korea prosecutors raid the offices of Volkswagen and Audi as part of their probe into the emissions case.

Mexico's Profepa environmental protection agency imposes a 168M peso ($8.9M) fine on Volkswagen Mexico for importing and selling 2016 model vehicles in the country without the mandatory environmental certificate showing emissions standards compliance. Volkswagen Mexico blamed an administrative error for the oversight.

The EPA requests information from Mercedes-Benz in response to a class-action lawsuit filed earlier in the month accusing the automaker of deceiving consumers with false representations of vehicles marketed as "the world's cleanest and most advanced diesel."

February 22   *Inhabitat* says there is evidence that Volkswagen has deliberately misled the U.S. Environmental Protection Agency from 2014 to 2016, knowing that the altered vehicles could not, in fact, be made compliant with environmental regulations.

Reuters quotes German newspaper *Süeddentsche Zeitung* saying "development of software to cheat diesel emissions tests was an open secret in Volkswagen's engine development department."

February 23   *MotorBeam* magazine reports that the Ministry of Heavy Industries in India has stated that Volkswagen cars in India are also fitted with a similar defeat device as in the U.S. and that the emission levels of these cars are nine times higher than permitted levels in the country. The Ministry has asked the country's Road Transport Ministry to take action against Volkswagen.

February 25   Lawyers representing car owners affected by the emissions test cheating scandal file a consolidated complaint in U.S. federal court against Volkswagen AG, Robert Bosch GMBH (a supplier that helped develop emission controls for Volkswagen), the current and former CEOs of Volkswagen, and other Volkswagen executives. The complaint accuses them of various acts of misconduct, including racketeering, mail fraud, and wire fraud. The plaintiffs request that Volkswagen be ordered to buy back vehicles that do not meet emission standards and also pay "significant" damages.

Volkswagen AG hires a German law firm to advise it on the liabilities the automaker could face as a result of its cheating on diesel emissions tests.

February 26

In a report on the European automotive industry, Bernstein Research was less than optimistic. Their conclusion: "Europe is a market where unfortunately the auto industry has little hope of making any money, as it is beset with over capacity, very high structural costs, and is populated by too many automakers all offering technically sophisticated and expensive-to-build vehicles."

Two U.S. Senators and a pair of House Representatives introduce the CLEAN-UP Act in Congress, which will penalize automakers who violate the country's Clean Air Act. The bill will also prevent automakers from obtaining Corporate Average Fuel Economy (CAFE) credits and benefits if found in violation of the Act.

February 29

The German car regulator (KBA) says Volkswagen failed to notify U.S. and California environmental regulators in 2004 about a defect in an emissions-related part.

March 1

Volkswagen recalls 8700 cars in Australia to implement a fix to current pollution-masking software. These vehicles are part of the approximately 100,000 cars in Australia estimated to be equipped with the now infamous software cheat device.

March 2

The European Parliament begins a year-long investigation into the Volkswagen emissions scandal and into whether European regulators could have done more to prevent it.

March 4

Volkswagen sets new dates for its full-year news conference and publication of 2015 financial results (April 28) and its annual meeting of shareholders (now June 20), both of which have been delayed due to open questions relating to the costs of its diesel emissions test cheating scandal.

March 8

German prosecutors have reportedly expanded their investigation into Volkswagen's illegal manipulation of diesel emissions, raising the number of suspects to 17 from six. No suspects are current or former members of the Volkswagen management board.

CEO Mueller tells Volkswagen workers in Wolfsburg that the diesel emissions scandal will inflict "substantial and painful" financial damage on the company and that it will likely take years to fully gauge the financial implications of the scandal.

March 9   German insurer Allianz plans to sue Volkswagen to seek compensation for the severe drop in the company's share price stemming from the diesel emissions test scandal. The planned lawsuit by Allianz Global Investors (AGI) is the first legal action being taken by a major German institution against the country's automotive icon.

March 10   Michael Horn, President and CEO of Volkswagen Group of America, steps down "with immediate effect" to "pursue other opportunities." He had been with Volkswagen for 25 years and assumed the Volkswagen of America CEO role in 2014. The news does not resonate well with Volkswagen's U.S. dealers who say Horn was the one Volkswagen executive who understood their plight.

Various media reports state that Volkswagen plans to cut 3000 office jobs in Germany by the end of 2017 as the automaker looks for ways to offset the coming costs of the emissions test rigging scandal.

Volkswagen New Zealand pulls a television commercial after a complaint to the New Zealand Advertising Standards Authority said the advertisement promoted unsafe practices.

The central excise department of Pune, India penalizes three Volkswagen firms in the country Rs460M (US$7.4M) for allegedly evading taxes by undervaluing cars sold in India between 2010 and

2014. The three firms are Volkswagen India, Skoda Auto India, and Volkswagen Group Sales. A Volkswagen spokesperson said the company would appeal the fines.

March 11   The U.S. Department of Justice issues subpoenas under a federal statute that targets bank fraud. Doing so allows the Justice Department to investigate whether lenders suffered damages from financing Volkswagen vehicles at an inflated price, under the umbrella of the Financial Institutions Reform, Recovery and Enforcement Act (FIRREA).

A *Fortune* magazine article says researchers in Germany have found that Volkswagen improved its defeat device software at the end of 2014, or early 2015. The improvement created a more efficient cheating of emissions tests.

March 14   First reports emerge that a whistleblower is suing Volkswagen in Michigan after being fired by the company over a data deletion row. The whistleblower, a former employee, claims he was fired for refusing to delete Dieselgate data.

March 15   Volkswagen's financial services arm says it has taken a reserve of 335M euros ($391M) to cover potential declines in residual values on cars in its leasing fleet. It also took an additional 96M euros ($105M) to cover risks in its business in the United States as a result of the ongoing diesel emissions scandal.

March 18	Reuters cites a *Der Spiegel* magazine study that claims two senior Volkswagen executives were told in an internal meeting on August 24, 2015 that the company could face potential penalties exceeding $20B for the use of illegal software in its vehicles. Volkswagen AG refutes the story, saying any information *Der Spiegel* believed to have is "pure speculation" and any conclusions drawn were based on "a subjective description of events."
March 22	*Automotive News* reports state that Volkswagen has been wiring "discretionary" payments totaling tens of thousands of dollars to its dealers in the U.S. for the past six months, in addition to other financial programs being provided.
March 24	Volkswagen and the U.S. government are given another month to hammer out a settlement by U.S. District Court Judge Charles Breyer. The judge's previous deadline has been extended to April 21, one week before Volkswagen is scheduled to announce its 2015 financial results.
March 25	Kentucky joins New Jersey, Texas, West Virginia, New Mexico, and Harris County (Texas) in initiating its own legal action against Volkswagen. Kentucky Attorney General Andy Beshear says, "Volkswagen must be held accountable for its false and misleading promotion and sales of its vehicles." Investigations are now being conducted by 48 U.S. state attorneys.

March 29   The U.S. Federal Trade Commission (FTC) files a federal complaint seeking compensation for consumers allegedly deceived by false claims that Volkswagen's cars were low-emission, environmentally friendly, met emissions standards, and would maintain a high resale value. The FTC cited Volkswagen promotional materials in its suit that "repeatedly claimed its Clean Diesel vehicles have low emissions, including that they reduce nitrogen oxides (NOx) emissions by 90% and have fewer such emissions than gasoline cars."

Volkswagen recalls nearly 800,000 VW Touareg and Porsche Cayenne vehicles worldwide due to a malfunction in pedal construction.

March 30   *Motor Trend* cites analysts who estimate the diesel scandal could cost Volkswagen as much as $34B globally.

March 31   Members of the Volkswagen National Dealer Advisory Council meet in Germany with VW global brand boss Herbert Diess, newly appointed North America head Hinrich Woebcken, head of global sales Juergen Stackminn, and North America sales head Ludger Fretzen to discuss key issues and concerns of VW dealers in the U.S.

April 2   Volkswagen recalls 177,000 Passat sedans across the world due to a potential electrical fault. An *AP* report

322 • STEVEN B HOWARD

says wiring under the body can corrode, overheat, and potentially start a fire.

Volkswagen is now facing a potential class-action lawsuit by its U.S. car dealers, alleging breach of contract and fraud. The lawyer crafting the complaint on behalf of the group says no action would be taken until after the dealers meet with Volkswagen leaders at the National Automotive Dealers Association (NADA) conference later in the month.

Volkswagen has stopped the sale of its diesel variation of its Vento sedan car in India over inconsistent carbon monoxide emissions. Models with a manual gearbox were found to be exceeding threshold emissions limits during tests conducted by the Automotive Research Authority of India (ALAI).

Volkswagen of America is recalling over 5500 Golf electric vehicles due to a battery management issue that could cause an emergency shutdown of the car's high-voltage battery and the vehicle. Ironically it appears that this is a software issue causing the problem.

April 3 Volkswagen dealers in the United States form a 5-member committee and tell Volkswagen to talk with this committee to avoid lawsuits from the dealers.

April 5 The head of the VW car brand, Herbert Diess, meets with hundreds of VW auto dealers during the annual

National Automotive Dealers Association (NADA) conference in Las Vegas and promises to "redefine" the company's tarnished image and "relaunch" the VW brand. He also said Volkswagen would fast track much-needed products so dealers would have more non-diesel cars available to sell.

April 6 — Volkswagen recalls nearly 104,000 vehicles in China to replace a missing part, without which the brake pedals may dislodge.

April 11 — Volkswagen delays its recall of 160,000 cars in Europe after a software update aimed at fixing emissions violations fails to work properly. In fact, checks by the German Federal Motor Transport Authority (KBA) showed that fuel consumption of some 2-litre diesel engines had actually increased following the software update installed to fix the problem. The delay affects 160,000 Passat and Skoda cars.

A Chicago-area VW dealer is suing Volkswagen over a $5M loss claimed to have incurred because Volkswagen sold him the dealership on September 12, just days before the diesel emissions test cheating scandal was made public but well after EPA had made Volkswagen regulators aware of the testing issues.

April 13 — Ten of the top Volkswagen managers agree to forego a portion of their annual bonuses by at least 30%.

The National Labor Relations Board (NLRB) in the U.S. votes to uphold a December election in which a small group of workers at Volkswagen's Chattanooga, TN plant voted to join the United Auto Workers union. These 160 employees will become the first workers at a foreign-owned auto assembly plant to gain collective bargaining rights in the southern United States.

Volkswagen names Hinrich Woebcken as CEO of Volkswagen Group of Americas. He has been the interim CEO since Michael Horn resigned in early March. Woebcken will simultaneously remain head of the VW brand for the region, which he has been since January.

April 19   Volkswagen car owners in the U.S. are said to be ready to seek a trial if there is no fix in the emissions case soon.

April 20   The *Guardian* newspaper in the U.K. reports that the Volkswagen emissions test cheating software was created by Audi way back in 1999.

April 21   The proposed Volkswagen settlement in the U.S. will also be applied to over 100,000 vehicles in Canada. A Volkswagen Canada spokesman is quoted in the *Globe and Mail* as saying, "Rest assured that what happens in the U.S. will be mirrored in Canada."

Don Carder, the director for West Virginia University's Center for Alternative Fuels, Engines and Emissions, is named one of TIME Magazine's 100 most influential people in the world.

April 22   Volkswagen AG reports a full-year loss of $1.53B after taking an $18.2B charge to its 2015 financial results to cover the increasingly growing costs of the diesel scandal.

Volkswagen announces a delay in the publication of the internal probe by law firm Jones Day until late in the year.

April 23   German automotive regulator KBA orders almost all of the car industry's major players — both German and foreign-owned — to make changes to their motors to reduce levels of hazardous emissions. The regulator says tests show actual emissions are up to 50 times legal limits.

April 24   Volkswagen's powerful labor leaders accuse the company of betraying workers and trying to use the diesel emissions scandal as a pretext for job cuts.

Bosch earmarks $735M for Volkswagen-related legal risks. It emerged last year that Bosch had supplied Volkswagen AG with the engine management software that was eventually used to cheat on emission tests.

Volkswagen will appeal a National Labor Relations Board (NRLB) ruling earlier this month that upheld a unionization vote among 160 skilled workers at its only U.S. assembly plant (in Chattanooga, TN).

April 25   A British transport minister told a U.K. Parliament transport committee that the country's Serious Fraud Office is looking into the issue of compensation in Britain for owners of the 1.2 million cars affected by Volkswagen's diesel emissions scandal.

April 26   In its annual report to shareholders, Volkswagen admits it could face "further significant financial liabilities" beyond the $18.4B it has reserved for the diesel emissions scandal. It also stated that it may need to sell assets if necessary to pay for increased scandal-related costs.

Volkswagen CEO Matthias Mueller said he had a two-minute conversation with President Barack Obama in Hanover during which he personally apologized for the company's emissions test cheating scandal.

April 27   Germany's Economy Minister says that the German auto industry risks being taken over by foreign competitors unless it receives more government and domestic support. He also announced a 1B euro ($1.13B) plan to subsidize electric cars which includes customer rebates for purchasing electric vehicles, buying electric vehicles for the government's own car fleet, and investing in electric charging stations.

April 28   Volkswagen recalls 15,000 diesel Golf models in Europe for emissions fixes.

                  Volkswagen's Chief Financial Officer Frank Witter tells a news conference that Volkswagen is not currently contemplating selling any of its brands or business units to help pay for the costs of its diesel emissions problems.

May 1   *Automotive News* reports that VW brand chief Herbert Diess told reporters that "We believe that the USA has in fact the greatest potential for Volkswagen worldwide in the next decade," though he added, "naturally not in the near future, since we are starting from zero in the U.S."

May 7   Activist hedge fund TCI lashes out against what it calls excessive pay of the top executives at Volkswagen, claiming these top managers have been rewarded for years for mistakes. In a letter to Volkswagen, TCI founder Chris Kane writes, "Shockingly, in a six-year period, the nine members of the executive board will have been paid around 400 million euros ($456M) — that is corporate excess on an epic scale; management has been rewarded for failure."

May 11   The Volkswagen AG board announces that preliminary results of an internal investigation into the company's diesel emissions scandal have revealed no serious violations by past or present top executives. The company's leaders have previously blamed "rogue engineers" for installing the cheat device software that led to the scandal.

Volkswagen also says the "huge amount of information and data" being examined in the internal investigation led by the Jones Day law firm will not be published until late in the year, for fear that releasing details would disrupt the ongoing criminal investigation by the U.S. Justice Department. Previously, Volkswagen had indicated the findings would be made public before the annual shareholders meeting.

Volkswagen's supervisory and management boards vote to recommend that shareholders ratify actions taken by the company's management board in 2015.

May 19   Baltimore-based Paice LLC has filed a complaint with the U.S. International Trade Commission for infringement of its hybrid electric vehicles patents by Volkswagen. Paice LLC is seeking a cease-and-desist order, which would block the import and sales of Volkswagen, Porsche, and Audi hybrid models in the United States. The ITC announced it has launched an investigation, but had not yet made any decision on the merits of the case.

May 20   Reuters cites a *Der Spiegel* magazine report that says a power struggle has ensued on the Volkswagen supervisory board, with an attempt to dilute the voting power of Lower Saxony. The attempt was blocked when the Volkswagen Worker's Union, which has nine of the 20 supervisory board seats, sided with the two Lower Saxony representatives.

May 23

The *New York Times* reports that a former top developer at Porsche has been suspended in relation to the ongoing Volkswagen scandal.

German investor group DSW calls for an independent audit of Volkswagen's emissions test rigging scandal, to be done in addition to the automaker's internal probe. "When you have an independent investigation you can be sure that the findings will be publicized. With internal investigations you do not know whether everything has been made transparent," says DSW spokesman Jurgen Kunz.

Global investment advisor Hermes EOS calls for Volkswagen shareholders to vote against the company's board at the car giant's annual meeting of shareholders next month.

May 24

Volkswagen announces a $300M investment in Uber rival Gett.

May 25

In a stunning and surprising development, Volkswagen challenges the U.S. jurisdiction in the ongoing emission scandal, saying that cars in the United States were sold through local businesses and not the parent companies (Volkswagen AG and Audi

AG). In a response filing in U.S. Federal District Court to the U.S. Department of Justice suit, Volkswagen also claimed that the statute of limitations voided any conduct of Volkswagen prior to 2010.

May 26

The Executive Committee of the powerful IndustriALL Global Union adopts a resolution calling on Volkswagen to respect employee rights at the company's plant in Chattanooga, TN. In comments supporting the resolution, the President of IG Metall (which represents Volkswagen employees) said, "It is not acceptable that companies abide by the law in Germany but disregard it in other countries. Workers' rights should be respected worldwide — particularly by companies headquartered in Germany."

Media reports in Germany say that Volkswagen is mulling an $11B electric car battery factory in order to be independent and less reliant on Asian battery producers.

Audi Volkswagen Taiwan Co. is fined NT$55M ($154,000) by a Taiwanese regulator over false advertising concerning the emissions levels of certain vehicles.

Having slumped for eight consecutive months, Volkswagen AG's European market share hits a five-year low. The company's share of Europe's car sales in April was 25.4% and its market share for the first four months of the year was 23.9%, its lowest since 2011.

June 7

Volkswagen gets approval for diesel cheat fixes in Germany. The KBA grants approval for 800,000 of the 8.5 million cars affected.

June 8

German prosecutors are now investigating whether Volkswagen employees deleted data that could be harmful to the company in the week before the September 18 public announcement that it had cheated on diesel emission tests.

June 9

Daniel Donovan, an information manager for Volkswagen's data center in Auburn Hills, Michigan withdraws his unfair dismissal suit. Donovan had claimed he was fired when Volkswagen discovered his plan to report the company for obstruction of justice and data deletions related to the emissions scandal. A statement said the matter "has been resolved amicably to the satisfaction of both parties."

German media and the *New York Times* report that several Volkswagen employees have told investigators that in August 2015, just before the scandal broke, someone "in a supervisory position" told them indirectly to remove evidence of the emissions test cheating defeat device software. Because of ongoing investigations the employee cannot be named, thought the NYT cites an anonymous source who claimed the employee "was a member of Volkswagen's legal staff and had since been suspended from his job."

One German media report says that German prosecutors are indeed looking into a Volkswagen employee suspected of suppressing documents and obstructing their investigation by asking colleagues to "get rid of data, which was partially carried out." The state prosecutor's office said, however, that it was optimistic that some of the data would be recovered.

June 11   News reports indicate that Volkswagen AG's South Korea division is alleged to have manipulated 37 emissions and noise level tests submitted to the South Korean National Institute of Environmental Research to secure importation of its vehicles.

Volkswagen announces new investments in California, including a $4.5M new training center near Riverside and a new $6.8M parts distribution center near Sacramento.

June 17   Media speculation in two major automotive industry trade magazines surfaces that Volkswagen might consider selling off one or more of its non-core asset brands that do not manufacture cars. These non-car brands include Ducati motorcycles, MAN Diesel & Turbo (trucks), Scania (big rigs), and MAN Rent (propulsion engines for large ships).

Volkswagen will make a huge shift to electric vehicles, self-driving cars, and shared ownership as core components of a new 2025 strategy.

June 18   Volkswagen says it will phase out more than 40 current car models in the coming year as part of its new strategy. The automaker currently produces around 340 models across its various marques of SEAT, Audi, Porsche, Skoda, Bentley, and, of course, VW.

June 19   The *Guardian* newspaper in the U.K. says the European Commission was warned of car emissions test cheating five years before the Volkswagen scandal became public.

June 20   Volkswagen's majority stockholders close ranks at the company's annual meeting of shareholders, defying the ire of minority investors. The three main shareholders — the Porsche-Piech families, the Lower Saxony regional government and the Arab Gulf state of Qatar — which control almost 90% of the voting stock in Volkswagen AG, backed the company's management during the annual general meeting over criticisms and complaints from small investors calling for an independent inquiry into the emissions test cheating scandal and how this had been handled by the carmaker's senior executives.

During the annual general meeting of Volkswagen AG stockholders, CEO Matthias Mueller apologized to shareholders saying, "On behalf of the Volkswagen Group and everyone who works here, I apologize to you shareholders for your trust in Volkswagen being betrayed. This misconduct goes against everything Volkswagen stands for."

Volkswagen management board member Christine Hohmann-Dennhardt tells shareholders at the annual general meeting that the company remains convinced it did not violate German capital market disclosure rules

Former Volkswagen CEO Martin Winterkorn is now under investigation in Germany for alleged stock market manipulation. German prosecutors in Braunschweig said the investigation of Winterkorn and another former board member is focused on "sufficient real signs" that Volkswagen executives did not alert investors and the market as soon as they were made aware of the possible financial damage that could result from the emissions test cheating scandal. The Braunschweig prosecutor's statement said this new probe was opened on behalf of Germany's Federal Financial Supervisory Authority, the country's main financial watchdog.

Volkswagen says the German prosecutor's probe offers no fresh facts on former CEO Winterkorn.

The Boston Retirement System, the public pension fund for Boston municipal employees, files the first bondholders proposed class-action suit against Volkswagen AG. Filed in the U.S. District Court for the Northern District of California, the lawsuit seeks to reverse damages for bondholders who purchased Volkswagen bonds between May 23, 2014 and September 22, 2015. The lawsuit names Volkswagen AG, Volkswagen Group of America Inc., and Volkswagen Group of America Finance Inc. as respondents.

June 21

The United Auto Workers released a signed 2014 agreement stating Volkswagen would recognize the UAW as the representative of its members in exchange for the union dropping a challenge to the outcome of a union election at the Volkswagen plant in Chattanooga, TN. The UAW said that Volkswagen was now reneging on this deal.

International law firm Quinn Emanuel has filed the first in an expected wave of class-action suits against Volkswagen AG on behalf of shareholders who lost "hundreds of millions of euros" following the EPA's announcement last year that the automaker had been cheating on pollution emissions tests. The move is being led by legal funding firm Bentham, which says it has gathered major Volkswagen shareholders, including sovereign wealth funds, global asset managers, and major pension investors who suffered losses when the company's share price dropped dramatically in the wake of the emissions test cheating scandal.

Germany's financial watchdog, BaFin, calls on prosecutors in Germany to investigate Volkswagen's entire former management board over the time it took to disclose the automaker's emission test cheating. BaFin believes the entire former management board should be held collectively responsible for how the scandal was communicated to investors and the financial markets.

The Oklahoma Attorney General sues Volkswagen AG.

June 22   Volkswagen Human Resources Chief Karlheinz Blessing says the Volkswagen management board will not assist the efforts of the United Auto Workers (UAW) union to organize at its auto assembly plant in Chattanooga, TN. The company also reaffirmed its resistance to the union's requests that it start talks over wages for a small fraction of the factory's 1500 hourly workers.

Volkswagen receives approval for fixes on another one million vehicles from the German motor vehicle authority KBA. This brings the technical solutions approved by KBA to over 3.7 million cars. CEO Matthias Mueller says the company "expects the recall campaign to really pick up speed now."

June 23

The German investor's association DSW announced it was going to court to push for an independent investigation of the Volkswagen diesel emission scandal. In a statement DSW said it was convinced that such an investigation was the right tool for cleaning up the scandal, even after its motion for an independent probe was voted down at the recent annual meeting of Volkswagen shareholders.

A South Korean court issued an arrest warrant for a Korean-based Volkswagen AG executive in connection with an investigation into the company's auto emissions test cheating. It is the first known arrest warrant leveled against a Volkswagen executive anywhere in the world in connection with the 9-month old scandal.

June 24

Norway's $850B sovereign wealth fund, the world's largest, files a complaint against Volkswagen as part of a joint legal action in the Braunschweig District Court in Germany.

June 28

Volkswagen and the U.S. Department of Justice (on behalf of the EPA and the FTC) file a Proposed Settlement Agreement with U.S. District Court Judge Charles Breyer in which Volkswagen agrees to buy back 2-liter diesel vehicles it cannot fix, pay compensation to car owners, and set aside funds to promote infrastructure development for electric vehicles. The cost to Volkswagen could be up to $15.3B and this proposed settlement does not cover the 85,000 3-liter vehicles also fitted with defeat device software.

Judge Breyer accepts the Proposed Settlement Agreement for review and schedules a hearing for late July in which a preliminary agreement will likely be given.

U.S. Attorney General Loretta Lynch said a Department of Justice investigation into the Volkswagen emissions scandal was continuing and that it was important to look at the actions of the individuals involved. The proposed $15.3B settlement has no impact on these investigations.

June 29   Porsche Automobil Holding SE, the majority shareholder in Volkswagen AG, said it has no plans to sue the carmaker for damages over the diesel emissions scandal. Porsche Automobil Holding SE owns 52% of the voting rights in Volkswagen AG. It told its own shareholders that no claims would be filed because an investigation by Braunschweig prosecutors against former Volkswagen CEO Martin Winterkorn has not uncovered evidence of misconduct.

Europe's Industry Commissioner Elzbieta Bienkowska says Volkswagen should replicate its U.S. settlement agreement in the European Union and voluntarily provide the same compensation to its European customers who bought vehicles with the emissions testing defeat device software program.

July 1   A lawyer for Volkswagen AG told a U.S. District Court that the German automaker believed it could fix 85,000 polluting 3-litre Volkswagens, Porsche, and Audi diesel cars and SUVs. The lawyer told District Court Judge Charles Breyer that the company believed that the vehicles were fixable and that the fix will not be complicated or negatively impact vehicle performance.

July 4   VW brand chief Herbert Diess is not planning to step down even though he is now the subject of an investigation by German public prosecutors. Volkswagen said Diess is part of a probe into whether any of the automaker's executives or managers violated disclosure and financial market manipulation rules in Germany by taking too long to inform investors it had cheated on emission tests in the U.S.

Volkswagen CEO Mathias Mueller said the company could not afford US-style damages payments in Germany as doing so would overwhelm Volkswagen.

Germany's financial watchdog BaFin has widened its probe of Volkswagen leadership for misleading shareholders. *DW* reports BaFin has seen "real signs" that the Board failed its collective responsibilities to warn investors of the impending Diselgate scandal.

July 6   Volkswagen is recalling almost 6000 gas-powered Touran multi-purpose vehicles (MPV) worldwide to replace gas bottles with potential risks that corrosion might cause the gas tanks to burst and create considerable injury risk.

July 7   A U.S. law firm, representing a large pension fund for California teachers as well as other investors, files a lawsuit with the Braunschweig district court in Germany against Volkswagen for damages caused by the Dieselgate scandal.

The German Ministry of Transport announces that Volkswagen will not have to pay any fines for the millions of emissions test cheating diesel cars it sold in the country. But the company will be required to "return the cars to a legally compliant condition," according to the German Transport Minister Alexander Dobrindt.

News reports emerge that Volkswagen, along with BMW, Daimler, and two other firms were raided by the German anti-trust regulator at the end of June in relation to a probe into steel price fixing allegations.

July 8   European consumer watchdog BEUC claims that one of its Italian partners has discovered that deactivating the defeat device on an Audi Q5, which they claim is the Volkswagen proposed solution, actually increases, not decreases, nitrogen oxide (NOx) output.

The Spanish High Court rules that Volkswagen AG will be liable to answer any charges over emissions fraud. Volkswagen had argued that a Spanish probe should be directed at its Spanish affiliates SEAT, Volkswagen-Audi España, and Volkswagen Navarra.

Volkswagen will pay an additional $86M in civil penalties to California to resolve claims made by the state under its unfair competition law.

July 12

Some Volkswagen shareholders want to recall bonuses paid to the company's executives.

German prosecutors have notified Volkswagen management that they will be seeking punitive damages in addition to the four criminal investigations already underway. If Volkswagen is forced to pay damages in Germany, the costs could be enormous — potentially running as high as the profit Volkswagen earned on each of the 11 million vehicles sold worldwide with the emissions test cheating software.

July 13

The California Air Resources Board (CARB) flatly rejects Volkswagen's proposed fix for 16,000 3-litre diesel engine cars from Audi, Porsche, and VW that were outfitted with illegal, emissions. CARB called the plans submitted by Volkswagen "substantially deficient and vague." The regulator also said the plan "falls far short" of meeting legal requirements. If Volkswagen is not able to find a fix amenable to CARB, the company may be forced to buy back the 85,000 3-litre diesel engine vehicles sold nationwide, adding to the $15.3B it has already agreed to pay owners of its 2-litre diesel models and the U.S. and state governments.

July 14   A committee of U.K. lawmakers said Britain should consider prosecuting Volkswagen over the diesel emissions scandal. The British Transport Select Committee also said Volkswagen should be punished to avoid a repeat of the scandal.

July 18   German newspaper *Handelsblatt* reports that Volkswagen could be liable for up to $2B if it reaches a settlement in Canada similar to the proposed U.S. settlement.

Media stories report that Volkswagen executives in the U.S. have promised restitution within a month for American franchise car dealers damaged by the automaker's diesel scandal. The reports cite dealers who attended a meeting in New Jersey with senior Volkswagen of America executives.

Christian Science Monitor reports that Volkswagen will stop selling diesel cars in the United States, blaming increasingly difficult federal emissions standards.

July 19   Truck maker MAN, owned by Volkswagen AG, is one of five European truck manufacturers cited by the European Union's Competition Committee for price fixing and operating a secret system aimed at delaying the installation of pollution-curbing exhaust pipes and engines. MAN avoided being fined, however, as it had revealed the existence of the cartel.

July 20   The attorneys general for the U.S. states of New York, Massachusetts, and Maryland say in a court filing that the Volkswagen scandal reaches all the way to the top of the company and, for the first time, connect Volkswagen CEO Matthias Mueller to the scandal, saying he was aware of a 2006 decision to not outfit Audi vehicles with equipment needed to meet U.S. clean air standards.

July 22   Volkswagen will halt the sales of most of its vehicles in South Korea. Sales are already down 33% in the first half compared to the first six months of 2014.

Various media outlets report that Volkswagen has an emissions test cheating fix ready. The solution reportedly includes a software update and a larger catalytic converter to trap harmful nitrogen oxide (NOx) particles. The reports are based on comments from car dealers briefed at a regional dealer meeting in Newark, NJ by Volkswagen of America Chief Operating Officer Mark McNabb.

July 25   Europe's Commissioner for Justice is working with EU consumer groups to pressure Volkswagen into compensating customers across Europe as it proposes to do in the U.S. Volkswagen has rejected calls to do so for the 8.5 million affected vehicles in Europe, where different legal rules weaken the chances of car owners winning any kind of payout. Options will be discussed when the Commission organizes a meeting with consumer groups in Brussels in September.

New York, Massachusetts and Maryland file separate, but nearly identical, lawsuits in their respective state courts accusing Volkswagen of violating each state's environmental laws.

The Law Office of Thomas L. Young, a plaintiff trial law firm in Tampa, FL releases a statement saying "We suspect Volkswagen may be forced to pay hundreds of millions, likely billions more, after all the unresolved litigation is better understood and accounted for."

July 26   Prosecutors in the German city of Braunschweig said they had widened their probe into the diesel emissions test cheating, with 21 current and former Volkswagen staff now under investigation. In March prosecutors had indicated that only 17 people were under investigation.

Volkswagen recalls 6000 cars for failing child locks.

July 27   Federal District Court Judge Charles Breyer grants preliminary approval to the Volkswagen settlement plan with U.S. and state regulators. The proposed settlement requires Volkswagen to buy back or modify 85% of the cars sold with defeat device software between 2009 and 2015. The automaker must also pay owners who agree not to sue the company an additional $5001 to $10,000 each. Volkswagen is to set aside $10B to cover costs related to fixing, buying back vehicles, and/or compensating U.S. car owners.

Volkswagen must also establish two environmental remediation funds, one to take older diesel vehicles off the road and another to pay for the infrastructure necessary to encourage sales of zero-emission vehicles. These two funds will total $4.7B.

The proposed settlement will now be made publicly available for review and comment. Judge Breyer is expected to grant final approval, pending any new issues or public comments, in late October.

Volkswagen must still work out a separate settlement plan with the EPA and the California Air Resources Board (CARB) for 85,000 vehicles from Audi, Porsche, and VW that were fitted with defeat device software in 3-litre V6 diesel engines.

July 29   First half operating profits for the VW brand, the largest division by sales for Volkswagen AG, plunged by more than a third to 900M euros ($998M) as costs for its diesel engine emissions scandal and falling car sales outweigh gains from cost cuts. The 1.5B euros set aside under the VW brand as additional provisions to cover costs related to the scandal is roughly two-thirds of the additional 2.2B euros in reserves taken by Volkswagen AG in the first half.

The Department of Ecology in Washington State has fined Volkswagen $176M, saying people's health was put at risk when Volkswagen vehicles emitted up to 40 times the allowable amount of harmful nitrogen oxides (NOx) while being driven in the state. The fine was based on the 21,000 Volkswagen diesel vehicles registered in the state.

July 30   Volkswagen becomes embroiled in a fresh scandal in the U.K. over false safety rating claims made by some of its car dealers.

August 1   Volkswagen and the California Air Resources Board (CARB) are reportedly testing a fix that could bring the automaker's 2-litre diesel engines into compliance with U.S. emissions laws. Along with the EPA, CARB must approve any modifications or fixes before they are implemented by Volkswagen. However, if the new hardware and software solution is successful, Volkswagen might avoid having to buy back some 475,000 2-litre diesel engine cars it sold in the U.S. between 2009 and 2016. This could potentially save the company billions of dollars, but only if car owners also agree to the fix.

August 2

South Korea suspends sales of 80 Volkswagen Group models and fines the company 17.8B won ($16.1M), accusing the automaker of forging documents on emissions or noise-level tests. Affected car models are under the Audi, Bentley, and VW brands. The ban was announced before a ship in Seoul's harbor carrying 3000 new Volkswagen Group vehicles for South Korea could be unloaded.

Additionally, news reports surface that Korean authorities in July indicted a local Volkswagen executive on charges of submitting manipulated emissions data to authorities and violating the country's air quality laws.

The *Wall Street Journal* reports that a district judge in Germany last week dismissed Volkswagen's objections and ruled that local owners of tainted diesel vehicles had a right to return their cars to dealers for a full refund because of Volkswagen's "massive fraud."

Volkswagen requests dismissal of a U.S. investor's class-action suit since the company's shares trade mostly in Germany.

The German state of Bavaria announces plans to sue Volkswagen for damages. Bavaria's state pension fund for civil servants lost approximately $784,000 after Volkswagen AG shares plunged following last September's diesel emissions test cheating scandal announcement. Bavaria will be the first of Germany's 16 federal states to seek legal action against Volkswagen AG over the scandal.

August 5

In comments filed on the proposed Volkswagen settlement agreement, *Consumer Reports* said the buyback offer undervalues retail prices and urges the use of values that "would lead to buyback offers for consumers that will be at least several hundred dollars higher." The magazine also wants owners who opt for a fix to be able to change their minds and be allowed to sell their cars back to Volkswagen because the cars may perform differently after any software fix is installed.

August 6

28 electric vehicle charging companies write to the U.S. Department of Justice requesting an independent administrator be appointed to oversee the $2B Volkswagen AG is required to invest in clean car infrastructure as part of the proposed settlement plan. Their written concerns are reportedly that Volkswagen should not have the power to shape the development of the electric car charging market as a result of the settlement.

August 7

U.S. authorities have found three unapproved software programs in 3-litre diesel engines made by Volkswagen's Audi unit, according to a report in the German weekly newspaper *Bild am Sonntag*. The software reportedly shuts down emission control systems after 22 minutes in the turbocharged direct injection (TDI) engines used in Audi Q7, Porsche Cayenne, and VW Touareg models. The magazine says that official methods to test and measure emissions usually last about 20 minutes.

August 8   The district court in Braunschweig, Germany has sent 170 investor lawsuits, claiming up to 4B euros ($4.5B) in damages against Volkswagen, onward to the regional court for selection of a model plaintiff. The model plaintiff's case would represent and then be applied to the other suits filed by hundreds of private and institutional investors who held, or continue to hold, shares in Volkswagen AG.

Italy's anti-trust agency has fined Volkswagen 5M euros ($5.5M) for allegedly misinforming car buyers about diesel emissions results. Volkswagen said it plans to challenge the fine at an administrative court.

August 9   The Federal Trade Commission releases two blogs to help ensure consumers and businesses know the facts surrounding the $10B proposed settlement agreement for car owners. In one blog post the federal regulator states, "The FTC will be watching closely to ensure that the compensation process is unsullied by deception." The FTC also advises car owners to visit VWCourtSettlements.com, where by entering a car's vehicle identification number (VIN), they can find out how much they are entitled to under the proposed settlement agreement.

August 11   Lawyers representing the plaintiffs in the various lawsuits against Volkswagen bundled together in U.S. District Court, which led to the Proposed Settlement Agreement, say they will seek up to $332.5M in legal fees and costs from Volkswagen.

August 12   A team of researchers from the University of Birmingham in England finds that the entire ensemble used to lock and unlock Volkswagen vehicles with a remote control key fob is vulnerable to being hacked. This vulnerability impacts over 100 million Volkswagen cars built since 1995, along with several other car models.

August 13   Federal Judge Charles Breyer signs an order authorizing Volkswagen to conduct a test program for scrapping 2-liter diesel engine cars. The test program will involve 20 vehicles owned by Volkswagen or its finance company. Volkswagen requested the tests so it can understand the process of scrapping the cars and salvaging parts.

August 15   A *Wall Street Journal* report says U.S. prosecutors and Volkswagen are negotiating a settlement that could result in significant financial penalties after Justice Department officials found evidence of criminal wrongdoing related to the automaker's diesel emissions test cheating.

August 18   Volkswagen has received approval by German motor vehicle authority KBA for technical fixes on another 140,000 2-liter diesel cars with illegal emissions control software. This brings the number of vehicles cleared for repair by KBA to 5.2 million.

August 23   Robert Bosch GmbH said claims it was a knowing participant in Volkswagen's decades-long scheme to evade U.S. anti-pollution laws were "wild and unfounded." The statement was made in a filing in U.S. District Court in San Francisco in response to a lawsuit filed on behalf of U.S. car owners.

Fortune reports that Volkswagen has agreed to hold settlement talks with several U.S. states that have sued the company for hundreds of millions of dollars over state environmental law violations. Volkswagen said settlement talks will begin no later than November 1st.

August 25   Volkswagen tells a court hearing that it plans to compensate car dealers in the United States. Volkswagen did not specify the amount of compensation, but the Reuters news agency reported it could be close to $1.2B.

August 26   The National Labor Relations Board orders Volkswagen Group of America to recognize and bargain with the United Auto Workers Local 42 as the representatives of a portion of workers at the

Volkswagen assembly plant in Chattanooga, Tennessee.

August 30   *Motor Trend* cites a Bloomberg report saying Volkswagen recently briefed its U.S. car dealers on how it plans to boost sales. One strategy, according to the Bloomberg report, is to lower the prices on its vehicles by slashing MSRPS and embracing a "volume mindset" targeting mass-market brands from General Motors and Toyota.

Volkswagen has decided not to sue the South Korean government over its sales ban of the automaker's cars. Instead, Volkswagen will try to achieve certification for the 80 models of VW, Audi, and Bentley vehicles banned last month.

August 31   CEO Matthias Mueller tells a briefing in Hamburg, Germany that it will take Volkswagen 2-3 years for its wide-ranging revamp and restructuring to start paying a return. He said the Volkswagen management board is working on 60 projects to overhaul the company, including a cultural shift to get the automaker's 12 brands and numerous divisions to cooperate.

September 1   Germany's Transport Ministry has asked the European Commission to investigate exhaust emissions of Fiat Chrysler for potential illegal manipulation devices. This direct approach to the European Union comes after KBA, the German motor vehicle authority, began testing the vehicles of several auto manufacturers last year. The German Transport Ministry previously raised concerns over Fiat with Italian authorities earlier in the year, but received a rejection of claims that Fiat and Chrysler vehicles used illegal exhaust manipulation devices.

Volkswagen has filed an appeal of the National Labor Relations Board decision on its dispute with the United Auto Workers (UAW) union in the U.S. Court of Appeals for the District of Columbia. Jörg Hofmann, head of the powerful German union IG Metall, which has members on the Volkswagen supervisory board, calls for Volkswagen to "no longer act contrary to American labor law and to seek talks with UAW without delay."

Australia's Competition and Consumer Commission (ACCC) is suing Volkswagen's Australian subsidiary for lying about the emission of its diesel vehicles. Volkswagen has sold more than 57,000 diesel engine vehicles in Australia over a five-year period. The ACCC says it wants Volkswagen Group Australia to make public declarations of misconduct, pay unspecified financial penalties, and issue corrective advertising in relation to its actions over a five-year period.

September 5   European Union Consumer Commissioner Vera Jourova told a news conference that Volkswagen AG may have violated two EU consumer laws: the

Consumer Sales and Guarantees Directive, which "prohibits companies from touting exaggerated environmental claims in their sales pitches," and the Unfair Commercial Practices Directive. Volkswagen said it considered the allegations of the EU Consumer Commissioner unfounded and rejected them.

September 6   The former CEO of Bentley and Bugatti, Wolfgang Schreiber, is suing Volkswagen in a Munich court over $100M in royalties, which he believes he deserves for having played a key role in developing Volkswagen's ubiquitous Direct-Shift-Gearbox (DSG) transmission.

Lawyers for U.S. car owners allege in a new filing in U.S. District Court in San Francisco that automotive supplier Robert Bosch GmbH concealed the use of Volkswagen's secret defeat device software that it helped design. The filing also said Bosch demanded in 2008 that Volkswagen provide legal protection to Bosch if the software is used. Citing a January 2008 email, the filing said Bosch demanded that "Volkswagen indemnify Bosch for any legal exposure arising from work on the defeat device."

The majority of the 210,000 car owners in the U.S. who have signed up for the proposed Settlement Agreement program have indicated they want their vehicles bought back by Volkswagen, Elizabeth

Cabraser, the lead plaintiff attorney in the settlement, says in an interview with Bloomberg.

September 7   Volkswagen AG buys a 16.6% stake in Navistar for $256M to strengthen its truck business. *Motor Trend* reports the move should help Volkswagen gain access to the North America truck market and reduce development costs for its truck and bus division.

September 9   James Liang, a long-time Volkswagen engineer, pleaded guilty to charges of violating the U.S. Clean Air Act, conspiring to defraud the United States, and wire fraud as part of a plea bargain with the U.S. Department of Justice. He faces up to five years in prison and up to a $250,000 fine when sentenced. He is the first individual charged by U.S. authorities for actions relating to the diesel emissions test cheating scam. As part of the plea agreement Liang will cooperate with the Department of Justice in its ongoing criminal investigation.

September 13   A Frankfurt-based law firm has filed 12 lawsuits against Porsche SE, the main shareholder of Volkswagen AG, claiming Porsche did not disclose the financial risks of Volkswagen's emissions test cheating scandal to its shareholders.

September 15   Asset manager Blackrock, the world's largest money manager, is joining a group of institutional investors suing Volkswagen for $2B euros ($2.2B) over the drop in the automaker's stock price after the emissions scandal broke publicly.

September 18   On the 12-month anniversary of the EPA announcement of the first Notice of Violation Volkswagen has reportedly fixed less than 10% of the 8.5 million affected diesel cars in Europe and none in the United States.

Various news media report that the Audi head of development, Stefan Knirsch, will be suspended from duties. The media reports say internal investigators at Volkswagen have shown that Knirsch, an Audi board member, knew about the use of the cheat software in the Audi 3-liter diesel engines and gave a false promise under oath.

Over 6000 additional investor lawsuits are expected to be filed in the Lower Saxony district court in Braunschweig. This is in addition to the 1400 cases already filed which seek 10.7B euros ($11.9B) in civil redress from Volkswagen for investment losses sustained when the diesel emissions test cheating became public a year ago. The surge in new lawsuit filings is because investors are concerned that the one-year anniversary of the EPA announcement of the first Violation of Notice may be the deadline to file.

September 19   Volkswagen super luxury brands Bentley and Lamborghini will skip the annual Paris Motor Show this month as Volkswagen AG reins in spending and exhibition attendance in a belt-tightening move to help cover the increasing costs of its emissions scandal.

The *Guardian* newspaper reports that new research reveals that all major diesel car brands are selling models that emit far higher levels of pollution than Volkswagen's vehicles. The research by Transport & Environment (T&E) found not a single car brand complies with the latest Euro 6 air pollution limits when driven on the road.

September 22   Detlef Stendel, who heads Volkswagen's emissions certification, is questioned by South Korean prosecutors investigating cheating of pollution tests by the carmaker.

September 23   MAN SE, in which Volkswagen is the majority owner, announces plans to cut 1400 jobs at its diesel engine unit.

Volkswagen is "awarded" the Chemistry Ig Nobel Prize for "solving the problem of excessive automobile pollution emissions by automatically, electromechanically producing fewer emissions whenever the cars are being tested." These tongue-in-cheek scientific awards were first established at Harvard in 1991.

September 25   Citing an article in Germany's *Bild Zeitung* newspaper, *Forbes* and Bloomberg report that former Volkswagen CEO Martin Winterkorn was "well aware of the Dieselgate scandal long before it was made public." Documents referenced by *Bild Zeitung* reportedly also "appear to prove that Winterkorn initiated or attempted a cover-up." These documents reportedly include an internal Volkswagen memo dated July 30, 2015 instructing two Volkswagen employees to only "partially disclose" issues with Volkswagen's diesel engines in forthcoming discussions with CARB.

September 26   A senior EPA official tells a European Parliament committee that Europe's car emissions tests have been seen as inadequate for decades. He also said much stronger enforcement will be needed to stop cheating by automakers.

Stefan Knirsch, the Audi head of technical development, resigned "with immediate effect," a week after the *Bild am Sonntag* newspaper reported that the internal investigation by the Jones Day law firm had found he knew that Audi's 3-liter diesel engines were equipped with the defeat device cheating software before the scandal was made public. Knirsch, who had been in the job for only 10 months, had previously led the group's engine development work.

Volkswagen AG hires former EU Commissioner for Climate Connie Hedegaard to join its nine-member Sustainability Council. Other members include former Belgian Prime Minister Yves Leterme, Secretary General of the International Red Cross Elhadj As Sy, and former Executive Director of the United Nations Global Compact Georg Kell.

September 30

VW brand chief Herbert Diess tells Bloomberg TV that it will take "three to four rough years ahead of us to really restructure the company and getting more profitable and more competitive." He said by 2020 "we will have finished the hard work."

Volkswagen has asked a U.S. federal judge to reject requests from groups representing European investors and customers for documents related to the diesel emissions scandal.

Porsche Automobil Holdings SE, the major shareholder in Volkswagen AG, may face an investor test case over how quickly it informed investors of the implications of the Volkswagen diesel emissions test cheating.

Volkswagen CEO Matthias Mueller tells *Automotive News* at the Paris Motor Show that he is hopeful Volkswagen will reach a settlement with the U.S. Department of Justice on their criminal investigation with an agreement on the size of a fine.

Volkswagen has agreed to pay $1.21B to its 652 car dealers in the United States. Each dealer will receive an average of $1.85M over an 18-month period.

October 4	*Handelsblatt* reports that some Volkswagen car owners in Germany are planning legal action, believing that the software updates installed to fix diesel emissions are harming vehicle performance.
October 6	Volkswagen will not sell any diesel vehicles in the United States for model years 2016 and 2017. The company has been banned from selling any diesel vehicles in the U.S. since late 2015.
	An article in *Car & Driver* notes that Volkswagen will be subjected to additional payments if less than 85% of vehicle owners in the United States sign up for the Proposed Settlement Agreement.
October 7	Roughly two-thirds of affected U.S. car owners have registered to receive settlement benefits, according to a memorandum filed in U.S. District Court by the law firm representing them. Only 3,300 people thus far have opted out of the settlement program.
October 8	The German legislature votes to ban new gasoline and diesel powered vehicles from European Union roads starting in 2030. Only zero emission vehicles would be allowed to be sold after that time. This resolution, however, has no binding authority over the EU or its member states.
	Congresswoman Anna Eshoo (D-CA) writes publicly to EPA Administrator Lisa McCarthy saying the proposed $2B settlement with Volkswagen on zero emissions vehicle infrastructure gives the automaker

too much authority on how to spend these funds. "A particular concern," she notes allows Volkswagen to make "possible investments in its own proprietary technology and subsidiaries."

The U.S. Department of Justice said it received 1195 comments on the Proposed Settlement Agreement from private citizens, state and local government offices and agencies, businesses, institutions, and associations. DOJ said it urged the U.S. District Court to approve the Proposed Settlement Agreement with only minor changes.

October 9   Volkswagen recalls 281,500 VW and Audi branded vehicles in the U.S. due to a potential gas leak. Volkswagen did not say if the recall will affect vehicles outside the U.S.

October 10   The German newspaper *Bild am Sonntag* reveals that the Jones Day internal investigation has shown that current Volkswagen CEO Matthias Mueller had no knowledge of the automaker's diesel emissions test cheating before it became publicly known. He had been CEO of the Porsche division before replacing Martin Winterkorn as CEO of Volkswagen AG a week after the scandal broke.

October 12   ChargePoint, the world's largest electric vehicle charging network, has asked U.S. District Court Judge Charles Breyer to amend the proposed agreement between Volkswagen and the U.S.

Department of Justice requiring Volkswagen to invest $2B over 10 years to increase the zero emissions vehicle infrastructure in the U.S. ChargePoint claims the settlement threatens its survival and that of other charging station companies.

October 13   The Investor Expectations of Automotive Companies report, published by the Institutional Investors Group on Climate Change (IIGCC), warns car manufacturers to address climate change by moving to low emission vehicles or face a sell down of their shares. The IIGCC is a network of over 250 global investors with assets in excess of $24 trillion.

October 14   News reports indicate that Audi may drop out of the World Endurance Championships (WEC) after 2017, as the Volkswagen Group continues to seek cost saving opportunities to help pay for the diesel emissions test cheating scandal. One report said the budgets for both Audi and Porsche to compete in the WEC are $219M each.

Car sales in Europe hit an all-time high for the month of September, totaling 1.455 million vehicles sold, an increase of 7.2% over September 2015. While Volkswagen Group remained Europe's biggest selling carmaker, its market share for the first nine months of 2016 dropped to 23.8% compared to 24.9% for the same time period the previous year.

Volkswagen Group sales rose 7.1% in September, its largest monthly increase in 30 months. This sales growth was spurred by a 20% increase in sales in China, Volkswagen's biggest market, and a 6.3% improvement in Europe (where roughly 40% of its vehicles are sold).

Lawyers in the class-action lawsuits against Volkswagen in the U.S. will receive $175M in legal fees and other costs from the automaker, according to media reports. The lawyers had requested up to $332.5M in fees and costs in their initial proposed payment structure. This increases the total cost of the Proposed Settlement Agreement to $16.7B.

October 15   Volkswagen CEO Matthias Mueller has demanded heightened belt-tightening at the automaker, inclusive of 10% decreases in material costs and overheads in the 2017 budget, according to trade publication *Automobilwoche*.

October 17   The British government was scathing in its official response to the U.K. Transport Committee Special Report on the emissions test cheating scandal. It concluded that Volkswagen's response to date has been "unacceptable" and that "the treatment of U.K. consumers has not been acceptable and that vehicle owners should be compensated for the inconvenience, uncertainty, and worry" caused by Volkswagen's cheating and for any loss in the value of affected vehicles. The government also clearly indicated it was willing to pursue legal action against Volkswagen in the future.

Missouri becomes the 17th U.S. state to take legal action against Volkswagen. In filing the state's civil suit, the Missouri attorney general says, "Volkswagen's actions demonstrate a flagrant disregard for Missouri's environmental laws, as well as the health and welfare of Missourians."

October 18   U.S. District Court Judge Charles Breyer grants preliminary approval to the $1.21 settlement between Volkswagen and its 652 dealers across the U.S.

Judge Breyer also holds a three-hour hearing on objections to the Proposed Settlement Agreement. Over 450 written objections to the deal have been filed with the court.

Volkswagen has reportedly hired 900 people to handle the buybacks of affected vehicles and will have a dedicated person in each of the 652 dealerships to oversee the purchases.

October 20   Volkswagen AG is targeting 3.7B euros ($4.1B) in cost saving cuts at is flagship VW brand division by 2021. The savings are reported by *Fortune* to be needed for funding a shift to electric cars and self-driving vehicles, as well as the cost impact from the diesel emissions test cheating scandal.

October 21
Der Spiegel reports that Audi will buy back 25,000 diesel engine cars that cannot be brought into compliance with U.S. Clean Air Act emissions regulations. These older generation cars are part of the 85,000 3-liter vehicles not covered by the Proposed Settlement Agreement between Volkswagen and the U.S. Department of Justice slated for final approval in coming days.

October 25
U.S. District Court Judge Charles Breyer signs an order approving the court settlement between the U.S. Department of Justice (on behalf of the EPA and FTC) and Volkswagen AG that includes Volkswagen spending up to $10B to buy back affected VW, Porsche, and Audi 2-liter vehicles, paying compensation to U.S. car owners, and establishing two funds to provide infrastructure development for electric vehicles. According to Reuters Volkswagen will begin buying back the affected vehicles around the middle of November.

October 26
European Union champion Vera Jourova asks for proof that Volkswagen can fulfill its pledge to make vehicles comply with limits on nitrogen oxide (NOx) by the fall of 2017. "We need Volkswagen to guarantee, in a legally binding way and without any time limit, that the repairs will work and do not have any negative impact," she says in a letter to a Volkswagen official.

October 29   Karlheinz Blessing, Volkswagen's Human Resources chief and a member of the automaker's management board, says the company expects the shift to electric cars to result in 25,000 fewer jobs over the next decade. He reaffirms that there would be no forced dismissals at the automaker, but that older workers who retire would not be replaced. The job reductions will come as the assembly of electric engines requires fewer workers than making combustion engines.

Volkswagen says 190,000 of the 1.2 million affected diesel vehicles in the United Kingdom have been fixed and that a solution for another 478,000 vehicles has been identified. That leaves around 700,000 vehicles in the U.K without an approved solution.

Operating profit for the VW brand plummeted to $396M for the third quarter, down over 50% from the $801M recorded for the same 3-month period last year.

November 1   Citing substantial progress in talks between the U.S. Department of Justice and Volkswagen, U.S. District Court Judge Charles Breyer sets a December 1 deadline for a report on a resolution fix for the 85,000 3-liter VW, Audi, and Porsche vehicles fitted with the defeat device software.

Several media outlets report rumors that Volkswagen flagship brand VW is likely to immediately quit the World Rally Championship in a cost-saving move. VW has won the World Rally Championship manufacturer's title four years in a row.

Sales for the VW brand in the U.S. dropped 18.5% in October over the same month last year and are down 13.1% for the year. VW sold a paltry 256,047 vehicles in the U.S. for the first 10 months of 2016.

Two U.S. House of Representative Republicans have requested the EPA provide Congress with more details on the settlement agreement with Volkswagen and to disclose how much excess pollution the automaker's vehicles sold in the U.S. since 2009 have emitted. The two Congressmen also expressed concerns that "Volkswagen may be able to obtain substantial competitive benefits, if not a monopoly, on electric vehicle infrastructure," which they write is a "curious outcome for the settlement of a cheating scandal."

November 3   More than 375,000 Volkswagen car owners have registered on the Settlement Website and nearly 200,000 people have already submitted claims an attorney for Volkswagen told a federal court judge in San Francisco.

Volkswagen AG chairman Hans Dieter Poetsch is now under investigation by German prosecutors for allegations involving securities law violations for "failing to notify shareholders quickly enough of the financial risks of the diesel emissions cheating scandal." Poetsch was the Chief Financial Officer of Volkswagen when the automaker was first informed of the EPA Notice of Violation of the U.S. Clean Air Act. He became chairman a few weeks after the emissions test cheating became public knowledge.

Volkswagen will have a historian investigate the automaker's practices in Brazil during the country's military dictatorship between 1964 and 1985. This follows a civil lawsuit filed by former employees last year claiming 12 Volkswagen workers were arrested and tortured in a Volkswagen factory near Sao Paolo.

November 4   Volkswagen says the software allowing its diesel vehicles to evade emissions rules does not violate European law. In an email statement the automaker proclaimed, "The software contained in vehicles with an EA-189 engine in the view of Volkswagen represents no unlawful defeat device under European law. The efficiency of the emissions cleanup system will not be reduced in those vehicles which however would be a prerequisite for the existence of an unlawful defeat device in the legal sense."

The Volkswagen statement on European law compliance drew criticism from Lower Saxony premier Stephan Weil, a member of 20-person Volkswagen supervisory board. His office released a statement saying, "This manipulative action is inexcusable in the opinion of the prime minister, regardless of whether the software is legal due to varying national legislation."

Volkswagen receives approval from the German Federal Motor Transport Authority (KBA) for technical fixes for another 2.6 million vehicles. These are cars with 1.6-liter TDI engines. KBA has previously approved fixes for around 5.6 million Volkswagen Group models with 1.2-liter and 2.0-liter engines.

November 6   *Bild am Sonntag* reports that the California Air Resources Board (CARB) has discovered several Audi vehicle models running illegal software to bring carbon dioxide (CO_2) emissions within legal limits under laboratory test conditions. The software has apparently been found in both gasoline and diesel Audi models with automatic transmissions produced up until May 2016. The paper also reports that Audi has suspended several engineers after being informed of this matter by CARB earlier this year.

November 7   Environmental groups in Colorado urge the state's Department of Public Health and Environment to use a portion of the $9.2M the state will receive from the Volkswagen Settlement deal to build out a zero emissions vehicle charging network. This would be enough to build around 60 new electric charging stations and electrifying 3000 miles of major highways in Colorado.

November 8   Volkswagen CEO Matthias Mueller says he hopes "the (U.S.) election results won't have more negative consequences for Volkswagen." He also said, "I think we're at a point where a consent decree could be reached, but that's the Department of Justice decision, not mine."

A class-action suit on behalf of owners of more than 100,000 Audi vehicles is filed in Chicago federal court. The suit accuses Audi of installing defeat device software into at least six models of 3-liter gasoline powered engines since February 2013 and possibly earlier. The suit also alleges Audi executives encouraged the use of the defeat devices in gas powered vehicles as recently as May, a full eight months after the diesel cheating was publicly revealed by the EPA. This is the first civil suit in the U.S. concerning gasoline engines instead of diesel engines.

November 9   The Illinois Attorney General hits Volkswagen with a lawsuit claiming the automaker violated the state's pollution protection laws. An estimated 19,000 Volkswagen vehicles fitted with the defeat device cheating software are registered in Illinois.

November 10   Volkswagen starts offering a $1000 loyalty bonus to current brand owners in the U.S.A. who own or lease any 2001 or newer VW model. Owners are not required to trade-in their existing car and the offer is extended to members of the same household.

French investigators have referred automaker Renault to the country's prosecutor for possible indictment over abnormal nitrogen oxide (NOx) emissions from some diesel engines.

A senior manager at Volkswagen attending the launch of an updated version of the VW Golf hatchback in Wolfsburg tells a Reuters reporter, "It's undeniable that cost discipline has become the name of the game at VW."

According to NHTSA recall data analyzed by iSeeCars.com, the Volkswagen Group had the highest auto recall rates over the past three decades. The data for the Volkswagen Group (excluding the Porsche brand which is reported separately by NHTSA) shows 1805 vehicles recalled per 1000 cars. The industry average is 1115 cars recalled for every 1000 sold.

November 11   Reuters reports that the Jones Day law firm conducting the internal investigation at Volkswagen on the diesel emissions test cheating will now question Audi CEO Rupert Stadler regarding the new cheat software device that lowers CO_2 emissions during testing on some Audi diesel and gasoline models.

The U.S. Federal Trade Commission has asked a federal judge to allow the agency to take additional testimony from Volkswagen AG staff over allegations some of the automaker's employees destroyed documents last year related to the diesel emissions test cheating software.

In a court filing, lawyers for the Volkswagen dealer network in the United States seek legal fees up to $36.2M

November 12   Volkswagen AG and Audi AG confirm that U.S. and European regulators are investigating fresh irregularities related to carbon dioxide (CO_2) emissions levels in a number of Audi automatic transmission vehicles.

November 13   Volkswagen admits that Audi automatic transmission software in some models can change test behavior in a manner that minimizes CO_2 emissions during testing and return to normal settings when driven on the road.

November 14   Litigation funding company Bentham Europe plans to bankroll a potential 100B euro ($110B) damages claim against Europe's biggest truck makers after they admitted to operating a 14-year price-rigging cartel. The truck manufacturers include Volvo, Daimler, Paccar's DAF, CNH Industrial's Iveco, and Volkswagen's MAN.

November 15   Numerous media report that Volkswagen has reached an agreement with the EPA and CARB on a resolution to the 85,000 3-liter vehicles fitted with defeat device software. The resolution reportedly includes Volkswagen buying back 20,000 older Audi and VW sports utility vehicles (SUVs) and a software fix for 65,000 newer Porsche, Audi, and VW cars and SUVs. Talks are continuing with regards to additional compensation to be provided to affected car owners.

November 17   Volkswagen announced it will invest $2.2B in Brazil by 2020 to overhaul its production facilities and to pave the way for a new family of vehicles for the Latin America market.

November 19   Volkswagen plans to cut 5000 jobs in Brazil and 2000 jobs in Argentina within the next five years.

Volkswagen said it no longer expects the German government to make tax demands to recover revenue losses related to the automaker's diesel engine emissions test cheating. In Germany, motor vehicle taxes are linked to the volume of carbon dioxide emissions, as well as other factors.

November 20   The Mayor of London writes to Volkswagen requesting the automaker reimburse Transport of London £2.5M ($3.12M) in lost congestion charge revenue from its vehicles which were known to be contributing to pollution levels. He also requested

Volkswagen to "fully compensate" the approximately 80,000 London residents who "bought VW cars in good faith, but whose diesel engines are now contributing to London's killer air."

November 22   Volkswagen will build its Atlas TDI SUV in the USA for export to Russia.

November 25   *Automotive News* reports that Porsche is planning to fix the emissions test cheating defeat device software in the nearly 1500 new Cayenne vehicles sitting on dealer lots and then selling these as low-mileage used vehicles. The plan is dependent on Porsche receiving regulatory approval of their proposed fix for these vehicles and the other 85,000 3-liter Volkswagen vehicles already sold to consumers.

Volkswagen says it will not sell any diesel vehicles in Canada for the 2017 model year.

Audi appoints Peter Mertens, R&D Chief at Volvo, as its new head of technical development. This fills the position vacated by former R&D Chief Stefan Knirsch, who left the automaker in September under a cloud of suspicion regarding his knowledge of the emissions testing defeat device software.

November 27   VW brand chief Herbert Diess signals that the automaker is all but done with diesel engine cars in the U.S. He told reporters at the Los Angeles Auto

Show that, "At the moment we assume that we will offer no new diesel vehicles in the U.S."

Porsche is targeting around 10,000 electric car sales a year for its Porsche Mission E vehicle, which is slated for a 2019 release. Porsche will reportedly create 1400 new jobs to develop, build, and sell its first electric vehicle.

November 29   U.S. Federal Court Judge Charles Breyer postpones a hearing on Volkswagen's 3-liter violations until December 16th, citing progress between the automaker and the U.S. Department of Justice on a plan that includes a mixture of fines, compensation to car owners, and buybacks for the 85,000 3-liter vehicles equipped with emissions test cheating software.

South Korea's government announces it plans to ban the sales of some vehicles made by Nissan Motor Co, BMW, and Porsche after it found these automakers manipulated documents to make their vehicles road certified. The automakers also face a combined $5.6M in fines and have until mid-December to "clarify their positions."

VW, Audi, Porsche, BMW, Daimler, and Ford's European division announced a joint venture to fund the establishment of ultra-fast charging stations for electric vehicles across Europe, starting in 2017. The goal is to boost the acceptance of electric cars throughout Europe, as well as to compete with U.S. rival Tesla.

November 30

The U.S. Environmental Protection Agency (EPA) is considering locking in new fuel efficiency benchmarks before the end of the Obama Administration. The proposed goals would be to double fuel efficiency to 54.4 miles per gallon by 2025. The EPA says this will lead to over $1 trillion in fuel savings and keep six billion metric tons of greenhouse gas out of the environment. Transportation is now the largest source of carbon emissions in the U.S., recently surpassing the electricity sector.

December 1

Volkswagen Truck & Bus will invest $420M euros ($446.5M) in Brazil over the next five years in order to offer new products, modernize its manufacturing plant, and develop connectivity services.

December 2

Athens, Paris, Madrid, and Mexico City reportedly will ban all diesel cars by 2025 within their respective city limits in an attempt to improve air quality in these polluted cities. The officials cited a World Health Organization (WHO) figure that three million deaths a year are directly related to air pollution, mostly in large cities.

December 4

South Korea fines Volkswagen $31.9M for falsely advertising its diesel-engine vehicles as environmentally friendly. South Korea also said criminal complaints will be filed against current and former executives of Volkswagen in the country.

December 5

Volkswagen executives have been told to pay back millions of euros for use of company planes for private and family holidays.

Media reports state that Volkswagen executives in Germany have started hiring criminal defense lawyers as U.S. Department of Justice (DOJ) authorities travel to Germany to conduct interviews and seek cooperation in their criminal investigation probe.

Concerns surface that the DOJ may not be able to complete its criminal probe and reach a resolution with Volkswagen before the Trump Administration takes over in late January. Whether this would be good or bad for Volkswagen is unknown.

However, Jeff Sessions, appointed as the new Attorney General by President-elect Trump, said in 2010 when he was a U.S. Senator that he would not back away from charging a major company if there was evidence of criminal conduct. At the time, the U.S. Department of Justice was investigating BP over the Deepwater Horizon oil spill in the Gulf of Mexico. Sessions, a former federal prosecutor in Alabama, also stated at the time that the Justice Department should not be swayed or influenced by concerns that criminal charges against BP might harm those who depend on the company for jobs. "They are not too big to fail," he stated. If he brings that same attitude to his role as head of the Justice Department, Volkswagen and its executives may be in for a long and rough journey ahead.

December 6   The California Air Resources Board (CARB) lays out its rules for how the $800M Volkswagen investment in zero emissions vehicles infrastructure will be used. CARB plans to maintain strict oversight of how these penalty funds will be used.

A U.S. House of Representatives panel grills the EPA over the Volkswagen settlement agreement and zero emissions vehicles guidelines.

Audi promises no forced redundancies in its German workforce before 2020, extending its job guarantees for 61,000 workers by two years.

December 7   Volkswagen launches Maia as its rider-hailing brand. This becomes the 13th brand in the Volkswagen AG stable. The name comes from the Sanskrit word for magic.

December 8   Paris faces its worst winter air pollution in a decade and the city government bans half of all cars from traveling within the city limits and makes public transportation free for three consecutive days. Similar action is planned for Lyon as well.

The European Union says it will take legal action against seven countries, including Germany, Spain, and the United Kingdom for failing to police car emissions. The move reflects growing frustration in Brussels over how national governments have failed to clamp down on the widespread air polluting emissions of automotive manufacturers exposed by the Volkswagen Dieselgate scandal.

The U.S. Federal Trade Commission (FTC) is seeking more information on whether employees at Volkswagen destroyed cell phones in an effort to hide evidence related to the emissions test cheating defeat device software. Some 23 phones are missing and constitute "a bright red flag" the FTC said in a court filing.

In an attempt to clean up London's deadly air, the mayor announced that the city will no longer buy diesel buses for its famed public transportation network. It is estimated that London's dirty air kills up to 9500 people a year.

December 9   Swiss prosecutors have opened criminal proceedings and seized evidence from Swiss car importer AMAG after an appellate court ruled Swiss investigators must conduct their own investigation of the Volkswagen emissions scandal. Some 2000 criminal complaints have been filed in Switzerland related to the emissions test cheating scandal.

December 12   German regulators are now investigating whether Porsche illegally manipulated fuel economy data by installing devices allowing its gasoline engine cars to sense whether they are being tested for fuel consumption and carbon dioxide (CO_2) emissions.

December 14   Volkswagen will switch to English as the group's future official language. The automaker also said it is changing how it develops managers and will place more emphasis on foreign assignments and knowledge gained in different areas and brands. It will also help more women reach top positions by ensuring they get the experience needed for appointment to upper management positions.

Lab tests conducted by the European Commission Joint Research Center show the latest Audi diesel engine emits double the statutory levels of NOx. The results threaten to embroil Audi, the main profit contributor to Volkswagen AG, in another cheat device scandal.

December 18   Beijing and 22 other Chinese cities impose emergency measures, including ordering cars off the roads and closing schools, after air pollution levels soared to more than 10 times safe levels. Flights were canceled or delayed due to poor visibility.

December 19   Volkswagen Canada agrees to a C$2.1B ($1.57B) deal to settle a class-action lawsuit. About 105,000 Canadian owners of VW and Audi vehicles will receive between C$5100 and C$8000 each in compensation. They will also be able to sell their cars back to VW and Audi. In addition, Volkswagen agreed to pay a fine of C$15M ($11.2M) to the Canadian Competition Bureau. Approval of the settlement by the Ontario Superior Court and the Superior Court of Quebec is expected in March 2017.

December 20

German auto supplier Robert Bosch GmbH has agreed in principle to pay $300M to settle a civil lawsuit filed by U.S. car owners related to the Volkswagen emissions test cheating scandal. In doing so, the company says it does not accept liability nor admits to the allegations made in the lawsuit that said the company was a knowing and active participant in the Volkswagen emissions test cheating scheme.

Volkswagen agrees to a $1B settlement that includes buying back or repairing the 85,000 3-liter diesel-powered vehicles in the U.S. fitted with defeat device software to cheat emissions testing. As part of the agreement Volkswagen will pay $225M into an environmental trust fund to remediate the excess emissions produced by its vehicles. It will also pay $25M into a fund to support the use of zero emission vehicles in California.

Germany's Federal Motor Vehicle Authority (KBA) has cleared Volkswagen to begin repairing cars with the emissions test cheating software installed. In a statement Volkswagen said the KBA "confirmed that implementing the technical solution for the affected models will not adversely affect fuel consumption, engine performance or noise emissions."

December 30   The U.K. government's chief medical officer says diesel cars should be phased out to reduce the tens of thousands of deaths caused each year by air pollution.

The U.K. Transport Minister, John Hayes, says over a million Volkswagen drivers in the country have been "taken for a ride" over the diesel emissions scandal and must be compensated. He also revealed that Volkswagen has agreed to reimburse the U.K. government £1.1M ($1.4M) for the cost of vehicle emission tests on other automotive manufacturers conducted by the government earlier in the year.

2017

January 2   Volkswagen has commissioned an expert to examine if the carmaker allowed the arrest and torture of employees in Brazil during the country's former military government.

January 3   Sentencing for James Liang is delayed until May 3 by a U.S. Federal District Judge "to allow more time for defendant's cooperation in the investigation."

January 4   German consumer rights champion myRight has filed the first legal test case in Germany against Volkswagen. The lawsuit asks to force Volkswagen to repurchase vehicles with the emissions test cheating defeat device software at the original price.

South Korea has halted the sale of 10 car models from three brands — BMW, Nissan, and Porsche — after they were found fabricating certification documents related to emissions tests.

January 5   A South Korea court sentenced a Volkswagen executive to 18 months in jail for falsifying documents enabling Volkswagen vehicles to be imported into the country. Two other employees were convicted on related charges.

U.S. District Court Judge Charles Breyer rules that Volkswagen AG and former CEO Martin Winterkorn must face an investor lawsuit filed in California. The suit accuses Volkswagen and a handful of senior executives of not having informed investors in a timely fashion about the emissions test cheating scandal or about potential financial liabilities.

January 6   The EPA and CARB said they have approved a fix for around 67,000 2-liter Volkswagen AG vehicles from the 2015 model year.

January 7   A Volkswagen executive, Oliver Schmidt, who had headed the automaker's regulatory compliance office in the U.S. from 2014 until March 2015, was arrested by FBI agents at Miami International Airport before he could board a flight to Germany. He was charged with conspiracy to defraud the U.S. government.

January 8   A British law firm has commenced legal action against Volkswagen, seeking thousands of pounds of compensation for each U.K. driver affected by the Diselgate scandal. The firm says 10,000 drivers have already signed up to the legal action.

Volkswagen recalls 50,000 vehicles in China due to brake problems. The recall includes imported VW Golf vehicles and VW Beetle models.

January 11   The U.S. Department of Justice (DOJ) and the Environmental Protection Agency (EPA) announce that Volkswagen has agreed to a $4.3B settlement to resolve the U.S. government's civil and criminal investigations. Volkswagen also pleaded guilty to three federal felony charges and has agreed to cooperate with the DOJ's ongoing investigations.

Additionally, the DOJ announced that six Volkswagen executives and employees have been indicted by a federal grand jury on conspiracy and other charges related to the diesel emissions test cheating scandal. This includes Oliver Schmidt, who was taken into custody by FBI agents a few days earlier.

Volkswagen has agreed to sweeping reforms, new audits, and oversight by an independent monitor for three years as part of its most recent settlement deal with U.S. regulators.

South Korea's Fair Trade Commission, the country's corporate watchdog, fines Volkswagen nearly 37.2B won ($32M) for false advertising on vehicle emissions. The FTC said it would also file criminal complaints against five current and former VW executives. It is the largest fine ever imposed in South Korea for false advertising.

Simultaneously, Seoul prosecutors indicted seven current and former executives of Volkswagen's Korean operations on charges of fabricating official documents and alleged violation of the Clean Air Conservation Act.

Volkswagen Group of America recalls 136,000 vehicles for an anti-lock brake fix.

U.S. environmental regulators accuse Fiat Chrysler of installing defeat device software on rough 104,000 Jeep and Dodge Ram diesel-powered vehicles to cheat on emissions tests.

January 12   French prosecutors say they are investigating Renault for possible cheating that may have damaged the public's health. The investigation centers on the possible use of defeat device software and vehicle emissions test cheating.

January 14   The five Volkswagen executives under criminal indictment in the U.S. for their alleged roles in the Dieselgate scandal have been advised not to leave Germany as doing so risks arrest and extradition to the U.S. Other executives have been advised to stay away from the U.S. in case charges are pending against them.

January 15

In a published interview in the German newspaper *Bild*, U.S. president-elect Donald Trump warns German automakers he will impose a 35% border tax on vehicles imported to the U.S. market. In the interview he criticizes BMW, Daimler, and Volkswagen for failing to produce more cars in the U.S.

The French Environment Minister says the judicial investigation into diesel emissions testing in France could widen beyond Renault after tests showed other automakers had also exceed authorized emission levels.

January 16

A report in Germany's *Bild am Sonntag* newspaper says former Volkswagen CEO Martin Winterkorn knew about the automaker's diesel emissions test problems two months earlier than previously stated. Citing confidential documents the newspaper says Winterkorn was presented with evidence in July 2015 that the Volkswagen Group was using special software to manipulate diesel exhaust reading during tests to cheat environmental regulations in the U.S.

Less than 67,000 of the 475,000 VW and Audi 2-liter diesel vehicles with emissions test cheating software have been returned to dealers as buybacks or lease terminations, according to a lawyer for Volkswagen during a federal court hearing. That figure is expected to rise to around 96,000 by the end of January.

January 18   Volkswagen says it will appeal a German court ruling that the automaker must buy back at full purchase price a German customer's diesel car equipped with the emissions test cheating defeat device software. The judges in the ruling said Volkswagen acted "indecently" by installing the software and compared the automaker's deceit to previous cases of winemakers mixing antifreeze in wine or food manufacturers putting horse meat into lasagna.

January 19   Former Volkswagen CEO Martin Winterkorn denies early knowledge of the diesel emissions test cheating during two hours of testimony to a German parliamentary committee. Declining to be specific about when he was informed because it is a matter still being investigated by German prosecutors, he said he also is "looking for satisfactory answers."

January 21   Volkswagen will halt production at one of its biggest factories in Germany for 11 days in January and February due to shrinking demand for its Passat saloon and estate models. The factory in Emden employs about 9000 workers.

January 26   U.S. District Court Judge Charles Breyer approves the $1.2B settlement agreement between Volkswagen and its 652 franchised dealerships in the U.S. The total settlement is valued at $1.6B, including $1.2B in direct payments, $270M through a provision for prior payments, and $175M in continued incentive payments based on sales volumes.

Christine Hohmann-Dennhardt, who joined the Volkswagen AG management board as head of integrity and legal affairs a year ago, is leaving the board by mutual consent "due to differences in their understanding of responsibilities and future operating structures within the function she leads." She had been recruited to join Volkswagen from Daimler shortly after the Dieselgate scandal became public.

The European Commission issued guidance on how European Union member states should be policing automotive manufacturers. The 11-page guidance, while not legally binding, is an attempt to clarify how existing EU rules should be implemented. It could form the basis for legal action against EU countries that do not crack down on excessive, health-damaging vehicle emissions.

January 27   Prosecutors in Germany announce they are expanding their probe once again into Volkswagen's emissions test cheating scandal. An announcement